THE PHILOSOPHY OF GEORGES BASTIDE

THOMAS KOENIG

THE PHILOSOPHY OF GEORGES BASTIDE

A Study Tracing the Origins and Development of a French Value Philosophy and a French Personalism against the Background of French Idealism

MARTINUS NIJHOFF / THE HAGUE / 1971

ISBN-13: 978-94-010-3047-2 e-ISBN-13: 978-94-010-3045-8
DOI: 10.1007/978-94-010-3045-8

GRATITUDE

is expressed

to Gerald Kreyche of DePaul University for encouragement,

to my professors, especially Albert Dondeyne and André Wylleman of Louvain University, under whose direction this work was undertaken,

to the United States Educational Foundation in Belgium for its financial assistance during the two years of my Fulbright fellowship and to Mrs. Dorothy Moore Deflandre, Executive Director of the Foundation,

to the Augustinian priests of Chicago and to Tolentine College for granting me a sabbatical leave in order to complete this study,

to F. van der Zande for his assistance with the final draft,

to my mother, Marion, and my father, Louis.

TABLE OF CONTENTS

To
GEORGES BASTIDE
one who gave witness

PREFACE

The axiological idealism of Georges Bastide, which is itself an attempt to come to grips with basic philosophical problems in a form wholly in accord with the preoccupations of our times, offered a unique opportunity for coming into contact with two new horizons – critical idealism and axiological personalism. An examination of the intimate relationship between these two viewpoints promised to be of special interest and worthy of research. A similar theme is encountered in the philosophy of R. Le Senne and a number of works have been devoted to the study of his philosophy. However, in Bastide's axiological idealism the emphasis is on the relationship between the problem of spiritual conversion and the problem of the transfiguration of values and, as far as I know, no major study has been made of Bastide's philosophy.

This study also opened up the possibility of a deeper understanding of the philosophies of Descartes and Kant, as well as the philosophies of Brunschvicg and Bergson. Bastide's philosophy offers new possibilities for reflection on the past in the light of contemporary problems, just as his own work can be understood only in the light of the philosophies which are the chief inspiration for his axiological idealism.

In this regard we have devoted three chapters of historical background in order to introduce the main influences on Bastide's philosophy. At the same time we introduce in these chapters the principal factors involed in Bastide's own development, especially as regards the object, method and doctrine of axiological idealism. In Bastide's philosophy the orientation towards a critical idealism as grounded in the philosophies of Descartes and Kant remains throughout the principal underlying force. The practical philosophy of Kant seen in the light of the *Cogito* gives the metaphysical framework to the reflexive method and grounds as well the doctrine of Bastide's spiritual personalism.

The second chapter of Part I is devoted to the philosophies of Brunschvicg and Bergson, mediating influences between Descartes and Kant and Bastide's axiological idealism. In fact, a study of Bastide's major and original work *De la Condition humaine* shows that these are the four authors around whom he centers his own philosophy. With the philosophy of Brunschvicg there is a new appreciation of Descartes' spiritualism and a purification of Kant's critical idealism through an emphasis on the function of reflection as found in the third Critique, freed, as Brunschvicg says, from the structure of *a priori* forms. Brunschvicg came to a new appreciation of the creative dynamism of spirit intimately connected with its own experiences and history. Bastide's metaphysics of action can be seen to develope under this influence. It is an attempt to ground the incarnational aspect of human freedom and thus avoid formalism. Along these same lines there is a constant effort to avoid dogmatism and an undesirable subjectivism. The life philosophy of Bergson gives support to Bastide's axiological idealism in more than one point, but especially in the notion of consciousness as genesis and the method of a reflection obtained genetically at the heart of spiritual activity itself.

The third chapter of Part I hardly does justice to the difficult problems raised by philosophies of reflection, such as that of Nabert. However, since we had already dealt with the major influences in Bastide's philosophy, it was felt that a brief chapter of transition would not be out of place, even though the author regrets not having had more time to gain a better knowledge of these philosophers. No doubt there are many points of comparison between Bastide's axiological idealism and the philosophies of Lavelle, Le Senne, Madinier and Nabert. Such a comparison admittedly would not be without interest. At the same time it was not deemed necessary for fulfillment of the original project and in some ways may even have distracted from it. The time ahead, it is hoped, will offer other occasions for new studies in this regard.

The plan of construction for the central part of the thesis is simply an attempt to follow the philosophical itinerary of Bastide himself in order to see in its genesis, as it were, his own philosophical project: the development and implications of a philosophy of spiritual conversion in an axiological idealism. Why, in other words, must philosophy be axiology? Why must the philosophical method be one of reflexive analysis in the strict, idealist sense? How is personalism the necessary outcome of axiological idealism?

The human situation constitutes a basic existential whole which can be attained only through two series of cognitive elements irreducible to one another. The main question is concerned with the relationship between spiritual conversion (reflexion) and its pre-reflective roots. Put in another way, the question to be examined in Bastide's philosophy concerns the nature of the *Cogito* in the sense of the irreducible first truth as well as its character in spiritual conversion (the personal, free Cogito) together with the metaphysical *experience* which grounds it.

Thus the second part of the thesis begins with Bastide's own description of the original affirmation of consciousness and the basic problematic which it is said to yield, namely the relationship between the constituent factors of the first certitude – being, truth and value. The effort to resolve this problematic – expressed in terms of authenticity – yields, for Bastide, the metaphysical primacy of value and the subsequent necessity of an axiological metaphysics. But axiology itself is problematic, for what are the true values?

The first chapter, then, leaves us in need of a method, a method for determining the authentic use of axiology. We are brought naturally to the second factor present in all philosophy, the nature of the metaphysical experience which grounds the Cogito. This is studied in the second chapter under the notion of alienation, for Bastide's examination of the pre-reflexive experience of man, as we might suppose already, leads to a discovery of man's original situation in the world as an alienating one, one of inauthentic existence. The second chapter is a description of those factors leading up to the spiritual conversion.

The third chapter is brief, but it presents, along with the aspect of axiology, the central intuition of Bastide's philosophy. For just as the notion of value enables the philosopher to find once again the ethical dimensions of human existance, uniting the clarity of intellectual analysis with the depth of lived experience, so the spiritual conversion, says Bastide, is centered around the central philosophical problem of the basic attitudes (the engagement of the whole man) which orientate the philosophical search itself. It is precisely here in an axiology where the perennial problem of spiritual conversion manifests itself as connected with the problem of a transfiguration of values. This connection proves to be the second contribution of Bastide's philosophy, the first being the application of axiology to the problem of man as such.

The final chapter concerns the doctrine of an axiological idealism, namely, spiritual personalism. Admittedly, it is all too short to represent the full richness of Bastide's moral philosophy as found in his *Traité de l'Action morale*. But our main purpose was to follow the philosophy of Bastide along the principal lines and problems involved in its development. The author hopes that further study will reap the benefits of having first come to grips with the basic philosophical problems involved in an axiological idealism. It is in this spirit also that this modest contribution and research is offered to the reader.

Chicago, Illinois
June 6, 1970.

character in spiritual conversion (the personal, free Cogito) together with the metaphysical *experience* which grounds it.

Thus the second part of the thesis begins with Bastide's own description of the original affirmation of consciousness and the basic problematic which it is said to yield, namely the relationship between the constituent factors of the first certitude – being, truth and value. The effort to resolve this problematic – expressed in terms of authenticity – yields, for Bastide, the metaphysical primacy of value and the subsequent necessity of an axiological metaphysics. But axiology itself is problematic, for what are the true values?

The first chapter, then, leaves us in need of a method, a method for determining the authentic use of axiology. We are brought naturally to the second factor present in all philosophy, the nature of the metaphysical experience which grounds the Cogito. This is studied in the second chapter under the notion of alienation, for Bastide's examination of the pre-reflexive experience of man, as we might suppose already, leads to a discovery of man's original situation in the world as an alienating one, one of inauthentic existence. The second chapter is a description of those factors leading up to the spiritual conversion.

The third chapter is brief, but it presents, along with the aspect of axiology, the central intuition of Bastide's philosophy. For just as the notion of value enables the philosopher to find once again the ethical dimensions of human existance, uniting the clarity of intellectual analysis with the depth of lived experience, so the spiritual conversion, says Bastide, is centered around the central philosophical problem of the basic attitudes (the engagement of the whole man) which orientate the philosophical search itself. It is precisely here in an axiology where the perennial problem of spiritual conversion manifests itself as connected with the problem of a transfiguration of values. This connection proves to be the second contribution of Bastide's philosophy, the first being the application of axiology to the problem of man as such.

The final chapter concerns the doctrine of an axiological idealism, namely, spiritual personalism. Admittedly, it is all too short to represent the full richness of Bastide's moral philosophy as found in his *Traité de l'Action morale*. But our main purpose was to follow the philosophy of Bastide along the principal lines and problems involved in its development. The author hopes that further study will reap the benefits of having first come to grips with the basic philosophical problems involved in an axiological idealism. It is in this spirit also that this modest contribution and research is offered to the reader.

Chicago, Illinois
June 6, 1970.

PART I

HISTORICAL PERSPECTIVES AND PHILOSOPHICAL METHOD

CHAPTER I

BASIC POINTS OF REFERENCE IN DESCARTES AND KANT

The *Meditations* of Descartes and the moral philosophy of Kant are the two principal remote sources for the axiological idealism of Georges Bastide.* Not that the idealism of Plato and the ideal of Socrates are not also present to his own reflections. On the contrary. But they are not the main sources for the philosophical principles that found his philosophy. The spirit of a Pascal, a Montaigne, a Spinoza receives a most sympathetic understanding from Bastide, and he gleans several important principles from each of them. But they do not determine his thought like the philosophies of Descartes and Kant do. It is the purpose of this chapter to discuss in the light of Bastide's philosophy the philosophies of Descartes and Kant, in order to better understand Bastide's philosophy in light of the past, and, perhaps, find new possibilities for reflection on the past in the light of contemporary problems.

1. The influence of Descartes

The starting point and, in a sense, the end point of Bastide's philosophy is the *Cogito* of Descartes. His own metaphysical *Meditations* begin with the formula "Consciousness exists and I am its witness." And the same *Meditations* end with the affirmation: "God exists and I am his witness." [1]

What interests us here is the fact that Bastide is attempting to come to grips with contemporary problems, of which he is keenly aware, by having recourse to essentially the same basic philosophical principle espoused by Descartes over three hundred years ago. For Descartes the *Cogito* is the first

* Professor Bastide was born April 5, 1901 at Cournonterral, France. For many years he was professor of Moral Philosophy at the University of Toulouse as well as Dean of the Humanities Department. He was also director of the philosophical review *Les études philosophique* and president of the *Société de philosophie de langue française*. He died suddenly at the opening of the philosophical congress at Nice, September 1969.

[1] G. Bastide, *Méditations pour une éthique de la personne*, p. 1 and p. 198.

principle of philosophy. It is not simply the starting point of all our knowledge, but is the primary intelligible along with the immediate evidences contained in it. But just what are the immediate evidences of the *Cogito* and how does Bastide interpret them?

Bastide presupposes the general facts concerning the nature of Descartes' first principle that have been distilled by the most competent interpreters over the centuries. The structure of the *Cogito* is an act of intuition.[2] It is the first judgment of existence that cannot be called into doubt. It is the aperception of the existence of the subject in the act of thinking.[3] It is the bridge between the ideal order of mathematical analysis to the real order of the subject judging.[4] It is contact with and affirmation of the spirit present to itself, "consciousness bearing witness to itself." [5] Most of all it is the real, first principle, able to ground a metaphysics, the unique and privileged evidence logically anterior to every other judgment of existence, the most known and most certain of all truths, even the ideal truths of mathematics.[6]

Bastide, firmly committed to idealism, accepts this *Cogito*. But Bastide wishes to go deeper existentially and spiritually. An interpretation of Descartes "according to the spirit" and not just according to the letter reveals the real context of the *Cogito* and gives new dimensions to the critical problem. This dimension is essentially ethical.[7] The *Cogito* reveals the true human situation of man in the act of finding himself as spirit, as freely alienated from authentic vocation which is perfection, as being called to accept responsibility for his condition and engage himself in the search for wisdom in the clear direction pointed out by the *Cogito*. The full problematic of Descartes's first principle, then, is viewed by Bastide as *practical* and not merely theoretical.[8]

[2] "'*Cogito ergo sum.*' The Cartesian 'therefore' is a new kind of intuition which, on the one hand, contains the immediate evidence of the simple mathematical relation and, on the other hand, implies the incontestable certitude of reality." Leon Brunschvicg, *Le progrès de la conscience dans la philosophie occidentale*, Paris, 1953, p. 139. The translations from the French throughout this work are those of the author.

[3] Cf. R. Verneaux, *Les sources cartésiennes et kantiennes de l'idéalisme français*, Paris, Beauchesne, 1936, p. 87.

[4] "The passage from the order of mere possibility to the order of existence is made within the act of judgment, but only on condition that we modify the point of application of the judgment, no longer demanding that it justify the existence of its object, but rather to manifest the existence of the subject who judges." Leon Brunschvicg, *La modalité du jugement*, Paris, Alcan, p. 53.

[5] G. Bastide, *Méditations*, p. 1.

[6] Cf. R. Verneaux, *op. cit.*, pp. 95-97.

[7] Cf. G. Bastide, "The Metaphysical Dimensions of Man," *International Philosophical Quarterly*, 1962, pp. 351-366. Cf. p. 356.

[8] *Ibid.*, p. 352.

The problem of philosophy is how to give adequate expression to a consciousness that is ethical as well as theoretical, a philosophy that will shed light on our actions, a philosophy that will follow life in its real conflicts and tensions, a philosophy, in other words, of authenticity.[9]

But is this the philosophy of Descartes? Or is it only Bastide's philosophy? To this question Bastide would without doubt reply that it is essentially the philosophical itinerary of Descartes' own spiritual conversion provoking in Bastide himself a similar conversion which is the source of authentic philosophy. All authentic philosophy must follow the same itinerary of the *Cogito.*[10]

Bastide wishes to integrate the moral philosophy of Descartes with his metaphysics in one philosophy of spiritual conversion. Perhaps the basic text in which Bastide conceives this possibility is the passage in the *Discours* where Descartes remarks the separation between the firm and solid foundations of the mathematical sciences ("upon which nothing more significant had been built than the technical arts") and the uncertain foundations upon which something so important and necessary as morality was based.[11] "All Descartes is in germ in these lines," remarks Bastide.[12] That is, the real problematic of Descartes' philosophy, according to Bastide, is that of a practical humanism, the personal discovery of the authentic reasons for living by which a man takes upon himself personal responsibility for his own life and so begins to restore the "dislocated values" by drawing them together in the original source of their unity, which is the spirit.[13]

In order that these remarks do not remain "up in the air," it would seem necessary to follow briefly Descartes' own reflections wherein the meditations of Bastide take root.

9 "... to bear witness to consciousness at the personal level is to be in the act of seeking an existence known with certainty to be of value; and since existence at this level is constituted by the search itself and since it is a question of living and bearing witness, we can say in a word that it is the search for a worthwhile existence that constitutes the person and that this search is essentially the search for authenticity." G. Bastide, *Méditations*, Paris, 1962, p. 352.

10 Cf. G. Bastide, *Traité de l'action morale*, Paris, P.U.F., T.I., pp. 353-359.

11 "I took pleasure above all in the mathematical sciences, because of the certitude and evidence of their reasonings; but I had hardly noticed their real use when, thinking that their only purpose was the mechanical arts, I was surprised at the fact that although their foundations were so very stable and solid, no one had established anything more important on this base. While on the other side I compared the writings of the ancients who wrote ethical treatises to really superb and magnificent palaces built on sand." R. Descartes, *Le discours de la méthode*, in *Collection nouvelle des classiques*, Editions "Labor," Brussels, 1935, p. 36.

12 Cf. G. Bastide, *Les grands thèmes moraux de la civilisation occidentale*, Grenoble, Bordas, 1944, p. 132.

13 *Ibid.*

The model of a pure mathematics transposed into a philosophical method, combined with the ideal of a universal, apodictic science left Descartes with a "problem of knowledge." Idealist in method, realist in intention – Descartes had to face the "problem" of man's relationship to the world. The reality of spirit is revealed in the *Cogito*. The ideal world of spirit as well. But the method had rendered impossible the "naive" acceptance of sense intuition and a direct contact with reality other than spirit. There was no way of return to the "things in themselves." [14]

There is no need here to go into the proofs given by Descartes in order to affirm with certitude the existence of objects other than spirit. In the end Descartes' proofs are based in their point of departure in the spirit and the ideas which the spirit discovers in itself, especially the idea of God and his veracity.[15] What is of interest to us is to determine the Cartesian foundation for a central thesis in Bastide's philosophy, namely, that the original relationship of man in the world is naive, bound to lead up to the experience of alienation, a *necessary* presupposition to spiritual conversion and the discovery of the spiritual values.[16]

For Descartes the necessity of experience is related to the life of the spirit. But the role of experience is only secondary.[17] It becomes a kind of necessary evil. For in fact, sensation begets only confused ideas, ideas which must be reduced into simple natures, which, in the end, only serve as stepping stones to the discovery of spirit. Experience itself must be finally verified in the spirit.[18] The proper function of the senses is purely practical.[19] Experience brings nothing that is not already to be found in thought itself. But thought needs experience as the condition (occasion) of its coming to life. The passage from sensation to intellectual knowledge is not by way of abstraction of a concept; it is simply a progress in clarity of thought.[20]

For Bastide the native relationship of man to the world is not a natural one.[21] It is to be surpassed in the discovery of the *Cogito* and the *interior*

[14] "Let us begin by considering the things which are most common and which we think we know with greatest clarity, namely, the bodies we touch and see . . . and what is to be noticed most of all is that perception or the act by which we perceive is not a seeing or touching nor an imagination (nor was it ever, although it may have seemed so at one time), but rather an inspection of the mind alone . . ." R. Descartes, *Méditations Métaphysiques* in *Les grands textes*, Paris, 1966, pp. 45 and 48.

[15] *Méditations*, III, 40.

[16] Cf. G. Bastide, *De la condition humaine*, Paris, Alcan, 1939, pp. 268-269.

[17] Cf. R. Verneaux, *op. cit.*, p. 169.

[18] *Méditation* VI, 15, 16, 21, 27.

[19] Cf. R. Verneaux, *op. cit.*, p. 173.

[20] Cf. R. Verneaux, *op. cit.*, p. 177.

[21] Cf. G. Bastide, *La conversion spirituelle*, Paris, P.U.F., 1955, p. 8.

transcendence the *Cogito* reveals. The original contact with the world is naive and eventually alienates man from himself. Man is revealed to himself in his authentic humanity, in his human situation, only after the purification by way of the experience of alienation and the resulting conversion and transformation of values.

Thus, for Bastide, none of the limitations of Descartes' philosophy (his mechanism, the body-soul dualism, the problematic relationship of divine and human freedom) affect the "essential point," the "essence of his message," which is the discovery of "interior transcendence," after "the heroic and fruitful struggles of consciousness throughout the *Méditations*." [22] The discovery of the *Cogito* reveals man to himself and, at the same time, the "nothingness" (as regards value) of the "external" world.

Already in the *Regulae* Descartes had pointed out the necessity of going from "those objects of which our spirit is capable of acquiring a certain and undeniable knowledge," for "there is only knowledge when there is evidence." [23] But the light of true knowledge was not to be found in those objects which appear to us *of themselves*, but in the spirit of men under the direction of a method. Here we have the foundation for that fundamental opposition of idealism to realism. Realism seeks a method (chemin vers) already regulated in some way by the *intelligible* object, an emphasis reiterated by Husserl and much of contemporary philosophy. Bastide, true to the idealist position, opposes this return to the things in themselves.[24]

Descartes sought examples of such objects (which could provide certain knowledge) in the pure objects of mathematics untouched by experience.[25] Mathematics offered, therefore, an example of the method he was looking for, because the "pure triangle" is not an object of experience but of intuition. The foundation of knowledge was sought here, because Descartes was convinced it was the only way to find "not what others declared or what we ourselves conjectured, but what we have a clear and evident intuition

[22] G. Bastide, "The Metaphysical Dimensions," pp. 357-358.

[23] R. Descartes, *Règles pour la direction de l'esprit*, trad. by J. Sirvin, Paris, Vrin, 1945, p. 5 (première règle).

[24] "That is why we think that the expression 'bracketing' the world of objects by which Husserl's phenomenology translates his opposition to naive realism is still insufficient for expressing spiritual conversion. Intentionality is still direction towards an object, obtained by bracketing the object, but still maintaining a direction towards it. But it is precisely this direction towards an object which is still suspect, for the will is still turned away from itself. What is required is a complete conversion of the will so that it can become conscious of the spiritual values. Spiritual conversion is not only bracketing the object; it is also and above all a calling into question the subject." G. Bastide, *De la condition humaine*, p. 276-277.

[25] R. Descartes, *Règles*, III.

of . . ." [26] Bastide's philosophy of spiritual conversion is nothing more than the effort to ground the constituting activity of the spirit as the ground of all authentic philosophy. His search for the *raisons d'être* parallels the Cartesian search for the first irreducible knowledge and the "universal science" of the fourth rule.[27]

The *Méditations* provide the link between method and metaphysics. Descartes sought here to establish the ultimate foundation of truth in which the method itself will necessarily appear. The itinerary of Bastide bears notable resemblances. From the problematic of the authentic values (once he has established that metaphysics is axiology) arises the crisis of the "conscience malheureuse" and the subsequent spiritual conversion, wherein is revealed the nature and necessity of the reflexive method.

For Descartes the problem of method is the problem of the value of the clear and distinct ideas, the value of the evidential truths, the possibility of the spirit itself being functionally sidetracked by another spirit, an evil spirit more powerful than man.[28] The fact of error motivated calling into doubt the naive certitudes we have concerning material things; [29] in the *Méditations* even the model truths of the *Regulae*, the mathematical certitudes, are made the object of a willed doubt – since Descartes seeks an absolute metaphysical foundation beyond the principles themselves.[30] It is precisely the character of the metaphysical doubt that Bastide emphasizes in an ethical context, since it is especially deliberately willed on the part of Descartes. As Verneaux had already noted, the fact of the doubt being willed is not a sign of its fictitious character, but rather a sign of its reality.[31] But Bastide would maintain that the reasons behind this willed doubt are not only psychological and pedagogical, but eminently moral.[32]

Bastide, then, sees a central role in the willed supposition of an evil spirit. For it gives an "intrinsic restlessness" to the problem posed by Descartes,

[26] R. Descartes, *Règles*, III.

[27] "But what is above all lacking in Bacon and what characterizes his empiricism is a sense of the mathematical law. It is here above all that we feel the real difference from Cartesian science. With Descartes the reflexive conversion of values places mathematics in the first place as model and instrument for truth. The absence of this conversion with Bacon leaves his science as no more than a prolongation of common sense, purified only of its own idols and prejudices. Descartes was concerned about a solid point of departure where Bacon was impatient for the rewards of the finished product." G. Bastide, *Les grands thèmes*, p. 168.

[28] *Méditations*, I, 12.

[29] *Ibid.*, I, 3.

[30] *Méditations*, I, 9.

[31] R. Verneaux, *op. cit.*, p. 73.

[32] Cf. G. Bastide, "Le malin génie," 1958 (43), pp. 233-245.

that is, it grounds an ontological experience, an ontological anxiety.[33] Descartes, says Bastide, was the first of the moderns to experience the "loss of the immediacy of being," and thus the first to be thrown back on his own subjectivity. Thus the hypothesis of the evil spirit is not the supplementary scene of the first act, but the original ground for all that follows and a necessary part of the revelation of the method.

It is here, then, that philosophy takes on the character of the "metaphysical drama" which, for Bastide, constitutes the human condition.[35] As such the doubt of Descartes is seen as a "reflexive doubt" already containing the presence of what is being sought. The attitude of Descartes is not at all one of irresolution, but a generous will seeking light. The doubt is an essential moment in the movement of spiritual conversion. Descartes is viewed as a man who was not only seeking knowledge, but above all authentic existence, one based on certitude but also ordered to the Good.[36]

In the second *Méditation* Descartes affirms the existence of the thinking subject: "I am, I exist." The existence of the "I" cannot be contested, not even by the evil spirit, since the "I" affirms only its own presence to itself. The object is the subject. There is coincidence between existence and thought. The "I" is, however, not an embodied subjectivity, but a substance who thinks.

Next Descartes affirms the various activities of the subject, abstracting from their objective correlates which he has called into doubt. This analysis of the *Cogito* has for its goal the affirmation of thought as conscious activity,

[33] Bastide cites Descartes' response to Mersenne who had objected that Descartes had not sufficiently made clear in the *Discours* the connection between the attitude animating his whole search and the metaphysical principles which receive the sense of their spirituality from this attitude. Descartes' answer was that he did so "on purpose and with good reason, principally because I had written in ordinary language for fear that weaker minds, welcoming at the outset the doubts I felt I had to propose and then afterwards confusing in the same way the reasons by which I tried to remove the doubts, would blame me for having engaged them in a direction that was not good without, perhaps, being able to draw them out of it."

Bastide emphasizes that the role of the evil spirit in Descartes functions in the same way as in his own philosophy, namely, as an essential moment in the spiritual conversion: "Descartes is the Father of Idealism not so much for his realism as regards subjectivity, as one most often thinks, but most of all by reason of his hypothesis of the evil spirit which is the refusal to adhere to the values of exteriority." G. Bastide, *De la condition humaine*, p. 276.

[34] Cf. G. Bastide, "Le malin génie," p. 234.

[35] Cf. G. Bastide, "The Metaphysical Dimensions," p. 354.

[36] But even here the Good is viewed as the good use of reason and will in the attaining of wisdom and the contemplation of truth. Cf. G. Rodis-Lewis, *La morale de Descartes* ("Initiation Philosophique" 27), Paris, P.U.F., 1962 (2nd edition), p. 124. We have hardly the metaphysics of action which Bastide seeks.

the auto-determination of the spirit determining itself in ideas. For Descartes it is the immanent act of consciousness (affirmation, negation, willing, not willing, feeling etc.) that is said to be attained. In the conscious act (judgment), what is primarily known is the spirit, that is, as long as the judgment frees itself from sensible appearances and grasps the intellectual idea itself.[37]

Again Bastide reflects on the "I" of the *Cogito* to assert the ethical nature of this metaphysical experience. Granting that the notion of substance retained by Descartes is an unhappy fact, he insists on the legitimacy of the *Cogito* being expressed in the first person. It is precisely the experience of the dubito-cogito that reveals the personal nature of the "I" in all the force of the term. It is precisely here that Descartes' philosophy can be said to be a practical humanism and a personalism, for it is in the act of conversion that man grasps his true nature as spirit, that he knows himself as man and knows that he knows it.[38]

This knowledge is not given as a contemplation of spirit (in representational or conceptual knowledge), but in the *act* of reflection itself.[39] It is the result of a struggle between the doubt and the subsequent affirmation of spirit, because "we never know what we are except in the act of authentic existence." [40] It was for this reason we said that, for Bastide, the evil spirit is not simply a methodological function, but above all a "search for authenticity," [41] a kind of dual between the otherness which denies my existence and my will which affirms it.

In the fourth *Méditation* Descartes poses the problem of the "true and the false." His solution to the problem of error is the distinction between the will (an infinite power wherein man is God's image) and the understanding (wherein is grasped the finiteness of man along with his distance from God). The will is the nerve of the judgment. It mediates the logical and the existential.

For Bastide, it is by the will that man must turn to the true values and constitute himself as person. The will being the organ of belief (and faith being an integral part of the willed act of affirmation or denial), man is at

[37] *Méditations,* II, 18.

[38] Cf. G. Bastide, *De la condition humaine,* p. 319.

[39] "It is one with that act which has no comparison in any fact of nature and which we call reflection ... but this light is almost always refracted through the material aspects of our empirical problems, although we see rather that which has been illuminated rather than the illumination itself." G. Bastide, "La nature, la conscience et la vie de l'esprit," in *La vie, la pensée,* Actes de VII Congrès des Sociétés de philosophie de langue française, Paris, 1954, pp. 27 and 31.

[40] Cf. G. Bastide, "Le malin génie," p. 239.

[41] Cf. G. Bastide, "Le malin génie," p. 239.

the cross-roads of a dual dialectic: the bad faith of naive realism geared to judge according to the empirical values or the acquired faith of spiritual conversion. The source of nothingness and the source of being (that is, the real as being attached to its *raison d'être*) is man himself. The problem of his existence as person is the problem of his freedom and its use.[42]

It is in this context that we must understand Bastide's interpretation of the *Cogito* as a real spiritual conversion and a consequent transformation of values. There has been a *change of orders* and not just a simple passage from the false objectivity of empirical exteriority (which produced the crisis of the doubt) to an equally erroneous solipsistic interiority. Bastide sees the *Cogito* as a discovery of the self as a personal, spiritual being, infallibly able to resist (if willed) the powers of dissolution (empirical attitude represented by the evil spirit) and, at the same time, to understand (in the idea) its vocation of being called to perfection. The *Cogito* is an experience of immanence, but not the immanence of solipsism; it is rather the immanence of the spiritual person that is at one and the same time vocation and transcendence.[43]

The affirmation of God in the third *Méditation* is not, says Bastide, an escape from solipsism or a final clean sweep of the evil spirit. For the evil spirit, says Bastide, is really the place of our alienation, the object of our temptation (to realism) and the cause and effect of our sin (the dislocation of the spiritual values). The affirmation of God, seen in the ethical context which is coloring the whole of Bastide's reflection, is the affirmation of the interior transcendence opened up in the spiritual conversion. The idea of the God "deceiver" of the third meditation is the idea of God formed by the uncritical mixture of the ideas I have of corporeal things with the idea of God. It is because of the evil spirit (consciousness in its unconverted state) that there is falsity in the intellect and error in the will. In other words, it seems that for Bastide, what Descartes is doing in the third *Méditation* is not simply trying to ground knowledge of something outside himself (although this is Descartes' method of questioning himself, just as the evil spirit was a certain obstacle presented to thought), but trying to establish once and for all the *idea of Perfection* present in the *Cogito*. Descartes is attempting to discover the ultimate source of value (Value itself) as regards the intelligible ideas, that is, the ultimate assurance of the authenticity of the activity of the spirit when it is employed in the analysis and the constitution of its ideas and the continually expanding relations made possible by them. It is not so much a question of finding an idea which will force me to go out of myself

[42] Cf. G. Bastide, "Le malin génie," p. 239.
[43] Cf. G. Bastide, "The Metaphysical Dimensions," p. 358.

into a world of existence. It is rather a question of discovering the ultimate *raison d'être* of all the *raisons d'être* that the reflexive consciousness can say of things in the act of judgment.

The problem of error coupled with the existence of God that is discussed by Descartes in the fourth *Méditation* leads us into another aspect of Bastide's interpretation of the *Cogito*. If the God, who cannot deceive, is the guarantee for the eternal truths, how is it that error is possible? [44] Descartes solves the problem by showing that the idea of the infinite is not only a positive and real idea of God, but also a negative idea, that of nothingness, that of being at an infinite distance from his Perfection.[45] This is a central idea, as we shall see, in Bastide's own *Cogito*, "consciousness exists, and I am its witness." Man, in so far as he participates in non being, is subject to error. The opposition of being and non-being is represented in man by the dualism of the twofold character of understanding and will, the latter being the infinite power of freedom by which man is the image of God,[46] the understanding, as a power of passive receptivity, representing man's finiteness.[47] For there are degrees of understanding (between the clear and distinct ideas and the mixed ideas wherein the intelligible qualities are confused with the sensible qualities); [48] the will (as a faculty of assent or denial), in giving assent or denial to what is not clear and distinct, becomes the source of error.[49]

Only the knowledge of the eternal truths gained in the spiritual conversion makes possible the authenticity of action. For the discovery of the *Cogito*, maintains Bastide, is a discovery of the God who is immanent (thus assuring the value of spiritual activity) and transcendent (as the goal of perfection yet to be conquered). The effort of the spiritual conversion (turning from the empirical values to the spiritual values) is the continual effort required of my freedom. "The consciousness of this responsibility is the meaning of my freedom." [50]

The judgment, then, is the result of two causes: the understanding and the will – the former proposing, the latter disposing; the understanding conceives the ideas I can affirm or deny with my will; the understanding is susceptible of degrees, the act of the will is absolute and indivisible. This

[44] *Méditations*, IV, 3.
[45] *Ibid.*, 5.
[46] *Ibid.*, 9.
[47] *Méditations*, IV, 13.
[48] *Ibid.*, 11 and 13.
[49] *Ibid.*, 13.
[50] Cf. G. Bastide, *Les grands thèmes . . .*," p. 138.

disproportion of the two factors of judgment makes me ultimately responsible both for the errors as well as for the truth and wisdom I seek.

An example is at hand. In the "duel" between the act of doubt and the "generous affirmation of spirit" the will (the will of indifference, "the lowest degree of freedom") [51] could have assented prematurely to the doubt and fallen into error; this same liberty of indifference was the refusal of the doubt, however, and issued in the "triumphant intuition" of the Cogito.[52] The clarity of the *Cogito* is followed by an equally free inclination of the will and this new freedom, "never indifferent," [53] becomes the ideal of autonomy.

The *de facto* union of will and understanding in error (therefore without value), or their separation in doubt, is opposed to their perfect union *de facto* and *de jure* as experienced in the *Cogito* and guaranteed by God. The subsequent search for wisdom and autonomy (the accord of will and clear ideas) is an imitation of God himself, "in whom it is one and the same thing to understand, to will and to create." [54]

Bastide follows closely this itinerary of Descartes in the fourth *Meditation.* He regards it as "one of the most profound descriptions of the spiritual activity." [55] It is in the fourth meditation, he insists, that the personal character of the *Cogito* is seen in its true fulness, that is, not only as the rejection of empirical individualism, but also as the assertion of a free will, than which "nothing is more personal." The *Cogito* is perceived in the *dubito,* the suspension of which is a free act of the will and not just a negative absence of the clear ideas. This is the real ground of Bastide's own moral idealism. He seeks "like Descartes" a practical intellectualism and a speculative voluntarism.[56] Speculative voluntarism – because of the necessity of will in knowledge; practical intellectualism – because of the necessity of the presence of intelligence in authentic action. "From this point of view there is no automatic knowledge; science is to be gained by an effort of the will." [57] For it is the will alone which can make the spirit pure and at attention.[58] The will exercises its function in the *dubito,* by a constant critique of the merely given in exteriority; it renders the spirit attentive by the continual

[51] *Méditations,* IV, 9.
[52] B. Bastide, *Les grands thèmes,* p. 139.
[53] *Méditations* IV, 9.
[54] R. Descartes, *Les principes de la philosophie,* ed. by P. Lemaire, Paris (A. Hatier), 1933, p. 42 (I., 23).
[55] G. Bastide, *La conversion spirituelle,* p. 89.
[56] Cf. G. Bastide, *Les grands thèmes,* p. 140.
[57] Cf. G. Bastide, *Les grands thèmes,* p. 140.
[58] *Méditations* IV, 15.

tension of reflection (spiritual conversion and transfiguration of values) by which every clear idea is made to share the certitude of the *Cogito.*[59] In this context science is regarded as a work of the spirit freely building its thoughts in the methodical chain of ideas.

The whole moral effort of man, then, must be directed toward the union of the will and the understanding through the sciences and philosophy. "The separation of my understanding and my will is my fault and their union is my work." [60] This is the central theme of Bastide's axiological idealism. It finds its origin here in Descartes' theory of liberty and is again supported in Kant's philosophy. The vocation of man is to use the very obstacles of his human condition in order to rise, degree by degree, to that perfect autonomy where the idea that determines our action is the product of that autonomy which aims at attaining itself. The ideal of Descartes and Brunschvicg – "regard the highest and look to the most just" – is the mark of Bastide's philosophy as well.[61]

In conclusion, there are two Cartesian moralities which eventually find their meaning in the life of the spirit.[62] Once having obtained the "correct order" (the order of the spiritual values and the order of person) guaranteed by the metaphysical certitudes (the Cogito as spiritual conversion and the transformation of values) man is ready to carry out his search for truth in the self-mastery of self and the conquest of nature. "By science for the sake of wisdom." Bastide's own vision can be compared to Descartes' tree of knowledge. It seeks to have its roots in metaphysics and its goal the "most perfect moral . . . which is the highest degree of wisdom." [63]

Metaphysics becomes Ethics,[64] and that Ethics is an employment of the reflexive method in an ever greater extension of scientific knowledge that comes, finally, to coincide with the moral good.[65] Nothing is certain except the fact that reason (practical reason) is *the* worker and the work,[66] the

[59] "The three moments of reflection on being – the ideal being of the mathematical idea, the real being of human thought, the necessary being of the divine – mark the three moments of progress in consciousness which Descartes accomplishes within one and the same intuition." L. Brunschvicg, *Ecrits philosophiques,* I, Paris, 1951, p. 46.

[60] G. Bastide, *Les grands thèmes,* p. 141.

[61] Cf. G. Bastide, "Leon Brunschvicg, Lecteur de Descartes et de Pascal," *Revue Internationale de Philosophie,* 1951 (51), p. 98.

[62] Cf. G. Bastide, *Les grands thèmes,* p. 142.

[63] R. Descartes, *Les principes de la philosophie, op. cit.,* p. 27 of preface.

[64] Cf. G. Bastide, "De la situation de l'homme et des fonctions de la philosophie," in *Les philosophes français d'aujourd'hui,* textes recueillis par G. Deledalle et D. Huisman, Paris, 1963, p. 256.

[65] Cf. G. Bastide, *Les grands thèmes,* p. 144.

[66] Cf. G. Bastide, *De la condition humaine,* p. 8.

source of wisdom and truth in the minds and hearts of men. It is man who must, by the correct use of reason and will, "give value to values" in the ever greater convergence of truth.[67] Full rein is given to a *moral of invention*. There is, to be sure, a moral of retrospection. But it works in the human condition, building on it, "not as a source of value but as an empirical trampline of my activity in the world." [68]

Bastide's reflections on the moral philosophy of Descartes inspire his own effort to weave a path between axiological subjectivism (creation of values) and objectivism, a morality of pure intention and a morality that is empirical. The first movement of retrospection is an effort to interiorize the given for myself, so that, having won back my alienation in spiritual conversion, I can give myself as person in the life of the spirit. Bastide makes his own the vision of Descartes in which the love and gift of self to the God of Perfection is not an alienation but a realization of oneself.[69]

II. The influence of Kant

The originality of Kant lies especially in the extent of the implications that critical philosophy begins to have due to the *Critique of Pure Reason*. The essence of Kant's critical method is the reflexive analysis of the spirit, beginning with its acts. This method "passed from Kant to Lachelier and Brunschvicg. It became the proper method of the critique of knowledge for the idealists." [70]

This method opened up, eventually, into a doctrine of spirit, its absolute spontanity, its free activity and autonomy, as a power for unity and an infinite possibility of progress in interiority and consciousness by way of reflection. All three critiques have a certain influence on Bastide's axiological idealism, but the moral philosophy of Kant seems to have had the greatest importance for Bastide. And not without reason.

It is not our purpose here to discuss the relationship between Kant and Descartes. Bastide tends to bring them together to support his own philosophy in those areas where comparison can be most fruitful to his own meditations. Above all Bastide emphasizes the reflexive method and the notion

[67] "That we have to give value to values, according to an ideal of total convergence of what is true, useful and good; that this convergence can only be the work of man, realizing in himself by virtue of the clarity of his ideas the coming together of understanding and will in the unity of the person: such are the principles of the great moral philosophy." G. Bastide, *Les grands thèmes*, p. 145.

[68] *Ibid.*, p. 149.

[69] G. Bastide, *Les grands thèmes*, p. 149.

[70] R. Verneaux, *op. cit.*, p. 297.

of autonomy which he finds supported by both Descartes and Kant, even though it is clear that the analytical method of Kant is not the mathematical, synthetic method of Descartes. Bastide's own critique of Kant, as well as that of Brunschvicg and the other idealists, touches essential points of Kant's philosophy, so that in the end we have a reflexive method that has gone far beyond Kant and, in a sense, hearkened back to Descartes.

The direct heritage of Descartes' philosophy was the classical rationalism of Malebranche, Spinoza and Leibniz. The real was regarded as intrinsically rational. For this reason the rationalists claimed that existential judgments could be analytic *a priori*. Kant accepted the notion of this kind of thinking for the intelligible world, but not for the world of sense. Kant broke with rationalism by rejecting the idea of a universal mathematical method as well as the passage from the order of the possible to the order of being, that is, to being as real. Metaphysics was to be sought, if possible, in another direction. Kant also broke with rationalism (the intellectualism of Leibniz) by a radical distinction between the sensibility (intuition) and the understanding, the difference being one not only of clarity, but of origin. But the very formality of the metaphysical method and the notion of sensation leave us still on this side of intellectualism when compared to more realist approaches to philosophy.

For Kant, then, the formal principles of sensibility and understanding are different and pertain, respectively, to different orders, the noumenal and the phenomenal. There is no way of closing the gap that exists between them (by abstraction for example). The sensibility is the receptivity of the subject by which its representational state can be affected by an object; the understanding tends to be pure spontaneous activity on the occasion of experience. It can of itself only represent the pure ideas (the idea of necessity and substance for example). The legitimate use of these touches the heart of the critical problem.[71]

In the *Critique of Pure Reason* Kant shows that these ideas make experience possible, but do not give a knowledge of the noumenal world. Know-

[71] "Thus all controversy in regard to the nature of the thinking being and its connection with the corporeal world is merely a result of filling the gap where knowledge is wholly lacking to us with paralogisms of reason, treating our thoughts as things and hypostatising them. Hence originates an imaginary science, imaginary both in the case of him who affirms and of him who denies, since all parties either suppose some knowledge of objects of which no human being has any concept ... nothing but the sobriety of a critique, at once strict and just, can free us from this dogmatic illusion ... such a critique confines all our speculative claims rigidly to the field of possible experience ... by an effective determining of these limits (of reason) in accordance with established principles ..." Immanuel Kant, *Critique of Pure Reason,* translated with an introduction by Norman Kemp Smith, New York, 1958, p. 200 (A. 395).

ledge is ultimately limited in the speculative area to the phenomenal world, the world as it appears to us and affects us. The reason for this is that the formal principles of the sensible world are structures of our subjectivity, the formal principles of the world in itself are not.[72] Since the intuited *a priori* forms of sensibility (space and time) limit already the field of knowledge, the notion of science (rational science) is limited to the sciences based on perception (space and time categories), namely, geometry, arithmatic and physics. The idealist prejudice against Ontology is greatly confirmed with Kant's critical method.

The knowledge of the intelligible world seems impossible, for how can the pure ideas be synthesized with the intelligible world they are aimed at? For the ideas do not produce their object of themselves nor is reason, according to Kant, affected by the world.[73]

In the physical sciences it was reason that questioned nature by determining beforehand the *a priori* laws (*a priori* synthetic judgments) to which nature corresponds. The *possibility* of these *a priori* synthetic judgments (transcendental knowledge, *a priori* knowledge of objects) is also the very question of the possibility of metaphysics, since it concerns its foundations.[74] Kant's critique concerns the essence and limits of pure reason (that is, reason as unmixed with empirical elements).

The transcendental critique, then, proceeds to examine the two aspects of knowledge, the reality as given and the *a priori* judgments. These two examinations constitute the transcendental aesthetics and the transcendental logic. The question is to determine how the intuited (sensible) is finally

[72] "All synthetic *a priori* principles are nothing more than principles of possible experience. The synthetic *a priori* principles can never refer to anything more than mere phenomena and can only represent that which makes experience in general possible, or which, inasmuch as experience is derived from these principles, must always be capable of being represented in some possible experience." I. Kant, *Prolegomena,* translated by C. Friedrich and published in *The Philosophy of Kant, Immanuel Kant's Moral and Political Writings,* ed. by C. Friedrich, New York, 1949, p. 85, 30.

[73] "Metaphysics has to do not only with concepts of nature which invariably have an application in experience, but also with pure rational concepts which can never be related to any possible experience. Therefore metaphysics has to do with concepts whose objective reality and with assertions whose truth or falsity cannot be confirmed or discovered by any experience." *Id.,* p. 93, 40.

[74] "For pure mathematics and pure natural science do not require a deduction such as we have just concluded for their own security and certainty; for pure mathematics rests upon its own evidence while pure natural science, though arising from the pure sources of the intellect, is dependent upon complete verification by experience... Both these sciences did not require the foregoing investigation for their own sake, but for the sake of another science, metaphysics... the comprehension of these rules (a priori rules of consciousness), which is independent of experience, belongs to the speculative understanding... Metaphysics is exclusively occupied with this latter kind of knowledge..." *Id.* pp. 93 and 115, 40 and the conclusion.

brought under the judgment, thus yielding knowledge. In the transcendental logic Kant determines the conditions of *a priori* knowledge (transcendental analytic) and abuses open to the wrong use of reason (transcendental dialectic). The central problem of the Critique is the demonstration (transcendental deduction) of the legitimate use of the transcendental concepts of the understanding in their *synthetic a priori* function, that is, in *objective* knowledge. The solution Kant gives is opposed to the empirical solution: for it is the category that makes the object possible and not vice-versa.[75]

The possibility of experience (objective knowledge) is not grounded in the *a priori* forms of sensibility, since the *unity* of knowledge is more than the diversity of extension in time and space. Therefore, even perception requires more. The categories are necessary for the possibility of knowledge even on the first levels of knowing.[76] Furthermore, the unity of the categories themselves is based on the original, synthetic unity of the Cogito (pure aperception).[77] The mediation between the empirical intuitions and the categories of the understanding is worked by the immagination and the transcendental schema.[78]

The conclusion of the critique is that the sensibility *realizes* and limits the understanding (categories).[79] Without the schema the categories represent no

[75] "The intellect does not derive its laws (a priori) from nature but prescribes them to nature." *Id.*, p. 91, 36.

[76] "All the manifold, therefore, so far as it is given in a single empirical intuition, is *determined* in respect of one of the logical functions of judgment, and is thereby brought into one consciousness. Now the *categories* are just these functions of judgment, in so far as they are employed in determination of the manifold of a given intuition. Consequently, the manifold in a given intuition is necessarily subject to the categories." Kant, *Critique of Pure Reason*, B. 143, p. 98 *op. cit.*

[77] "We must therefore look yet higher for this unity, namely in that which itself contains the ground of the unity of diverse concepts in judgment, and therefore of the possibility of the understanding, even as regards its logical employment ... it must be possible for the 'I think' to accompany all my representations; ... but this representation is an act of *spontaneity*, that is, it cannot be regarded as belonging to sensibility. I call it *pure apperception*, to distinguish it from empirical apperception, or, again, *original apperception*, because it is that self-consciousness which ... cannot itself be accompanied by any further representation. The unity of this apperception I likewise entitle the *transcendental* unity of selfconsciousness ..." Kant, *Critique of Pure Reason*, B 132, p. 92-93 *op. cit.*

[78] "Obviously there must be some third thing, which is homogeneous on the one hand with the category, and on the other hand with the appearance, and which thus makes the application of the former to the latter possible. This mediating representation must be pure, that is, void of all empirical content, and yet at the same time, while it must in one respect be *intellectual*, it must in another be sensible. Such a representation is the *transcendental schema*." *Id.*, A 138, p. 108-109.

[79] "We cannot think an object save through the categories; we cannot *know* an object so thought save through intuitions corresponding to these concepts. Now all our intuitions are sensible; and this knowledge, in so far as it is given, is empirical.

object; through the schema their meaning is given by the sensibility. Therefore it is only as directed to the sensibility that the understanding can direct itself to knowledge.[80] The possibility of the *a priori* synthetic judgments (in their legitimate role) is grounded in the original synthetic unity of the Cogito which unifies the diversity of the intuition by the mediation of the schema and categories and renders experience possible. Objectivity is grounded in the *a priori* synthesis at the heart of the Cogito. But this synthesis is ordered to possible experience. The judgments of metaphysics are "illusions" precisely because they are not possible objects of experience.[81]

In Kant's philosophy, therefore, the subjectivity is a condition for the reality of the object, for there is no object except what is given in intuition, but intuition is not possible except in conjunction with the internal *a priori* forms of sensibility. The reality of the object depends on the *activity of the spirit*. The unifying activity of the spirit is by way of the pure concepts (principles of unity) and the judgment (the expression of the unifying activity of the understanding). The absolute principle of unity of the logical functions (categories) themselves is the unity of pure consciousness.[82] The spirit is the original synthetic unity of apperception.

These various lines of Kant's thought bring us, then, to the heart of what is to be understood by a philosophy of spirit. The critical idea is wholeheartedly embraced by Brunschvicg and Bastide, even though the Kantian system of categories is rejected. Philosophy becomes *critique* in all its purity.

But empirical knowledge is experience. *Consequently, there can be no a priori knowledge,* except of objects of possible experience." *Id.* B1 66, p. 103.

[80] "To *think* an object and to *know* an object are thus by no means the same thing. Knowledge involves two factors: first, the concept, through which an object in general is thought (the category); and secondly, the intuition, through which it is given. For if no intuition could be given corresponding to the concept, the concept would still indeed be a thought, so far as its form is concerned, but would be without any object, and no knowledge of anything would be possible by means of it... now as the Aesthetic has shown, the only intuition possible to us is sensible; consequently, the thought of an object in general, by means of a pure concept of understanding, can become knowledge for us only in so far as the concept is related to objects of the senses... Our conclusion is therefore this: the categories, as yielding knowledge of *things*, have no kind of application, save only in regard to things which may be objects of possible experience." *Id.*, B 146, p. 98-99 *op. cit.*

[81] "But this extension of concepts beyond our sensible intuition is of no advantage to us. For as concepts of objects they are empty, and do not even enable us to judge of their objects whether or not they are possible." *Id.*, B 148, p. 99 *op. cit.*

[82] Cf. footnote 8 above. "The synthetic unity of consiousness is, therefore, an objective condition of all knowledge. It is not merely a condition that I myself require in knowing an object, but is a condition under which every intuition must stand in order *to become an object for me*. For otherwise, in the absence of this synthesis, the manifold would not be united in one consciousness." *Id.*, B 138, pp. 95-96 *op. cit.*

Its task is to know the spirit by reflecting on its acts of knowledge.[83] Knowledge is science, but science is always on the march. Therefore the spirit is also a continual becoming.[84]

Besides rejecting the Kantian categories, the idealists in France also purified the role of the sensibility, no longer making the knowledge of the spirit dependent on the existence of the thing in itself. Moreover, they reject in general the closed distinction of the two faculties (sensibility and understanding, passive faculty and spontaneous activity) in order to assert the complete autonomy of the spiritual activity itself. Modern science enabled Brunschvicg to view experience in a new way. It no longer furnishes the spirit with an objective content, but with a resistance encountered in the spirit itself, in the finite limitation of its own act. As we shall see for Bastide also, this new conception of experience and spirit, this notion of a spirit communicating with itself (without intrinsic dependence on an exterior world or on a separate and distinct faculty of sensibility) founds a new approach to reflection itself as "consciousness of consciousness," the reflexive knowledge of spirit of itself.[85]

It is by way of this route that the French Idealists make Kant, in a sense, more in accord with himself, by grounding the real primacy of the practical order. The spirit is free activity, really autonomous even in the speculative order, a virtual infinite possibility for progress. Reflection and freedom come to be the same thing.[86]

It is here in Kant's philosophy and in accord with the spirit of his transcendental idealism that is grounded the idealist notion of truth, the value factor of knowledge. The idealist notion of truth inserts itself in the Kantian notion of objective knowledge within the limits of possible experience. Concepts without application in the intuitions of sensibility are empty. A "new" conception of truth is born.[87] The idealists had only to do away with the thing in itself. Truth is no longer the accord between thought and the being of things, since the latter is never given to the subject, but only what appears, that is, the phenomenon. Truth is ultimately the accord of knowledge

[83] "Dès lors, la philosophie devient réflexion sur la conscience réfléchissante, redoublement réflexif par lequel la conscience aspire à s'éclairer elle-même dans toutes ses démarches: une philosophie de la philosophie ne peut-être qu'une philosophie de la conscience." G. Bastide, *De la condition humaine*, p. 3.

[84] "Elle est tout entière à son travail continu d'intime transformation; si elle cessait de devenir, elle cesserait d'être." *Id.*, p. 23.

[85] G. Bastide, *Méditations*, p. 1.

[86] "Moreover reflection and freedom are one and the same certitude of consciousness." G. Bastide, *Méditations*, p. 129.

[87] Cf. L. Brunschvicg, *L'Expérience humaine et la causalité physique*, Paris, 1949, p. 298.

with the subjective laws of its own constitution.[88] It is the connection of an object and a subject which mutually condition one another. In this sense are we to understand the *relativity of knowledge*.[89]

Ultimately, however, the final support for all knowledge and truth is the spirit itself.[90] For Brunschvicg and Bastide it is the spirit which constitutes being in its judgments. The problem of knowledge is to determine the validity, the value of this affirmation, that is, to determine the modality of judgment. And this must be sought in the subject giving the *raisons d'être* of its acts.[91] Being is of the ideal order. Philosophy is of necessity a philosophy of consciousness ... because it is a philosophy of man, who, by the very nature of his *human condition*, cannot leave his own subjectivity in the affirmation of the thing in itself.[92]

The *objectivity* of knowledge consists in the universal and necessary character of the *judgment of experience* (as contrasted with the judgments of perception).[93] It is the conformity of the spirit (judgment) with itself (universal laws of the mind). The norm for truth is the unity of spirit itself and of *spirits* in accord with one another. The essence of truth is the universal validity of the judgment. The spirit knows only itself, but it attains to the real in the act of judgment. Idealism becomes the way to realism.[94]

In the transcendental dialectic, Kant discusses the third element of knowledge, the *reason* or the faculty of ideas.[95] As such an idea is a notion which radically goes beyond the possibility of experience. Here Kant is made to

[88] Cf. R. Verneaux, *op. cit.*, p. 361.

[89] G. Bastide, *La conversion spirituelle*, p. 76.

[90] "But if the conditions for the existence of the phenomena are the very conditions for the possibility of thought, we overcome easily the embarrassing alternative: for, on the one hand, we can determine the conditions absolutely *a priori*, since they result from the very nature of our spirit." J. Lachelier, *Du fondement de l'induction*, Oeuvres de Jules Lachelier, Paris, 1933, p. 48.

[91] "To philosophize is to reflect and reflection is the attitude of consciousness in a subject questioning itself as to the reasons for its own being." G. Bastide, *Traité*, p. 354.

[92] "Nature cannot answer for man and man cannot answer for nature, nor does he have to." *Ibid.*, p. 630.

[93] "Empirical judgments, in so far as they have objective validity, are *judgments based on experience*; but those which are merely subjectively valid I call judgments based on perception ..." I. Kant, *Prolegomena*, 18, p. 71.

[94] In this regard Bastide often quotes Bergson: "Without playing at all on words, realism is at work when the spirit is idealist and it is only by virtue of idealism that we recover contact with reality." G. Bastide, *La conversion spirituelle*, p. 71.

[95] "Reason we shall here distinguish from understanding by entitling it the *faculty of principles*. Understanding may be regarded as a faculty which secures the unity of appearances by means of rules, and reason as being the faculty which secures the unity of the rules of understanding under principles." I. Kant, *Critique of Pure Reason*, A 302, pp. 162-163 *op. cit.*

think of Plato and *practical philosophy*, a metaphysics of action.[96] For Plato, says Kant, the ideas are especially operative causes.[97] The ideas are conditions in relation to which we judge a determined moral act, but in themselves they are unconditioned.[98] The illusory use of reason and the transcendental ideas is in believing that these yield an objective knowledge in the same way as the categories of understanding. The correct use of the ideas is *heuristic*, regulative.[99] As such they communicate *a priori* a *unity* to the different judgments of the understanding.[100] Reason is the source of all *progress* because it moves the understanding to greater and greater efforts of knowing. The idea, however, remains regulative, a simple "as if."

These reflections of Kant have been an original source, no doubt, for Bastide's axiology and for the notion of interior transcendence which he also discovers in Descartes. The interior presence of the Value of values (God), is also an absence, a Value which cannot ostensibly be shown to exist, a Value however which continues to function heuristically in the designation and orientation of man towards his authentic vocation. The *idea* of Perfection puts man on the road to grasping the ultimate unity of his person.

There is, then, a certain natural transition in idealism from the purity of the critical method to practical philosophy. Bastide's own axiological idealism asserts the primacy of practical reason; the spiritual conversion has to do with not only the faculty of knowledge, but above all the faculty of will.[101] "In the last analysis it is upon the *moral ideal* that the validity of the knowledge that consciousness can have of itself depends." [102]

[96] "Plato made use of the expression 'idea' in such a way as quite evidently to have meant by it something which not only can never be borrowed from the senses but far surpasses even the concepts of the understanding (with which Aristotle occupied himself), inasmuch as in experience nothing is ever to be met with that is coincident with it." *Id.*, B 370, p. 167 *op. cit.*

[97] *Ibid.*, p. 169-170 (316-319 A).

[98] *Ibid.*, p. 172 (A 322-323).

[99] "The principle of reason is thus properly only a rule . . . nor is it a *constitutive* principle of reason, enabling us to extend our concept of the sensible world beyond all possible experience. It is rather a principle of the greatest possible continuation and extension of experience . . . thus it is a principle of reason which serves as a rule, postulating what we ought to do in the regress, but not anticipating what is present *in the object as it is in itself, prior to all regress.* Accordingly I entitle it a *regulative* principle of reason . . ."

[100] "Reason is never in immediate relation to an object, but only to the understanding; and it is only through the understanding that it has its own specific empirical employment. It does not, therefore, *create* concepts of objects but only *orders* them, and gives them that unity which they can have only if they be employed in their widest possible application, that is, with a view to obtaining totality in the various series." *Id.*, A 643; pp. 300-301 *op. cit.*

[101] Cf. G. Bastide, *La conversion spirituelle*, pp. 72-73.

[102] Cf. G. Bastide, *La conversion spirituelle*, pp. 72-73.

The moral philosophy of Kant is found in the *Critique of Practical Reason* (especially for the method) and in the *Foundations of the Metaphysics of Morals* together with *The Metaphysics of Morals* which is divided into two parts *The Metaphysical Principles of Right* and *The Metaphysical Principles of Virtue*. All three works together give us a picture of Kant's moral philosophy.[103]

In the *Foundations* Kant seeks the "supreme principle of morality," a working principle that can be employed in our personal moral judgments and moral decisions.[104] His method is analytic (regressive) and aims at discovering the *Conditions* for ordinary moral judgments.[105] That principle is the categorical imperative, which is itself found to be the principle (*cognoscendi*) of autonomy, the ultimate principle (*essendi*) of morality. The notion of freedom, which is central to the philosophy of Bastide, follows the Cartesian notion of a liberty that is indifferent, but which, in reflection discovers the ideal of autonomy – that freedom which is never indifferent; but Bastide emphasizes also the development of the notion of autonomy as we find it in Kant's philosophy, related to the categorical imperative of duty.[106]

For Kant freedom is a transcendental idea.[107] As such it is the result of the spontaneity of Reason, that is, not restricted to or determined by the phenomenal order.[108] It is the *ratio essendi* of morality and is known by a con-

[103] In the *Critique of Practical Reason* Kant shows the unity of the speculative and practical reason under a common principle, the possibility of a synthetic *a priori* practical proposition, its real practical use as well as its limits. In the *Foundations* Kant treats especially the question of how a synthetic use of pure practical reason is possible, beginning with the phenomena of morality in order to discover its formula for action. The *Metaphysics of Morals* is more the practical system of Kant's moral philosophy. Cf. L. Beck, *A Commentary on Kant's Critique of Practical Reason*, Chicago (University of Chicago Press), 1960, pp. 46-52.

[104] Cf. H. J. Paton, *The Moral Law*, Kant's Groundwork of the Metaphysics of Morals, translated and analysed by H. J. Paton, London (Hutchinson University Library), 1966 (first printing in 1948), p. 57.

[105] *Id.*, p. 58. "None the less by mere analysis of the concepts of morality we can quite well show that the above principle of autonomy is the sole principle of ethics." I. Kant, *Foundations*, 88, p. 102 *op. cit.*

[106] Cf. G. Bastide, *Traité*, I., p. 152.

[107] "I understand by idea a necessary concept of reason to which no corresponding object can be given in sense experience. Thus the pure concepts of reason, now under consideration, are *transcendental ideas* ... they are imposed by the very nature of reason itself, and therefore stand in necessary relation to the whole employment of understanding ... metaphysics has as the proper object of its inquiries three ideas only: God, freedom and immortality ..." Kant, *Critique of Pure Reason*, A 327, A 337 (Cf. footnote a), pp. 174, 177 *op. cit.*

[108] "Since the mere form of the law can only be conceived by reason and consequently is not an object of the senses and does not belong to the class of phenomena,

sideration of duty (ratio cognoscendi).[109] Autonomy is a limit never attained in fact since it is a *variable function* with obedience to duty. It is the validity of the principle of autonomy which validates the imperative, and the problem of the *Critique of Practical Reason* is to firmly establish the former in its source in pure practical reason.

Can reason be practical? Can purely rational considerations (independent of facts of experience) be normative, not only of knowledge, but of action as well? The second *Critique* has the task of proving that pure reason does have a real use in practice and not just a logical use in the organisation of our experience for the sake of pragmatic success. Kant is asking, with regards to morality now, if morality as a metaphysics can exist or whether it must be reduced to one of the sciences.

The possibility of acting on a categorical imperative is equivalent to the possibility of an action that is not determined by the empirical order, one not moved by naive faith in what constitutes happiness.[110] The justification of the principle of autonomy and the possibility of a categorical imperative would provide the necessary proof for a strictly moral activity in its own right. For Kant, being morally right (like the objective knowledge of the first *Critique*) is based on the respect for the moral standards which the intelligence sets for itself. The categorical imperative defines the universally necessary criteria.

The parallel between knowledge and morality is worthy of note, since it comes up again in Bastide's philosophy.[111] Because there is no "intellectual

it follows that the idea of the law which determines the will is distinct from all the principles that determine events in nature according to the law of causality because in the case of the latter the determining facts must themselves be phenomena. If no determining principle can serve as a law for the will other than the universal legislative form, such a will must be conceived as wholly independent of the natural law of phenomena in their mutual relation, the law of causality. Such independence is called *freedom* in the strictest sense, that is in the transcendental sense. Consequently a will that receives its law from nothing but the mere legislative form of the maxim is a free will." I. Kant, "Critique of Pure Practical Reason" in *The Philosophy of Kant*, 5, problem 1, p. 220 *op. cit*.

[109] "The independent warrant of the moral law, which is the *ratio cognoscendi* of freedom, is the fact of pure reason. The independent warrant of the concept of freedom, the *ratio essendi* of the law, is found in its theoretical use." L. Beck, *op. cit.*, p. 174.

[110] "The sole principle of morality consists in moral law being independent of all substantive considerations such as a desired object; it thus consists in the accompanying determining of the will by the mere general legislating form of which its maxim must be capable." I. Kant, "Critique of Pure Practical Reason" in *The Philosophy of Kant*, 8 Theorem 4, p. 226 *op. cit*.

[111] For Kant the theoretical and practical reason are a unity, differing only in their applications. The Kantian distinction between reason and understanding highlights the task of practical reason to go beyond the order of things, as given, to an ideal

intuition" in Kant's philosophy, knowledge is dependent on the autonomy of the intelligence like morality is. To attain the true, as we have seen, is to judge *for truth's sake* according to standards which the intelligence autonomously determines for itself in the act of judgment. The reasons for respecting truth (truth itself) parallel the reason for being moral (duty as such, autonomy itself). In this sense autonomy cannot be denied and is considered established.[112] For even the denial of the autonomy of the intelligence (if it makes *sense*) is an endorsement of it – at least in what we are doing, if not in what we say.

Kant's ethics of autonomy, then, provides a bridge between two extremes: moral rationalism (of the Wolffian variety, where the law of nature is sovereign over man and is discovered by reason) and moral empiricism. Just as Kant had reversed the order of things on the speculative level, so here on the practical level. The source of the moral law is in autonomous reason.[113]

order of a systematic connection of experience, an object of *search* according to the *regulative* ideas. For Kant reason is spontaneous in formulating ideas that can never be adequately represented in our sense experience of the actual, even though this is categorized by the understanding. The understanding is restricted to a re-working of what is or can be given in perception.

[112] Whatever needs to draw the proof of its existence from experience must depend on principle of experience for the grounds of its possibility. Pure, yet practical, reason cannot be regarded as being so derived by its very concept. Furthermore, moral law is given as a fact by pure reason of which we are conscious *a priori* and which is apodictically certain, even though it is granted that no example of its exact fulfilment can be found in experience. Hence the objective reality of moral law cannot be proved through a deduction by any efforts on the part of theoretical reason, whether speculative or supported empirically. Therefore even if we renounced its apodictic certainty, it could not be proved by experience *a posteriori*. Yet the objective reality of moral law is firmly established by itself." I. Kant, "Critique of Pure Practical Reason," *op. cit.*, p. 239. The proof provided by the Critique is necessarily indirect, since it is itself the first principle of an entire area of knowledge (e.g. a practical system of morality) that needs to be established.

[113] "Kant's ethics, historically represents a transition between two great conceptions of the relation of man to the world. Against the eighteenth-century position that man is a part of nature and ought to be subservient to her laws, Kant reacted by inverting the order and making nature what she is because of how she appears to us. Then he transcended even this Copernican venture by daring to weigh nature in the scales of reason and to declare that she is wanting and does not contain the destiny of man. The practical – what man ought to be and how he ought to transform his existence – in this conception takes precedence over what nature is and what she demands of man as part of her order. Nature produced man but brought him to the stage where he can finally assert his independence of her."

Continuation of this development of the theory of the creative self is found in romanticism. For the romanticists, man stands above nature as her author and judge; but the judge has lost his law. The universality of law, which is Kant's heritage from the rationalists and naturalists of the seventeenth and eighteenth centuries, was maintained and even magnified by him, though he anchored it in the abstractly personal, in the *res cogitans*." L. Beck, *Commentary*, p. 125 *op. cit.*

The moral law obliges not only because it is *for* man, but also because it is *by* man. As such the practical order is beyond the order of nature and defines man's transcendent destiny – even though that destiny cannot be ostensibly defined or explained.[114] The practical – what man ought to be and how he ought to transform his existence – *takes precedence* over what nature is and what nature demands of man as part of her order.[115] The whole ideal of Bastide's philosophy is contained here.

This notion, found in Kant's *Idea for a Universal History*, is prominent in Bastide's philosophy of spiritual conversion where, as we previously noted, the state of naive faith (the original state of every man) is necessary, but only as the battleground, as it were, for acquiring the new faith of spiritual conversion. Nature is regulative of knowledge and practice, occasionally as it were; for it is not essential that action be identical, but that the different actions of men under the same maxim (or in the same spiritual conversion) are not in conflict (regulative principle of freedom) and even more, that they reciprocally promote each other (constitutive principle of freedom.)[116] What is important is that men impart to the sensible world the form of a system of rational beings (*raisons d'être*). Morality must be thought of in terms of this regulative function of nature.[117] Interaction mutually promotive of the spiritual values is the important thing, not uniformity of action.[118] The intelligible or supersensuous world is nothing more than the world of nature considered under the autonomy of practical reason.

Just as in the *Critique of Pure Reason* Kant had proceeded to show the necessary laws of the mind as necessary conditions for the validity of the

[114] "And thus while we do not comprehend the practical unconditioned necessity of the moral imperative, we do comprehend its *incomprehensibility*. This is all that can fairly be asked of a philosophy which presses forward in its principles to the very limit of human reason." I. Kant, *Foundations*, conclusion, p. 123 *op. cit.*

[115] "The discrepancy between what reason demands and what experience presents – this unsatisfied demand of theoretical reason – appears as the practical interest in the reign of a rational law that does not actually reign in nature." L. Beck, *Commentary*, p. 124, *op. cit.*

[116] "The regulative principle of freedom: that the actions do not conflict; the constitutive principle: that they reciprocally promote each other for the purpose of happiness." I. Kant, Reflexion 7251, cited by Beck, *op. cit.*, p. 99.

[117] "This Idea is that of a realm of ends, organized by the third category of practical relation, that of community of persons under common law, the whole being a *corpus mysticum* of rational beings. Such a world is archetypal, and the Idea of it 'determines our will to impart to the sensuous world the form of a system of rational beings.' This regulative conception of nature, believed by almost all eighteenth-century philosophers to describe the actual cosmos, is the model for our thought of the moral realm." L. Beck, *Commentary*, p. 161. Cf. I. Kant, A 808.

[118] This will be taken up again in our final chapter when we discuss Bastide's notion of understanding.

sciences, so in the *Critique of Practical Reason* he uses the moral law, the fact of reason,[119] as the undeniable starting point and *ratio cognoscendi* to conclude to autonomy. Freedom, an Idea of reason, is the given principle [120] and fills the role played by intuition in the first *Critique*.[121] For the fact of the pure practical reason (a synthetic *a priori* judgment) is the ground for the deduction of freedom, but the idea of freedom is also the credential of the moral law (but not in the same order, thus avoiding the vicious circle). For the moral law (moral consciousness, consciousness of duty) is the fact of pure reason; the concept of freedom can confirm the moral law because of its *theoretical use* where it is not only a possibility, but a *requirement of thought itself*.[122] That is, the fact of pure practical reason is precisely of the form required if the dialectic of theoretical reason is not to be irresolvable. The Idea of freedom, required but not confirmed in the first *Critique*, is confirmed practically in the second *Critique* through the fact of pure reason and the primacy of moral philosophy is established.

In this way, Kant could conclude eventually to the contrast (rather than harmony) between the *two orders* of science and morality, a synthesis being grounded only in *the nature of man* himself (or as Bastide would put it, in the human condition). It is *man*, not nature, which merits first of all the title of sublime and the absolute respect accorded to the person. The universality of reason makes man pass not only from moral empiricism, but also from moral individualism, to the condition of the person. Again we have a central theme of Bastide's philosophy with its roots in both the Kantian critique and in his own moral philosophy.

For Kant the notion of *person* is intimately related to the noumenon self

[119] "Moral law is given as a fact by pure reason of which we are conscious *a priori* . . ." I. Kant, "Critique of Pure Practical Reason" in the *Philosophy of Kant*, p. 289, *op. cit.*

[120] "For in the present case, we shall commence with *principles* and proceed to concepts, and only then, if possible, come to the senses. Whereas, in the case of speculative reason we began with the senses and had to end with the principles." *Id.* p. 210-211 (from the Introduction to the *Critique*).

[121] "A good will (sc. a pure practical reason) which has as its maxims only universal laws" is claimed to be a synthetic *a priori* judgment, for "by analysis of the concept of an absolutely good will, that property of the maxim cannot be found." How, then, can it be confirmed? Not by finding an intuition (which would be the obvious step in theoretical philosophy) but by *adducing some substitute for intuition*. It must be purely intellectual, and therefore a moral sense will not suffice. It must be *a priori* for otherwise the synthetic judgment would not be *a priori*. And it must, like intuition, have an *independent warrent*; that is, it must not be just a product of the thought it is to justify. This third thing, this substitute for intuition, is the Idea of freedom." L. Beck, *Commentary*, p. 173, *op. cit.*

[122] Cf. note 109.

under the imperative of autonomy. Free action must be related to person as agent, even though we can have no theoretical knowledge of this reality in itself. Acts have consequences for the state of the person. Respect for the law and respect for person go hand in hand. Personality is precisely that freedom from the mechanism of nature through a capacity to be subject to laws given by and for the person in autonomy. Man's dignity is grounded here. The phenomenologist interpretation of the self tends to be transcended "in a metaphysical personalism and activism, since the spontaneity felt in self-consciousness separates man from nature." [123] Such a metaphysics tends to be a metaphysics of action and we shall see this trend become thematic in Bastide's axiological idealism.[124] Bastide's own axiological interpretation of person as value seems to be, in part, grounded here in Kant's philosophy.

We can conclude this section on Kant's moral philosophy by a brief summary of the Kantian notion of faith, since this notion also plays an important part in Bastide's philosophy, being as it is a philosophy of value. As we have seen, the practical propositions of the moral law (coming from the imperative) have their corresponding object which is known, but not apodictically. The moral imperative demands an action, but this action is related to not only the possibility of such an action, but also to the subjective belief in this possibility. The doing and the recognition of what I ought to do are tied up with belief – since objective proof (theoretical and apodictic) is not possible. Rational belief is the epistemic mode of grasping the postulates of practical reason. With Kant there is a philosophical faith incorporated into philosophy itself. Belief, for Kant, is assent on grounds that are subjectively sufficient (therefore more than opinion) but objectively insufficient. Rational belief is based, as we have seen, on reason's needs for the satisfaction of duty.

Faith serves to orientate man beyond experience. Evidently, in Kant's philosophy a principle of orientation is needed especially in those matters which take man beyond possible experience. Faith, then, is a faith in the objects of practical reason. As such, it is "subjective," but not arbitrary or contingent. For the employment of reason has its *natural ends,* even though its *merely* natural use can involve man in illusions.[125] It was precisely to give

[123] L. Beck, *Commentary,* p. 226.

[124] "Meanwhile we may still retain the concept of personality – just as we have retained the concept of substance and of the simple – in so far as it is merely transcendental, that is, concerns the unity of the subject, otherwise unknown to us, in the determinations of which there is a thoroughgoing connection through apperception. Taken in this way, the concept is necessary for practical employment and is sufficient for such use." I. Kant, *Critique of Pure Reason,* A. 364, 366, p. 191-192 *op. cit.*

[125] Cf. I. Kant, *Prolegomena,* 59 and 60, pp. 106-107 *op. cit.*

reason full scope for development that Kant had to "deny knowledge in order to make room for faith." [126] The absence of knowledge of the supersensible leaves room for the mystery of God and man, while the respect for law introduces us into the presence of both. It is precisely the precariousness of "not knowing God but believing in his existence" that constitutes the dramatic character of the human condition and leaves room for the "merit" of spiritual conversion and the "effort" of the generous will. Bastide centers his own philosophy in this direction, but he seeks, it seems, to give them a more metaphysical foundation by placing them in the interior transcendence of Descartes' *Cogito.*

The third *Critique*, the *Critique of Judgment*, also presents certain important aspects worthy of note in reference to the philosophy of Georges Bastide. We are here interested in the faculty of judgment.

The importance of the judgment is necessarily central to a philosophy of spirit, the knowledge of whose *structure* is the principal goal of the *Critiques.* This is why Kant's philosophy is more a critique rather than a theory.[127] But critique is essentially a method.

Secondly the third *Critique* tends to approach one of the central problems of philosophy and certainly a central concern for Bastide, namely, the passage from the theoretic to the practical, from scientific knowledge to liberty.[128] In this problematic we find Kant's notion of the *judgment as reflection.* For previously, in the first critique, the judgment was considered in its role of subsuming the sensible intuitions under the pure concepts of the understanding.[129] This role is named "determinative judgment" in the third *Critique* to distinguish it from a new role of judgment, the "reflective judgment." [130] The particular laws of phenomena cannot be wholly derived from the categories and must be supposed by the understanding in its reflexive function. Here, instead of determining the object, the power of understanding turns from the object *towards itself* in order to determine a *new* law of

[126] Cf. I. Kant, *Critique of Pure Reason,* preface to the second edition, B xxx-xxxi, p. 22 *op. cit.*

[127] Cf. J. Meredith, *Immanuel Kant, The Critique of Judgment* translated by J. Meredith, Oxford University Press, London, 1964 (reprinting), p. 7.

[128] *Ibid.,* p. 38.

[129] "How then is the *subsumption* of intuitions under pure concepts, the *application* of a category to appearances, possible? A transcendental doctrine of judgment is necessary ..." I. Kant, *Critique of Pure Reason,* A 138, p.p. 108 *op. cit.*

[130] "Judgment in general is the faculty of thinking the particular as contained under the universal. If the universal (the rule, principle or law) is given, then the judgment which subsumes the particular under it is *determinant* ... If, however, only the particular is given and the universal has to be found for it, then the judgment is simply *reflective.*" I. Kant, *The Critique of Judgment,* Introduction, 179-180, p. 18 *op. cit.*

thought. The laws of thought are determined in the spirit, and it is these laws that permit "knowledge" of the subject. But in reality the principle of this knowledge remains wholly subjective.[131] That is, it remains contingent, but conceived as necessary. Like the ideas of the first *Critique* the reflexive judgment is regulative rather than constitutive of knowledge.

Experience, therefore, is in a purely negative role, the role of obstacle, occasion, even (as we shall see for Bastide) alienation. It is the dynamism and autodetermination of the spirit which reflects and invents the laws of thought.

In this framework science becomes the intelligible organization of facts by the laws determined by reflection on the occasion of experience. Philosophy is wholly a method, a critique, for *reflection is only regulative,* not constitutive. It is cognizant only of its own dynamism in the act of creating knowledge.

Therefore the *truth* of judgment in the final critique approaches the ideal of a spirit which is eminently *inventive,* that is, not concerned with any concept of nature or the possibility of the object. At the same time the spirit is in *harmony* with itself. It is not pure arbitrariness. *The objectivity of judgment is grounded in the accord of the faculties in their free play.* This objectivity is neither constitutive nor necessary, but *free* and *fruitful,* productive of the mutual harmony among men that is the goal of genuine morality.[132] Truth is seen, in this light, as being actively created by men in their spiritual works. For it is the *constitution of these works* that enables consciousness to become *aware of itself* in its free activity and interior harmony. The aesthetic intuition is one with the intuition of the spirit's own activity.[133] Here we find in Kant's philosophy what constitutes the central theme of the French idealism of Brunschvicg and Bastide, namely the immanence of the person who finds himself in spiritual conversion and in the spiritual activities of the spirit. But again, it is to Descartes, especially, that Bastide has recourse in order to find at the same time that this intimate presence of personal interiority is also the real presence of the highest transcendence.[134]

In this Bastide differs from Lachelier and Brunschvicg who tend to bring the immediate consciousness of our activity to its absolute conclusions in the assertion of perfect immanence (without transcendence) of the spirit to

[131] I. Kant, *Critique of Judgment,* Introduction, 185-186, p. 25 *op. cit.*

[132] "The assertion is not that everyone *will* fall in with our judgment, but rather that everyone *ought* to agree with it." I. Kant, Id., 22, p. 84 *op. cit.* Cf. *Critique of Pure Reason*: "The practical idea, therefore, is always in the highest degree fruitful, and its relation to our actual activities is indispensibly necessary." A. 328, p. 175 *op. cit.*

[133] Cf. R. Verneaux, *op. cit.,* p. 447.

[134] Cf. G. Bastide, *Traité* I., p. 724.

itself in the works of science and over the course of history. In this Brunschvicg is a descendent through Fichte and Spinoza with whom "idealism is definitely grounded on the notion of spiritual activity." [135] For Brunschvicg, the activity of spirit "par excellence" is the judgment.

In the last analysis, therefore, we have a view of nature as solliciting the efforts of the human spirit to greater and greater progress. It is the spirit's becoming aware of its own activity that founds the laws and knowledge of the world.

III. Summary

We have proposed to discuss in this first chapter certain points of reference for Bastide's philosophy in the philosophies of Descartes and Kant. In many ways contemporary French philosophy of spirit and reflection are continuations and developments of the philosophical spirit engendered by Descartes and Kant. The nature of philosophy as critique and as a spiritual conversion orientating philosophy towards the subject remain essentially in tact as received from Descartes. The "native" direction of the spirit towards a "naive realism" becomes reversed. Philosophy becomes first and foremost an analysis of the *Cogito,* its nature, activities and the conditions of its existence and exercise. The metaphysical work of Bastide, his own *Meditations* follows this order of analysis, with emphasis on axiology and spiritual personalism. At all times idealism remains his principle orientation.[136] The spirit becomes aware of its own dynamic development through its activities.

Bastide's own constant critique of the realist position is essentially grounded in the twofold critique of Descartes as regards sense knowledge and knowledge by way of concept. Knowledge of the world is approached indirectly by way of the spirit.[137] The original contact with being as the proper object of the intellect, as well as the theory of abstraction, are rejected for a philosophy of spirit in its free autonomy and spontaneous activity. In short, metaphysics as Ontology is deemed an illusion. Philosophy is wholly an analysis of the knowing subject, especially according to the model of the science of mathematics.[138] Eventually, as we shall see, these elements are made to serve a new and wider synthesis in a philosophy of value, "where

[135] R. Verneaux, *op. cit.*, p. 448. It is especially from Spinoza that Brunschvicg disengages the theme of the spirit's *progressive creation* of science. Cf. *Id.*, p. 393. Bastide follows Brunschvicg's lead in this.

[136] Cf. G. Bastide, *De la condition humaine*, pp. 375-391.

[137] Cf. G. Bastide, *Le moment historique de Socrate,* Paris, Alcan, 1939, p. 232.

[138] Cf. G. Bastide, *Le moment historique de Socrate,* Paris, Alcan, 1939, p. 133. This will appear more clearly in our discussion of the judgment of relation which Bastide makes central to his philosophy, following Descartes and Brunschvicg.

metaphysics becomes ethics following the imperishable model of Spinoza: ethics of the comprehensive activity itself, the redoubling of reflection upon itself, knowledge of the idea, or, what comes down to the same thing, knowledge of the value of values, whereby is effected a passage to the third grade of knowledge ethically connected with that third kind of life which is, properly speaking, the life of the spirit, that is, a life in spirit and truth." [139]

In Kant Bastide sees a further clarification of the reflexive method and a deepening of a philosophy of spirit. While it is true that Bastide takes exception to the regressive analysis of Kant in so far as it concluded to the *a priori* forms, thus giving a structure to human consciousness in general and, says Bastide, thereby missing the full creative dynamism of spirit,[140] nevertheless the practical philosophy of Kant puts in relief the legislating activity of spirit in its regulative and practical role, more conducive to Bastide's own concept of philosophy as an axiology and an ethical doctrine. But even to Kant's moral philosophy Bastide takes exception, again because of the prejudice of structure. The law constituting the moral order is inherent to the structure of the legislating consciousness. The truth of transcendence is compromised for the truth of immanence.[141] Bastide seeks to retain both. Spirit is, for Bastide, essentially tension, effort and is not to be identified with the footprints it has left in the course of history or with any abstract program whose course it must run. Liberty and efficacious action must not be presupposed, since they are revealed in their incarnational aspect in the act of constituting spiritual works.[142] In chapter II we will have occasion to note the mediation worked by the philosophies of Bergson and Brunschvicg between the philosophy of Kant and Bastide's axiological idealism. But even

[139] G. Bastide, *Traité*, p. 358. The philosophy of Spinoza, especially his *Ethics* and *On the Correction of the Understanding* (*De Emendatione*), serves as a particulary fruitful source of inspiration for the moral reflections of Bastide, as previously for Brunschvicg. But it is precisely because he "had learned from the humanism of Descartes" says Bastide, that his reflections are a fruitful source for meditation. Cf. 646, II *Traité*. It is this "philosophy of moral purity arising from intellectual clarity" that Bastide seeks for his own moral philosophy. Cf. *Id.*, p. 695. In general, then, Bastide finds in Spinoza the same radical affirmation of immanence of spirit, where the criterion of truth and source of truth is the spirit itself. Cf. G. Bastide, "Leon Brunschvicg, lecteur . . .," pp. 87-88. Again it is not the absolute idealism of Spinoza that Bastide accepts, but the orientation of his thought towards a spiritual conversion in a philosophy of reflection, something he already finds in Descartes. Cf. G. Bastide, "La conversion spirituelle," *Encyclopédie française*, XIX *Philosophie-religion*, Larousse, Paris, 1957. Cf. Chapter II, Sec. 2, p. 19.06-3.

[140] Cf. G. Bastide, *De la condition humaine*, pp. 297 ss.

[141] Cf. G. Bastide, *De la condition humaine*, p. 302.

[142] Cf. G. Bastide,*De la condition humaine*, pp. 302-303.

the philosophy of spirit in Brunschvicg, with its effort to restore the critical method in all its purity and independence, finds its basis, as we have noted, in the third *Critique* of Kant.[143]

[143] Cf. the conclusions of the section on Brunschvicg in the following chapter.

CHAPTER II

LEON BRUNSCHVICG AND HENRI BERGSON

In the introduction to his *Traité* Georges Bastide remarks that "it would be just to note that the orientation of our work is in the tradition of the idealism of Brunschvicg, while that of Le Senne came more directly under the influence of the idealism of Hamelin." [1] "But it is no less true," he continues, "that as far as the great names that preeceded are concerned, Maine de Biran, Ravaisson, Lachelier, Boutroux, Legneau and Bergson constitute our common heritage." [2] It is the purpose of this second chapter, then, to remark briefly the movement of French Idealism, especially as it came to be incorporated into the philosophy of Léon Brunschvicg, who, with Hamelin, represented the "principle movement" in contemporary French idealism.[3] Hamelin followed a more synthetic method, "confident in the stability of the dialectical, relational construction of nature and spirit." [4] Brunschvicg, on the other hand, followed a more analytic method, seeking the laws of the spirit and the conditions of their revelation in experience and history. The reflexive method of Georges Bastide, who had Brunschvicg as his teacher, follows Brunschvicg's approach in this regard. His own spiritual personalism and philosophy of interior transcendence, however, is a further development of Brunschvicg's philosophy of immanence.

The influence of Bergson, especially on contemporary French philosophy, has been both universal and important. Brunschvicg, whose orientation in many ways opposes Bergson's, dedicated his principle work, *le Progrès de la Conscience* to Bergson. Bergson's life philosophy has many links with French spiritualism and French idealism. His dynamic philosophy of becoming has much in common with a philosophy of spirit's self-realization in history and experience. Bastide's own axiological idealism tends to bring to-

[1] G. Bastide, *Traité*, p. 2.
[2] G. Bastide, *Traité*, p. 2.
[3] Cf. A. Etcheverry, *L'idéalisme français contemporain*, Paris, Alcan, 1934, p. 44.
[4] Cf. A. Etcheverry, *L'idéalisme français contemporain*, p. 44.

gether into one philosophy of spirit the life-idea philosophies of Bergson and Brunschvicg.[5] In fact, an examination of Bastide's fundamental philosophy of spirit in his major work *De la Condition humaine* can leave little doubt that the four major influences on his philosophy were Descartes, Kant, Brunschvicg and Bergson.

1. The influence of Brunschvicg

The method of Descartes and the critique of Kant were a major influence in French idealism. Today French idealism is not what it was at the beginning of the century. Nevertheless, it continues to manifest itself in the philosophies of reflection and the philosophies of spirit. The idealist principles of Descartes, Kant and Spinoza continue to exercise their influence.

The mathematical method continued to be the principle ideal of the reflexive method. The ideal of clear, distinct and apodictic knowledge within the limits of human reason inspired the search for the spirit itself which we find in the philosophies of Ravaisson, Renouvier, Lachelier, Lagneau, Hamelin and Brunschvicg. From Descartes idealism learned to follow the natural movement of the spirit in its infallible progress toward knowledge, once the true nature of spirit had been grasped in the spiritual conversion together with the essential method.

It is this dynamism of the intelligence which is taken up once again thematically in French idealism. For Brunschvicg, for example, the mathematical route opened up by Descartes and aided by the mathematical physics of Einstein gave access once again to the life of the spirit. In general, it can be said that he saw in the theory of relativity a confirmation of his own epistemology.[6] For Brunschvicg, however, it was not a question of grounding the synthetic activity of mind in a transcendent reality (like Descartes) or limiting spirit's activity within a structured framework of categories (as with Kant), but only in the spirit itself at work, the spirit whose principle function is the judgment. For Brunschvicg true philosophy had to be freed from all that was presupposed to the judgment. This is why the mathematical method of Descartes and the critical method of Kant could be asserted even more radically.

Already in the philosophy of J. Lachelier the new idealism had taken a more radical turn than either the philosophy of Descartes or Kant had permitted. Kant had denied that the spirit could pass on from subjective con-

[5] Cf. G. Bastide, *De la condition humaine*, pp. 305-323.

[6] L. Brunschvicg, "L'orientation du rationalisme," in *Ecrits Philosophiques*, II, Paris, 1954, p. 79.

sciousness to the affirmation of the thing in itself. Descartes had had recourse to the existence of God in order to attain to the absolute foundation he was seeking. But Lachelier sought to establish the integral autonomy of thought and the radical dependence of nature beyond the limits assigned to spirit by Descartes and Kant. In fact the proper role of philosophy was now defined in attaining to spirit in its "noumenal" reality.[7] Thought itself was to take on an absolute value. Reflection was to reveal not only the relation between thought and the phenomena which it supported, but with being itself. The distinction between phenomena and being would be surpassed.[8] The *method* is thereby highlighted more than ever, and this in a twofold way: for a reflexive analysis of the transcendental consciousness is followed by a progressive synthesis that permits the spirit to assert its own reality and that of its objects.[9] Lachelier sought to affirm the real, integrally grasped in its relationship with the unconditioned. The reflexive method is thus stated in all its purity and force. Metaphysics becomes the science of the light of reason in its very source.[10]

For Brunschvicg, no less than for Bastide, there is no immediate vision of spirit. Spirit is grasped in its works; consciousness is both the worker and the work.[11] Philosophy does not seek to know the profound reality constituting the universe, but limits itself to the reflexive study of the spirit *in its activity* of knowledge. Knowledge is defined in terms of itself as opposed to a knowledge of an order of reality existing in itself.[12] Thus Brunschvicg's philosophy is a "methodical reflection of the spirit upon itself" and as such is rightly called a philosophy of spirit.[13]

The originality of Brunschvicg is to have seen the progress of thought especially in its creative inventiveness as it *manifests itself* in experience and history. Without compromising its superior and eternal reality, he seeks to grasp it in its living movement. Philosophy is the metaphysics of judgment, or better, the metaphysics of the subject in the act of judgment.[14]

We have already noted how in Kant's third *Critique* especially we find a certain basis for this approach. Knowledge of the spirit in the reflexive judg-

[7] "The science of pure thought, of the light in its source, is what we mean by metaphysics." J. Lachelier, *op. cit.*, p. 129.

[8] J. Lachelier, "Annotation au vocabulaire de Lalande," in *Oeuvres*, II, p. 210.

[9] "Let us not fear to suspend in some way thought in a void; for it cannot rest except in itself: the final ground of support for every truth and every existence is the absolute spontaneity of spirit." J. Lachelier, in *Oeuvres*, I., p. 208.

[10] Cf. note 7 above.

[11] Cf. G. Bastide, *De la Condition humaine*, p. 23.

[12] L. Brunschvicg, *La modalité du jugement*, Paris, 1934, p. 4.

[13] Cf. M. Deschoux, *La philosophie de Leon Brunschvicg*, Paris, P.U.F., 1949, p. 1.

[14] L. Brunschvicg, *La modalité du jugement*, p. 236.

ment as revealed in its spiritual works is essentially the itinerary Brunschvicg seeks to follow. But Brunschvicg, having based his ideal of philosophy on that of science, rejects transcendental metaphysics and asserts the living, progressive nature of philosophy and truth. Philosophy not only points out the power of spirit in constituting knowledge, but it participates and shares the progress of knowledge itself. The nature of spirit is a mobile plasticity joined to scientific experience in history.[15] Reason has its own genesis, evolution and history. It forms and becomes conscious of itself in and by its contact with experience. Instead of proceeding science, it rather becomes enriched with its victories as products of its own invention.

It is precisely in the universal knowledge of the sciences that the spirit's reflection upon itself is said to escape the pitfalls of the complacent introspection of an autistic subjectivity as well as the false objectivity of empiricism. For the reflexive method, says Brunschvicg, is the effective exploration of the subject in the universal objectives of science and not the subjective impressions of an individual self.[16] At the same time Brunschvicg's vision goes beyond that of Comte's positive philosophy, for he sees in the progress of the sciences the "affirmation of the essential liberty of spirit transcending all sociological determinations." [17]

Thus we have the intimate connection between doctrine and method characteristic of idealism in general. The reflexive method and the dynamic conception of spirit go hand in hand. For Brunschvicg, for example, the autonomy of spirit is limited (as far as knowledge is concerned) to its manifestations in its activities. Kant had also related autonomy to a universal law and to a "variable incarnation" in accordance with the submission to that law.[18] The progression of synthesis is necessarily limited and relative to the analytic regression. The essence of the reflexive method is there, in the solidarity between the retrospective understanding and the prospective fecundity.[19]

Brunschvicg's philosophy, then, is an effort to stand between ontology and scientism. Like Kant, he refuses the transcendental speculations of traditional metaphysics and seeks to stay "within the human condition." At the same time, philosophical reflection is not of the same order as practical or scientific activity, but is able to judge the basis and process of verification

[15] L. Brunschvicg, *op. cit.*, p. 27.

[16] L. Brunschvicg, *De la connaissance de soi*, Paris, 1931, pp. x-xi.

[17] R. Boirel, *Brunschvicg* (coll. "Philosophes" P.U.F.), Paris, 1964, p. 34.

[18] Cf. G. Bastide, *Traité*, I., p. 151-152. Also J. Vialatoux, *La morale de Kant* (coll. "Initiation Philosophique" 22), Paris, P.U.F., 1966 (4th edition), p. 47. with note. Cf. also I. Kant, *Critique of Pure Practical Reason*, book I, chapter III.

[19] L. Brunschvicg, *Le progrès de la conscience dans la philosophie occidentale*, Paris, P.U.F., 1953, p. 741.

of the sciences themselves, going back to the original principles to which the sciences are subordinated. Furthermore, the very power of the spirit is taken beyond the limitations of the categories and made to be an "incessant revision of legislation" upon its own works.

The judgment is the "beginning and end" of the spirit.[20] The study of the judgment yields knowledge of the spirit. The relation established in the judgment is nothing more than the very life of the spirit. Therefore, philosophy is an effort to grasp this relation, that is, this activity of the subject in the act of constituting its object. Neither the object in itself nor the subject in itself is given before the *rapport* (judgment) which is itself the source of the other two terms.[21] There is neither spirit "en soi" nor nature "en soi." It is in the progressive constitution of the universe of perception and of science that the spirit – as a dynamic reality – is revealed and it is in the analysis of its work that we can find, by reflection, its true structure.

In Brunschvicg's philosophy, then, we do not have an opposition between reason and experience, but rather a "tension" of consciousness which is continually confronted by the provocation of experience.[22] It is this dialogue between spiritual dynamism and experience that gives occasion to the exercise of the indefinite power of invention on the part of the judgment. Knowledge, in other words, is a continual compromise between two forms of modality of the judgment – the form of internality lies in the reciprocal immanence of ideas (the unity of the spirit determining its own laws) and the form of externality (affirmation of an existence that is not the spiritual activity of the spirit).[23] From the start Brunschvicg opposed immediate realism. The intelligible world is an empty unity and sensation, only a simple "shock" which neither affirms or denies anything. The free activity of the spirit moves within these two ideal limits of pure logic and pure fact.

The affirmation of being is the judgment, the judgment being a mental relation established between ideas. Being is here *raison d'être*. The *raison d'être* of one idea is another idea which explains the first. The unity of ideas is constitutive of being. Being is the reciprocal interiority of ideas.[24]

But there is also an "outside of thought." This is being as such, that which is outside of the unity of spirit. It is an *a priori* affirmation of spirit and is

[20] L. Brunschvicg, *La modalité du jugement*, p. 24.

[21] L. Brunschvicg, *La modalité du jugement*, p. 80.

[22] L. Brunschvicg, "L'idée de la verité mathématique," in *Ecrits* III, pp. 71-72.

[23] L. Brunschvicg, *La modalité du jugement*, p. 81 and p. 90.

[24] For Brunschvicg the nature of being depends on the nature of the *affirmation* of being, since thought is considered as a function constitutive of being. Cf. p. 78 of *La modalité du jugement*.

called the form of exteriority.[25] Thus what is outside man is judged as there ... but it is of itself inexplicable and unable to be justified.[26] Furthermore, it in no way determines the spirit.[27]

The effort to raise oneself up to the level of rational life where the judgments participate in the form of interiority is the result of a *spiritual conversion*. In man there are two essential movements of thought, radically opposed to each other. Authentic reflection (true conversion) situates man in the act of thought itself where the spirit can be grasped in its unity. The other movement (false conversion) disassociates an *Ego* supposed given in its pure subjectivity and a *cogitata* supposedly given in its radical exteriority. Knowledge is seen in a framework of a philosophy of participation, where, says Brunschvicg, the nature of interiority as pure creativity is falsified Bastide brings the same critique to philosophy.[28]

Brunschvicg retains, then, the Kantian realism as regards sensation (as distinct from perception) and rejects the positing of a noumenal reality, since such a reality cannot be conceived outside its relation to the subject.

So far we have seen that, for Brunschvicg, metaphysics can be reduced to a theory of knowledge and that the constituting act of knowledge is the judgment, in the sense indicated above. The judgment is characterized by the affirmation of being. Brunschvicg's theory of truth must be centered in this framework.[29]

The intelligible, for Brunschvicg, does not exist before the act of thought. The intelligence is simply comprehension in act expressed in the judgment. The *real* is defined in terms of the real for us – there is only reality for the spirit.[30] Therefore only scientific reality is truth.[31]

Here Brunschvicg's positivism becomes apparent.[32] The true is that which has been verified.[33] The intelligence, as a power in continual progress and as a constant need for verification, attains the truth (objectivity) in the rationality of the judgment, that is, at the point where the judgment becomes *verified* and *universal*, that is, integrated with the judgments already established. It is the continual obstacle that experience poses that forces the spi-

[25] L. Brunschvicg, *La modalité du jugement*, p. 91.

[26] "Exteriority is not, for us, some thing; exteriority is only a principle of affirmation grounding the affirmation of being." *Ibid.*, p. 92.

[27] "There is no reason to seek a common measure between spirit and that which is not spirit." *Ibid.*, p. 92.

[28] Cf. G. Bastide, *Traité*, p. 277 ss.

[29] L. Brunschvicg, *La modalité du jugement*, p. 41.

[30] Cf. M. Deschoux, *La philosophie de Léon Brunschvicg*, p. 69 *op. cit.*

[31] *Ibid.*

[32] *Ibid.*, p. 77.

[33] Cf. note 22 of this section.

rit to exercise its infinite power of revisioning legislation; thus the power of judgment is continually constituting its own truth in its continual dialogue with experience. Truth is the unceasing development and verification of the connection between mathematics and experience. Descartes' ideal of the unity of science is seen operating here in Brunschvicg's ideal of the unity of scientific and philosophic truth. The abstract separation of the domains of science and philosophy is unacceptable to Brunschvicg as it was to Descartes.

For Brunschvicg, then, truth is scientific intelligibility, because intelligibility is the result of verification, the act of controlling reality. The progress of the intelligence is effected between two poles, empirical reality and ideal necessity.[34] Now the great difficulty for the philosopher is to determine the *authentic* figure of man's spiritual works. For the history of the sciences contains the nature of man's spirit. Spirit can be known by reflecting on the sciences as works of man. Of necessity, then, Brunschvicg's philosophy depends on the *interpretation* he gives to his critique of the sciences and the history of sciences. A similar remark can be made concerning Bastide's philosophy.[35]

Mathematical truth, then, is the ideal. Brunschvicg's critique of the philosophy of mathematics shows how the ideal had its different moments in the history of philosophy, always failing to arrive at a positive explanation of mathematical truth. The new mathematical physics made this possible. The mathematical *intuition* of which Descartes spoke, being interior to the intelligence, assures the unity of demonstration. It is this intuition which "liberates the intelligence from the tyranny of the categories and logical procedures" rejected by Descartes.[36] The new science discovers at the *interior of the movement of the intelligence itself* the different values of intuition. The notion of truth and of spirit is discovered at the origin of the constitutive notion of arithmetic and geometric truth. The problem of truth, therefore, looks not to a solution that philosophy itself must invent, but to the history wherein it is already a fact in progress.[37] Scientific truth does not presuppose a transcendent reality, but is directly related to the processes

[34] We shall see a further development of this notion of consciousness as tension in Bastide's axiology.

[35] Bastide proposes to study especially the historical movement of the spirit coming to reflection in his philosophy of consciousness (*De la condition humaine*), his study of the historical figure Socrates (*Le moment historique de Socrates*), in the determination of the authentic notion of civilization (*Les mirages et certitudes de la civilization*) and finally in the history of philosophy (*Les grands thèmes moraux de la civilization occidentale*).

[36] Cf. M. Deschoux, *La philosophie de Léon Brunschvicg*, p. 77.

[37] Cf. M. Deschoux, *La philosophie de Léon Brunschvicg*, p. 77.

of verification immanent to mathematical development. For the intelligence itself is "an indefinite capacity for progress and a perpetual restlessness for verification." [38]

To Descartes' ideal of a universal science based on the mathematical ideal Brunschvicg adds the qualification that the *effective realization* of this ideal interdicts all metaphysical realism.[39]

A critique of the natural sciences [40] leads to a similar conclusion, namely, that the only concrete system for knowing the *real in its universality* is the mathematical system.[41] Only mathematical physics is adequate to the real constitution of the objective universe. The figure of the world is designed for man in the lines of scientific thought. For the physician, in a world of relativity, the universe can be grasped only in function of the measures which determine it. It is necessary to take account of the conditions in which they are grasped, as well as the methods and place of observation. In other words it is necessary to *situate* the *center of reference* in relation to other possible centers.[42]

Positivism and idealism are, therefore, in a regime of mutually complementing one another once all logical realism has been abandoned.[43] Truth is not defined by a parallelism between the ideas of the subject and the realities of nature. It is a connection between a form precisely as finding its own existence in the matter to which it applies itself (matter itself existing only from the moment where it satisfies the double condition of *a priori* intuition and intellectual unification).[44] Here Brunschvicg remains faithful to the spirit of Kant.

Metaphysics, then, is born of science. It clarifies the authentic scientific notions. Idealism is not only the true mathematical philosophy; it is also the true philosophy of knowledge. For science is the natural reference point for the philosophical judgment. The knowledge of man, the ultimate object of philosophy, parallels the knowledge of the universe.[45]

[38] L. Brunschvicg, *Les étapes de la philosophie mathématique*, p. 561, *op. cit.*

[39] Cf. M. Deschoux, *op. cit.*, p. 83. Note also Brunschvicg's critique of Descartes in the *Modalité du Jugement*, pp. 51-62.

[40] Cf. *L'Expérience humaine et la causalité physique*, Paris, P.U.F., 1949 (third edition), 601 pp.

[41] L. Brunschvicg, *L'Expérience humaine et la causalité physique, op. cit.*, pp. 538-539.

[42] *L'Experience humaine et la causalité physique, op. cit.*, p. 537 under Brunschvicg's comments concerning Einstein.

[43] M. Deschoux, *op. cit.*, p. 98.

[44] M. Deschoux, p. 98 *op. cit.*

[45] "Moral progress therefore will demand the same reversal from immediate perspectives demanded by progress on the part of our intelligence, the same radical dis-

The philosophy of spirit culminates in a spiritualism, a practical humanism. Only here, says Bastide, can the rationalism and idealism of Brunschvicg be seen in perspective.[46] Both Brunschvicg and Bastide refer back to the humanism of Descartes, at this point, and note that his moral philosophy was far in advance when compared to his mechanism and the speculative idea of absolute deduction.[47] Brunschvicg and Bastide emphasize the profound unity between speculative and moral philosophy. Progress, whether in knowledge or in the evolution of moral life, is according to the critique of the "raison historique," between the reason which constitutes history and the reason which is registered *in* history. "The originality of Brunschvicg was to have brought together unequivocally the becoming of nature and the historical development of the intelligence. The progress of the human perspective and the cosmic structure are in the last analysis one and the same progress." [48]

As a humanism and a philosophy of spirit which is at the same time a *critique,* Brunschvicg's spiritualism can be called a philosophy of authenticity.[49] There is a way of thinking and a way of willing that is authentic and the whole purpose of Brunschvicg's critique is to discern, in some way, that authenticity and the norm which produces it.

The notion of spirit as judgment is only one step away from the notion of man as a *function of unity.* The essence of spirit is to be a unity begetting unity in the clarity of analysis. The *exigence* of unity is the principle motive force of progress ... both for science and morality. Thus the destiny of man becomes the responsibility of man. To preserve moral consciousness man must sharpen his intellectual consciousness, for in reality they are essentially one. For in the moral order, no less than in the scientific order, man must seek continually for the *real relations* that bind him together in a social context with other men. There is a moral invention no less than a scientific invention. The two go hand in hand.[50]

For authentic thought is creative of objectivity. It is, therefore, the power to disengage the spiritual meaning of reality, to give its *raison d'être* to

placement of our interests and our satisfactions." L. Brunschvicg, *La modalité du jugement,* p. v of the preface to the second edition, *op. cit.*

[46] Cf. G. Bastide, "La spiritualité brunschvicgienne," *Revue de Métaphysique et de morale,* 1945 (50), p. 43.

[47] Cf. Léon Brunschvicg, *Le progrès de la conscience,* pp. 145-154, p. 685, p. 694.

[48] M. Deschoux, *op. cit.,* p. 130.

[49] E. Brehier, "L'idéalisme de Léon Brunschvicg," in *Etudes de philosophie moderne,* Paris, P.U.F., 1965, p. 152.

[50] L. Brunschvicg, "Sur les rapports de la conscience intellectuelle et de la conscience morale," in *Ecrits philosophiques,* II., p. 153.

technology, to language, to art and to science, to moral, social and religious life as well. In Brunschvicg's spiritualism liberty, objectivity, rationality and historicity are made to come together in view of the perfect unity of spirit of which they are all functions. It is in the light of the determination of the authentic values that individualism is made to give way to the possibility of communion and community.[51]

The responsibility of man, then, is intimately connected with his scientific life, since it is upon this that his intellectual life depends.[52] So in the same way does the aesthetic life have its authentic and inauthentic modes. Our openness to others depends on our understanding of its authentic function.[53] The same is true for moral life. The moral life consists in giving active proof and verification, in reality, to the practical ideas conceived beforehand as hypotheses.[54] Like reason itself, the moral consciousness is engaged in a continual revision of itself in order to assure its authenticity and freedom from realism. Parallels with Kant's philosophy suggest themselves immediately.

Here also the notion of spiritual conversion, especially as further developed in Bastide's philosophy, plays its central role. Morality is the constant effort to find one's just place in the community and one's authentic relation with others. The same "finesse" required of man in the intellectual order is necessary also in the moral order. For since the moral act is creative of its object in conformity with the intention which orientates it, it becomes *all the more urgent* for man, in his moral life, to be honest without compromise and open to others on whom he depends for the orientation of his existence in authenticity.

Knowledge, aesthetic sympathy and moral effort – these are the three important areas open to the free choice of each one, and there is an urgency in the philosophy of Brunschvicg concerning this choice. Knowledge and morality cannot rest on the theoretical plane. Only man's freedom can bring them to their proper fulfillment. Liberated by reflection, man stands in his freedom faced with the necessity of choosing between the constant effort of spiritual conversion and the relapsing back into a primitive and naive realism.

Liberty is the spirit in act. It is not an object of speculation or demon-

[51] L. Brunschvicg, *La modalité du jugement*, p. 244.

[52] "The life of the spirit is found entirely in the scientific life." M. Deschoux, *op. cit.*, p. 143.

[53] M. Deschoux, *op. cit.*, p. 143.

[54] Both Brunschvicg and Bastide note their agreement with F. Rauh and the nature of moral experience. Cf. L. Brunschvicg, "Frédéric Rauh," in *Ecrits*, II, pp. 232-257. Cf. G. Bastide, *Traité*, p. 24, 386.

stration. Reason provides the differenciation between authentic freedom (autonomy) and the false liberty which alienates.[55] Man has a *task* to accomplish, for he is situated at the crossroads of being and nothing in his freedom. His vocation is to be a generous intelligence, a vigorous openness to understand other points of view, all in view of being able to give oneself more completely in love. Animated by a care for objectivity and reality, each one can be a moment of progress in history's course. The freedom which defines spirit is a freedom submissive in all things to reason, to the true ideas which give man his authentic vocation along with the power to use his freedom as a function giving value to life. The truth of action finds its verification in the harmony and understanding produced by them. For the authentic functions of science, art and morality, as well as philosophy, are only functions of the one spirit whose law and unique norm is unity itself.[56]

It is this ideal of unity, in the last analysis, which gives real sense to the existence and activity of man. That is why the humain condition is grasped as dualistic, for man is at the crossroads of two distinct possibilities: the ideal of autonomy in thought and action or the refusal to take upon oneself that responsibility upon which the promotion of spiritual unity depends. The life of the spirit is a matter of personal choice and the whole human condition is caught up in this decision. One might say that the starting point of Bastide's philosophy begins especially here with Brunschvicg's spiritualism.

II. The influence of Bergson

Despite the difference of its orientation as a philosophy of life rather than a philosophy of the idea, the philosophy of Bergson has many links with the philosophies of spirit. It was Emile Boutroux, Bergson's teacher, who had introduced Bergson to the French spiritualist tradition of Maine de Biran

[55] For Brunschvicg the functions of the spirit are not conceived in terms of faculties. Spirit is not to be conceived as divided between instinct, sentiment and will on the one hand and reflection, reason and liberty on the other. The problem of liberty takes its origin from the deep rooted sentiment of the *unity* of our interior, life. Thus we think and act with the totality of our being. The meaning of freedom, for Brunschvicg, must be found in this notion of our being taken us a whole. In other words there is nothing in us heterogeneous to reason. Our feelings can become permeated by reason just as emotion can engender abstract ideas. Liberty is activated in man's spirit in proportion as the spirit passes from unconsciousness to consciousness, that is, to reflection. Cf. "La notion de liberté morale," in *Ecrits,* II., pp. 164-182.

[56] In the tradition of Descartes, the unity and primacy of the spirit are among the central intuitions of Brunschvicg's philosophy. Cf. "La spiritualité," G. Bastide, pp. 98-99.

and Felix Ravaisson. Bergson's method of intuition in a metaphysics of real duration is, in its own way, a philosophy of spiritual conversion.

Bastide remarks that Bergson's philosophy marks a real progress of thought for having stressed in a particular way the notion of consciousness as genesis with the consequent corollary that the act of self-knowledge was to be obtained genetically, in the heart of spiritual activity.[57] It is this return to a concrete feeling for becoming that constitutes one of the chief merits of Bergson's philosophy.

As with the philosophies of idealism, method and doctrine are intimately connected in Bergson's philosophy. As a method of reflection the philosophy of integral experience has many similarities with the idealist method of immanence. Applying the method of intuition to the spirit, Bergson discovers the real self and in the self the metaphysical reality of real duration, a duration which is charged with a past of which nothing is lost and with a future subject only to creative liberty. It is at the heart of our own being that we discover the source of all existence and communicate with the original movement of creation. The philosophy of Bergson is also a philosophy of interiority.

In the beginning of this chapter we noted that the philosophy of Brunschvicg and the philosophy of Bergson can be brought together on several important points. Bastide sees them as mutually complementing one another by their corresponding emphasis on the two aspects of reality that constitute the essential duality of the human condition, life and thought. For Bastide, Bergson's intuition translates the effort of life becoming transparent to itself in the clarity of thought; the philosophy of Brunschvicg, on the other hand, translates the effort of thought to incarnate itself in a life of creativity and spiritual works. Bastide's own philosophy of spiritual conversion seeks to bring together these two points of view, by emphasizing the convergence of life and thought in the regime of spiritual conversion.[58] Bergson goes from intuition to historical criticism. Brunschvicg goes from historical criticism to the intuition of the living spirit.[59] The spirituality of Brunschvicg centers the drama of human existence in the continual scientific, moral and religious conflict between the fatal inertia and the deathly weight of the past and the internal progress and victorious continuity of the spirit, wherein the necessity of a spiritual conversion; [60] Bergson also speaks of the spiritual con-

[57] Cf. G. Bastide, *De la condition humaine*, p. 313.

[58] Cf. G. Bastide, *De la condition humaine*, p. 319.

[59] Cf. M. Deschoux, "Brunschvicg et Bergson," *Revue Internationale de Philosophie*, 1951 (15), p. 101.

[60] Cf. L. Brunschvicg, "De la vraie et de la fausse Conversion," *Revue de Métaphysique et de morale*, 1930-1932, pp. 270-297 (1930); 29-80, 187-235 (1931); 17-46.

version, the change of direction needed in order to contact the reality of spirit.

Both Brunschvicg and Bergson, then, are concerned with an authentic spiritual life grounded on the reality of experience.[61] While the tone of Bergson's approach is principally biological and psychological, for Brunschvicg, to be sure, it is more epistemological and historical criticism. For Brunschvicg the elan of life is more an elan of the intelligence. But for both philosophers the creative liberty of the spirit is a living thought which stands between intellectual formalism and empirical scientism. In short it is more the *interpretation* of the creative elan of spirit that separates the two philosophers. Nevertheless, both interpretations open up into a common vision of the indefinite progress of a practical humanism and life of the spirit.

Bergson's method then is one of intuition. It was precisely the intuition of real duration which showed the way of philosophy, as far as Bergson was concerned, the way of critique and the way of a positive elaboration of the fundamental intuition.[62] In other words, the search for a method and a new direction of thought was the result of this effort to determine and grasp the nature of real duration.

Rejecting the approaches of the associationists, such as Mill, Bergson concluded that the principle of all evolution, duration, could not be grasped in the divisive manner of the scientific or rationalist approach, but only by placing ourselves within the evolutionary movement itself.[63] A theory of knowledge had to be linked with a theory of life.[64]

Bergson, therefore, refused Kant's approach, since it made impossible the intuitive approach to metaphysics which he sought. The Kantian limitations concerning metaphysics or Descartes' ideal of a univocal scientific method were unacceptable to Bergson.[65] Instead, he insists on having recourse to the empirical plane of change in order to penetrate it, not by the quantitative analysis of the scientific method, but by a direct intuition of change and duration in their original mobility. The problem of metaphysics is to learn to

153-198 (1932). Cf. H. Bergson, *La pensée et le mouvant* in *Oeuvres* (édition du centenaire), 153, p. 1373: "Is not the role of philosophy to bring us to a more complete perception of reality by way of certain displacement of our attention? It would seem to have to do with turning our attention away from the pragmatically interesting aspect of the universe and turning it back towards that which is, practically speaking, of no use. This conversion of our attention would be philosophy itself."

[61] H. Bergson, *La pensée et le mouvant*, p. 1432 *op. cit.*

[62] Cf. H. Bergson, *La pensée et le mouvant*, p. 1255-1256 *op. cit.*

[63] *Ibid.*, p. 1255. Cf. also *L'Évolution créatrice*, xi, p. 494 *op. cit.*

[64] "That is to say that the theory of knowledge and a theory of life seem to us to be inseparable from one another." H. Bergson, *L'Évolution créatrice*, ix, p. 492, *op. cit.*

[65] Cf. H. Bergson, *L'Évolution créatrice*, 356 ss., pp. 796-801, *op. cit.*

use our powers in an attitude of consciousness that is not naive and utilitarian.

After distinguishing the two general orientations of the spirit towards science (homo faber) and philosophy (homo sapiens), Bergson concludes that the method for grasping real duration, the object of philosophy, is not by way of the practical intellect (the scientific mind whose object is inert matter and the spatial aspects of nature), but by way of instinct, but an instinct purified and reflexive, an intellectual sympathy.[66]

Thus we can see that Bergson's method is not without likenesses to the idealist approach in so far as it attempts to grasp the spirit in its metaphysical reality by way of a purification and detachment of mind, a spiritual conversion.[67] For this reason there can be a *moral* problem at the root of man's failure to become a philosopher and grasp the true nature of the spirit, and, at the same time, the principle of all cosmic evolution.[68]

Bergson's philosophy presupposes, then, the dynamic interconnection (by virtue of duration) between inner psychic duration and its secondary object – duration as the principle of the universe. But the primary object of the intuition is the grasp of the spirit by the spirit, the mind's attention to itself in the act of knowing some material object.[69] We have essentially the indirect realism already grounded in Descartes' philosophy and continued in the idealist tradition.

The metaphysical intuition, then, is a kind of intellectual sympathy whereby the unique and inexpressable reality of self is attained along with the knowledge of other things.[70] To philosophize is to learn to see everything "sub specie durationis." [71]

Like Brunschvicg, Bergson was careful that the notion of spirit as intuition should not be given an essential structure as, for example, in the

[66] "L'explication concrète, non plus scientifique, mais métaphysique, doit être cherchée dans une tout autre voie, non plus dans la direction de l'intelligence, mais dans celle de la "sympathie." L'instinct est sympathie ... Mais c'est à l'intérieur même de la vie que nous conduirait *l'intuition*, je veux dire l'instinct devenu désintéressé, conscient de lui-même, capable de réfléchir sur son objet et de l'alargir indéfiniment." H. Bergson, *L'Évolution créatrice*, 177-178, pp. 644-645 *op. cit.*

[67] Cf. H. Bergson, *La pensée et le mouvant*, p. 1395 and p. 1273 *op. cit.*

[68] The notion of purification continues to play an essential role in the philosophies of spirit. The way of self-knowledge through asceticism, already prominent in platonic and neo-platonic philosophy, is regarded as the way to Being itself, the source of absolute reality. The *Essai* of Bergson is also the declaration of a spiritual conversion and a free creation mediated by certain necessary purifications. Cf. J. Lacroix, in *Encyclopédie française*, T. XIX, p. 19.04-2.

[69] Cf. H. Bergson, *La pensée et le mouvant*, pp. 1273-1274 *op. cit.*

[70] *Ibid.*, p. 1361 *op. cit.*

[71] Cf. H. Bergson, *La pensée et le mouvant*, 142, p. 1365 *op. cit.*

categories of the understanding in Kant's philosophy. Bergson, like the idealists, affirms that knowledge is not necessarily given in a constructural framework.[72] At the same time, he attempts to avoid idealism by holding to a direct perception of material things in themselves.[73] But it is only under the aspect of duration that the source of all reality is attained.

We can say that in the light of these remarks Bergson's philosophy remains primarily a philosophy of consciousness. For in the last analysis, life is basically psychological in nature and conscious in origin – the movement of life tends towards reflexive consciousness in human experience. The vital elan is essentially a need for creativity that is realized only in the free act.[74] We shall see all these elements reappear in the axiological idealism of Georges Bastide.

The nature of duration and freedom, the relation between spirit and nature are examined, therefore, from the standpoint of a philosophy of consciousness.[75] As a result of spiritual conversion man can gain a knowledge of his true self in terms of real duration perceived as indivisible time. But because the notion of freedom, for example, is examined in the framework of duration as *the* metaphysical reality, we find that Bergson's approach eventually separates him from certain important points in idealism. For as a matter of fact, Bergson's notion of freedom is not a rational domination over the act of choice, but a spontaneity or movement of duration toward the future. Here is where Bergson's philosophy of memory comes to play its essential role in his philosophy of consciousness. To be truly free the real self must be attained by a deepened reflection by which we gain possession of ourselves in situating ourselves in pure duration. But this is also relative to the degree of attention we give to life itself.[76] Freedom is a fact of lived duration and as such it is a life in the spirit. Through the will contact is made between the individual consciousness and the vital elan of other consciousnesses and the material world. It is precisely the task of philosophy to introduce man into this life in the spirit and unify in conscious life the spiritual and corporal worlds.[77]

The functional duality of consciousness, which we find in Brunschvicg and Bastide, appears in Bergson's philosophy, especially in the *Les Deux Sources*

[72] *Ibid.*, p. 1421.

[73] *Ibid.*, p. 1420.

[74] Cf. H. Bergson, *L'Évolution créatrice*, pp. 716-718 *op. cit.* Cf. also *L'Energie spirituelle*, p. 824: "Consciousness is freedom. It is precisely freedom immersing itself in necessity and turning it to its own profit."

[75] *L'Évolution créatrice*, p. 724 *op. cit.*

[76] Cf. H. Bergson, *Matière et mémoire*, p. 166 *op. cit.*

[77] Cf. H. Bergson, *L'Évolution créatrice*, p. 724 *op. cit.*

de la morale et de la religion where consciousness itself is seen in its struggle between empirical and aspirational morality, between static and dynamic religion.[78] The notion of the two orders, as we shall see, is fundamental to Bastide's axiology and there are numerous similarities to be found between his own descriptions of closed and open morality. Bastide, however, attempts to surpass the naturalism of Bergson's philosophy in the axiological relationship of nature, culture and morality in a philosophy of spiritual conversion.[79]

[78] Cf. H. Bergson, *Les deux sources de la Morale et de la Religion*, p. 1024 and pp. 1029-29 *op. cit.*

[79] G. Bastide, *Mirages et certitudes*, p. 188.

CHAPTER III

PHILOSOPHIES OF REFLECTION AND PHILOSOPHY OF SPIRIT

Authentic philosophy reflects the age in which it is rooted as project as well as the past from which it is born. The search for truth will necessarily concern itself, in a special way, with the philosophical problems that define the particular "kairos" of the times. For the true philosopher will strive to meet the challenge which each age brings, to pass on the historical heritage new-formed, so that the future might reap the results of his own work.

The philosophies of reflection and the philosophies of spirit are by their very nature especially committed to this awareness, the awareness, that is, of the contemporary problems of man and the role philosophy can play in orientating them toward possible solutions. They are so committed by the very fact that they tend to be "practical philosophies," philosophies of action and philosophies of value. Man is more than ever the unique problem, and the metaphysical dimensions of his existence tend to be given an ethical framework, in the large sense of the word.

Therefore, to complete this historical introduction to the philosophy of Georges Bastide, it seemed necessary to indicate briefly the general tendencies of those philosophical movements of which Bastide's axiological idealism can be said to be a part. Two such movements stand out clearly, the movement of the philosophy of spirit begun by R. Le Senne and L. Lavelle in 1934 and the philosophies of reflection represented, for example, by J. Nabert and G. Madinier.

1. Philosophies of reflection

Philosophy is one of the many expressions of human life. It is existential, but it is also an ideal with unlimited possibilities. "To philosophize," said Maine de Biran, "is to reflect; it is to use reason everywhere, in the busy

[1] Cf. G. Bastide, *La condition humaine*, p. 3.

world as well as in the silence of our room." [1] Philosophy and reflection are intimately bound together. For Amiel, notes Bastide, "philosophy is the ideal reconstruction of consciousness understanding itself with all that it contains." [2]

Idealism attempted to show that spirit is initiative more than representation. But the experience of the self alone is not the complete description of man's project in the world. To discover our nature as spirit we must, say the contemporary philosophies of reflection, acknowledge at the very principle of our initiative *an interior dependence,* where our act is also *response,* as well as initiative. For the life of the spirit is also a submission to an appeal which is most interior to ourselves.[3] Reflection is not estrangement, nor is it identified with negativity; it is rather an experience of our being as spirit. The philosophies of reflection come to grips with idealism's claim to discover the reality of spirit; at the same time they strive to be fully aware of the demands and objections that phenomenology and existential philosophy have brought against the philosophies of idealism and the reflective method.[4]

Reflection is opposed to the immediately given, to perception and the pre-reflective movement of life. It is essentially division, "rupture," a leaving behind a certain easy and peaceful contact with life itself.

It is this fact that makes philosophy a scandal. The scandal of the "separated consciousness." The scandal of Socrates. The scandal of Descartes and Kant. The scandal of contemplation. And the philosophers themselves seem to hesitate at the very crossroads – not knowing whether to turn to Socrates or the pre-Socratics,[5] whether to follow Plato or Aristotle, Bergson or Brunschvicg, existentialism or axiological idealism.

No one has been more aware of the dangers of reflection than the philosophers themselves. Which one of the great philosophers, especially since Descartes, has not tried to make philosophy secure by a method that followed the true nature of man and the true elan which leads to salvation? Yet the danger remains. With the critique of Kant, philosophy, it seems, both tottered and strenghtened itself at the same time.

Can philosophy approach its ideal? Can it solve eventually the dilemma between action and contemplation, between liberty and nature, essence and

[2] Cf. G. Bastide, *La condition humaine,* p. 3.

[3] Thus is it an attempt to ground subjectivity in metaphysics. Cf. J. Robert, "Descartes," p. 378 where he notes the influence of Descartes and before him Plotinus and St. Augustine.

[4] Cf. for example J. Nabert's answer's to objections in his article previously cited in the *Encyclopédie française,* p. 19.06-2 to 19.06-3.

[5] Cf. M. Sauvage, *Socrate* (Coll. "Maitre spirituels" 9), Paris, Seuil, 1956, pp. 163-164.

existence? Must we make a choice between Socrates or the City? [6] Can life and thought be brought together? Or is philosophy only a necessary contradiction that man must impose on himself? Is it ever possible to find that authenticity of which Bastide speaks over and over again – where thought, belief and action are really one? [7] Is there hope for the ideal, if it is the ideal, namely, where thought is liberating life and life gives freedom to thought? [8] A life where the attention to what is truly ours becomes one with the context of what we live. Where sentiment itself is transfigured in reflection?

The *philosophies of reflection*, "par excellence" philosophies of interiority, attempt, it seems to me, to point out the real possibility of such a goal. Nor is it simply a question of dominating what is our life by a clarity of knowledge. It is more a question of a *new kind of existence*, a new possession of ourselves, a real spiritual conversion that remains wholly within the realm of philosophy and does not confuse the function of philosophy with the religious function.[9] At the same time philosophies of reflection are in a sense "philosophies of salvation" as much as the existential philosophies.[10] Philosophy is investigation, but it is also a way of life. And if "who I am" and "what can I know," are important questions concerning the reality of man, the questions concerning my salvation – "what must I do" and "what can I hope for" are no less philosophical.[11] Philosophies of reflection are, in the last analysis, methods and doctrines concerning the constitution of oneself as *person*. "Spiritual personalism is the normal and unequivocal result of moral idealism." [12]

Secondly, let us note the notion of reflection is here taken in its most strict sense.[13] The object of reflection is not simply an analysis of the given, but the very movement of the conscious act, the relation of the self to its act,[14] a passage from fact to value, a way of access to the real and the concrete by a grasping of the true self.[15] It is chiefly for this reason that Bastide insists that all idealism (philosophy of reflection) is essentially a *moral idealism*, an axiology, for it is only through the notion of value that we have

[6] *Ibid.*, p. 164-166.

[7] Cf. G. Bastide, *Traité*, pp. 208-209 and *Méditations*, pp. 15-17.

[8] G. Bastide, *La condition humaine*, pp. 319-323.

[9] Cf. G. Bastide, *Traité*, pp. 353-366.

[10] Cf. F. Copleston, *Contemporary Philosophy*, London, 1963 (4th ed.), p. 139.

[11] Cf. A. Dondeyne, "L'historicité dans la philosophie contemporaine," *Revue Philosophique de Louvain*, 1956 (54), p. 471. Cf. G. Bastide, *Traité*, p. 131.

[12] G. Bastide, *Traité*, p. 138.

[13] Cf. J. Robert, "Descartes," p. 381.

[14] Cf. L. Lavelle, *De L'intimité spirituelle*, Paris, Aubier, 1955, p. 270.

[15] Cf. A. Forest, "La signification du recueillement," in *Encyclopédie française*,

access to ourselves, to spirit.[16] Observation, notes Forest, has reference to a given, reflection to spiritual presence.[17] The given is *interior* to the presence which developes it and takes it in.[18]

Next, it should be emphasized at the outset that philosophies of reflection are also efforts to come to grips with man's situation as a being-in-the-world. They are well aware of the importance of the notion of intentionality. But there is an effort to go further than Husserl. There is an insistance on the interiority of the subject resulting from authentic spiritual conversion.[19] The aim of this method, however, is by no means to make man a stranger to his world. It is rather an attempt to situate and give equilibrium to the necessary tension of man's being in the world. Its fundamental goal is unity of the person and unity of humanity.[20]

It is axiology that preserves philosophies of reflection from being solipsisms or philosophies of introspection. For in authentic reflection, in genuine spiritual conversion, the spirit of man is open to value, to the Good, to infinite perfection; and this at the very moment when he knows himself. Self-knowledge, as we shall see, is not self-complacency, but openness to being, or better, to value and the reasons for being.[21] It is for this reason that the increase of immanence is not estrangement from the world, but, in the framework of an axiological metaphysics, it becomes the source of unity and enrichment, a growing experience of accord with oneself and the world in which we live. Authentic reflection is an orientation towards perfection. It is the promotion of spiritual values.

Philosophies of reflection differ from other philosophies, therefore, by their method. Instead of proceeding by deduction from an analysis of the

p. 19.08-10. Cf. also G. Madinier, *Conscience et signification*, Paris, P.U.F., p. 28 where Madinier clearly distinguishes two kinds of reflection, one intentional and another which is not able to "analyse the object about which it is thinking, but is able to understand the act which it accomplishes in thinking; here we are dealing with a thought reflecting back on itself in order to grasp itself in its own activity."

[16] Cf. Georges Bastide, *La conversion spirituelle*, p. 70.

[17] A. Forest, "La signification," p. 19.08-10. Also Cf. Madinier, *Conscience*, pp. 29, 30, 46.

[18] Cf. A. Forest, "La signification," *op. cit.*, p. 19.08-11.

[19] "If the subject is consciousness of the world and is nothing more than this intentionality which projects the subject towards things, then we can no longer speak of possession of oneself nor coincidence with oneself. There is no interior man, says M. Ponty. Consciousness has no interiority, says J. P. Sartre." G. Madinier, *Conscience*, p. 28; cf. also p. 48.

[20] Cf. G. Bastide, *Traité*, pp. 202 and 831.

[21] "If man reflects, it is in order to realize an authentic existence... the metaphysical function of the act of reflection is to awaken the moral consciousness to the source of value." G. Bastide, *Méditations*, p. 144; *Traité*, p. 106.

given to the absolute, it is the absolute which, it is said, reflects in a particular consciousness. It is reflection which constitutes the subject itself and *then* grasps the laws and norms of spiritual activity immanent to the operations of spirit.[22] At this point, notes J. Nabert, we can distinguish *two variations of the reflective method*. The first one is this: it is maintained that the regressive analysis is identical with the movement in which finite consciousness discovers its being as received from the Absolute reflecting in it and giving it the necessary elan to rejoin its principle. Here it is the *Absolute itself* which causes the ideas, normes and creates the needs of the finite spirit and the idea of Being. The *term* of the movement is present to consciousness from the start. But this presence can be a neglected presence. For only in and because of an existential restlessness, desire and experience of privation is the presence, the action of the Absolute, made apparent to consciousness. Reflection is this return of the finite consciousness to its principle. "Consciousness of self" is identified with the consciousness which the Absolute has of itself in a finite being.[23] The method, one of regressive analysis, describes the necessary propaedeutics for dissipating the illusions that cause our forgetfulness of ourselves and thus of being itself.

A second approach is one which terminates in the subject. Here the considerations are more with reference to an *individual* consciousness and a transcendent one,[24] after the manner of *Kant*, than the relation of finite to infinite thought, in the spirit of *Descartes*. It is the notion of a "constituting consciousness" which now grounds the opposition of act and event – in the same way that the opposition between internal necessity (spiritual) and the necessity of nature explains the difference between the ground for science and the ground for human freedom.

Philosophies of reflection are further distinguished, as we noted previously,[25] by that act of the spirit which is regarded as the "locus' 'of contact with the infinite or transcendent spirit. For Hamelin, reasoning itself is the proper operation of spirit,[26] for Brunschvicg the judgment,[27] for Biran the immanent apperception of self in the original experience of effort. But as Nabert brings out, two characteristics of this act are *common* to all philosophies of reflection: there is an elimination of intuition as such or of a re-

[22] Cf. J. Nabert, *Encyclopédie française*, p. 19.04-15.

[23] Cf. J. Nabert, *Encyclopédie française*, p. 19.04-15.

[24] I.e., the conditions of the appearance of things to the subjectivity of man, the conditions for the very life of man himself to whom things appear.

[25] Cf. p. 119.

[26] Cf. A. Etcheverry, *L'Idéalisme*, p. 97.

[27] Cf. A. Etcheverry, *L'Idéalisme*, p. 131.

doubling of reflection back upon itself in order to grasp itself; and, secondly, this act can be renewed by a decision of the will suspending the course of our spontaneous life to effect this contact with the eternal, the infinite or the transcendent. The subject attains the self, in other words, "without anything outside itself playing an *essential* role." [28] It is the reiteration of the idealist theme of the *radical initiative,* the perfect freedom of the act of reflection. This is not to deny the pre-reflexive role of the "immediate consciousness" but it is only to *limit* it to a role of prefiguration and foreshadowing.

These two directions of reflexive analysis that we mentioned earlier are not opposed to one another. Rather they indicate a difference of accent. Both are implicitly contained in the "Cogito" of Descartes. For it is possible to emphasize the relation of the self to self along the lines of a personalistic approach to philosophy; or it is equally possible to emphasize more the relation of thought to the infinite reality that is present as its principle. As we emphasize one or the other we take the path followed by Kant or that which is more in the spirit of Maine de Biran – both finding their common heritage in Descartes.[29] *What is important is to note a certain "passage" from strict impersonal idealism to a more existential approach which combines the idealist method with a philosophy of personalism.* Here lies the special interest of the study engaging our attention. Bastide's axiological idealism is itself an effort to go beyond the impersonalism implied in the philosophy of Brunschvicg, all the while retaining the reflexive method.[30]

The importance and originality of this movement is inherent in what Nabert says is the "just conception of the relationship between consciousness and reason." [31] It lies in the *solidarity* of these two directions of thought and not in their separation. For together they try to explain the relationship between an autonomy that is ruled by a norm without thereby becoming "less autonomous." As we shall have occasion to emphasize later in part two, the notion of spiritual conversion and the transformation of values (wherein lies the originality of Bastide's own effort),[32] while being able to retain the fundamental Kantian acquisition as regards the reflexive connection between duty (as universal law) and the autonomy of freedom, avoids the danger of rationalistic formalism or fideism in the implications of a phi-

[28] Cf. J. Nabert, *Encyclopédie française,* 19.04-16.

[29] *Encyclopédie française,* J. Nabert, 19.04-16.

[30] Cf. G. Bastide, *La conversion spirituelle,* p. 88; *Les grands thèmes,* pp. 129 ss.; "Le malin génie," pp. 238-240.

[31] Cf. J. Nabert, *Encyclopédie française,* p. 19.04-16.

[32] Cf. G. Bastide, *La conversion spirituelle,* p. viii.

losophy of reflection in an axiological metaphysics.[33] We have in this movement a unique effort to utilize the moral philosophy of Kant in the light of contemporary interpretations of Descartes and a deepening of reflection on the philosophy of Maine de Biran. For while Biran failed to discover from the experience of the "first fact" the forms and categories of objective knowledge and thus a guarantee of their value, still he favored a study of "consciousness at the level of sense" and perception.[34] On the other hand, the study of Kant on the *transcendental consciousness* with its demands for objectivity prevented the acts and ends of the concrete self from escaping the imperatives and norms of rational thought. It is the merit of the philosophies of reflection to have deepened the notion of *person* by insisting *both* on interiority and the constitutive operations of spirit, thus grounding autonomy in objectivity and universality.[35] The contribution of an axiological metaphysics seems to be, especially, its resulting in a *spiritual personalism*. There is an effort to reconcile once again the will and the understanding.[36]

Two goals, then, are to be brought into unity – a theory of knowledge and a way leading to self-possession and self-realization, a way, that is, to wisdom. The *idealists* traced out the way of knowledge, the way of philosophical reflection. Taking their cue from Kant and Maine de Biran, Lachelier and Lagneau, by an analysis of matter and perception, showed the immanence of intelligence in the sense consciousness, the former being the only means of passing from the order of fact to the order of spirit.[37] Brunschvicg, we saw, remained in the tradition, prefering the analytical method of Lachelier's *Fondement de l'induction* over the dialectic embraced by Hamelin. Seeking the laws of the spirit in the history of the sciences, he introduced the

[33] "Without going so far, as some, to deny too easily the distinction of the two orders, we admit, that for our part, the spiritual conversion and transfiguration of values characterizing the person can give us the key to this twofold register, empirical and prereflexive on one hand, idealist and spiritual on the other; in such a way that, keeping the fundamental insight of Kant, namely, the reflexive connection between duty conceived as universal law and freedom conceived as autonomy, we can translate the interior moral life of the person without giving occasion to the criticisms so often addressed to Kant when he was accused of rationalism in the pejorative sense of the word, of formalism, rigorism or fideism." G. Bastide, *Traité*, p. 151; cf. also pp. 149-163.

[34] Cf. J. Nabert, *Encyclopédie française*, p. 19.04-16.

[35] "The work of reflection is not to leave outside one another the interiority of consciousness and the universality of reason." J. Nabert, *Encyclopédie française*, p. 19.04-16.

[36] Cf. for example the interpretation of Descartes in the *Grands thèmes*, pp. 140-141 where Bastide speaks of his "speculative voluntarism and his practical intellectualism," which becomes the model for his own philosophy. Cf. also *La condition humaine*, pp. 274 ss. and *Traité*, p. 152.

[37] Cf. A. Etcheverry, *Idéalisme*, pp. 22-37.

dynamic and plastic aspect of spirit.[38] Thus, idealism sought to perfect the transcendental idealism of Kant who "concerned with justifying science, neglected somewhat the analysis of perception and of the spatializing function – thus risking to break the continuity between the exercise of thought at the level of sense knowledge and at the level of scientific knowledge." [39] Idealism sought to discover the action of the subject in the elementary forms of knowledge: "To find in the least object of thought, Thought itself." [40]

The contemporary *philosophies of reflection* (vd. J. Nabert, G. Madinier, L. Lavelle, R. Le Senne and G. Bastide) mark a further progress in the same direction, a passage to a more "existential" point of view.[41] Idealism, it is claimed, did not exhaust the possibilities of the reflexive method.[42] This is due, notes Nabert, to their *notion of subject*. Idealism tends to impersonalism and runs the danger of a relativistic humanism, a pragmatic spiritualism. Lagneau, in speaking of a "surmoi" tends to identify the self with a system of principles of knowledge.[43] Lachelier also tends to exalt thought over person.[44] In the spiritualism of Brunschvicg there is the same tendency to impersonalism as Bastide brings out in his criticism above.

"We must refuse to confuse 'interior life' and 'spiritual life'," says Nabert.[45] And here he points out the crucial ground upon which a passage can be built from the spirituality of a Brunschvicg to the personal spiritualism and axiological idealism of Georges Bastide. Here we are brought closer to the central claim of philosophies of reflection to further complete the notion of reflection and the notion of spirit in such a way as to surpass Kant and idealism without denying either their importance or the general validity of the orientation of their method. In short, it is an effort to ground the *incarnational* aspect of man's existence within the framework of an essentially idealist method.

Kant, and the idealists such as Hamelin, failed to provide an acceptable philosophy of self-knowledge. Their method for obtaining the real and the concrete, the spirit, is in the last analysis condemned to a certain sterility. For they failed to close the gap between the scepticism of an empirical self and the dogmatic formalism of a pure self. The doctrine of the latter, in turn,

[38] Cf. G. Bastide, *Traité*, p. 189; *La condition humaine*, pp. 313-315.

[39] Cf. J. Nabert, *Encyclopédie française*, p. 19.04-16.

[40] Cf. I. Alain, *Souvenirs concernant Jules Lagneau*, p. 136 cited by J. Nabert, *Encyclopédie française*, p. 19.04-16.

[41] Cf. J. Nabert, *Id.*

[42] *Id.*

[43] *Id.*

[44] J. Lachelier, *Lettres*, #81 cited by Nabert, *id.*

[45] Cf. J. Nabert, *Id.*

left open the possibility of a twofold interpretation of the activity of spirit – one rationalistic (Hamelin's idealism), the other irrational (Schopenhauer, the romanticists).[46] As Bastide remarks after his own critique of Kant's philosophy,[47] "... l'esprit ne se connaît pas du dehors ..." [48] The affirmation of spirit from a position of exteriority ("qui prétendrait en poser l'existence") [49] mutilates and deforms it, for the spirit is not "that which is affirmed but that which affirms." [50] Spirit cannot be affirmed in the notion of soul conceived in the category of substance. Nor can it be affirmed in its essence by empirical psychology by an examination of its different psychic phenomena transferred to the philosophical order. Nor is spirit "being" or "becoming" in the ontological (realist) or phenomenal sense of these words. But neither is spirit something of the "noumenal" order. Spirit can be grasped only in its very life.

Spirit can be grasped only in a position of interiority.[51] For the philosophies of reflection *Philosophy is eminently this maturing of the spirit being progressively revealed to itself, taking possession of itself and subsequently realizing itself in action and gradually becoming light and unity of life.*[52] Spirit must be grasped in its life, it is said, and this was the great merit of *Bergson* – to have pointed this out.

But how attain to the life of the spirit without fixing it in some kind of conceptual knowledge? By the effort to grasp it in its genesis. A spiritual conversion is necessary, a movement of the will rejecting an attitude of naive realism and at the same time and in the same movement realizing itself in genuine self-knowledge.[53] A way of uniting spirit in its transcendent reality and in its most concrete experiences through reflexive analysis – this is the goal which philosophies of reflection pose for themselves.[54] Maine de Biran, by his notion of the self, did not exhaust the whole truth of our being as spirit; nevertheless, his reflections and analyses of the "first fact" were based on an immediate consciousness of the connection between an act of the subject and the resistance it encounters. And even though Bergson had recourse to an intuitional grasp of life in its creative elan, rejecting the intel-

[46] Cf. G. Bastide, *La condition humaine*, p. 304.
[47] Cf. G. Bastide, *La condition humaine*, pp. 293-305.
[48] Cf. G. Bastide, *La condition humaine*, p. 305.
[49] *Id.*
[50] *Id.*
[51] *Id.*, p. 306: "... it cannot be grasped except from within, in its very own life."
[52] G. Bastide, "Nature, situation et condition humaine," in *Existence et Nature*, Paris, 1962, pp. 51-64.
[53] We will discuss this in detail in part two. For a brief summary cf. G. Bastide, *Traité*, p. 87 ss. Also chapters II and III of *La conversion spirituelle*.
[54] Cf. G. Madinier, *Conscience*, p. 40-41.

ligence as an instrument of authentic self-knowledge, nevertheless we know that it was an "intelligence-habitude" of which he spoke. But there is still the possibility, as we pointed out in the previous chapter, to think of an intelligence moving dynamically toward a rational ideal of universality and unity, an intelligence having many of the characteristics of Bergson's intuition.

Therefore, it is not surprising that the philosophies of reflection, in their own effort to surpass the impasses of idealism, have had recourse to the philosophies of Maine de Biran and Henri Bergson.[55] It is through them that a way is open for a doctrine of the self that would not be lacking in that dimension of interiority (dimension de l'intimité) which is missing from the transcendental consciousness of critical idealism. It is here that we see a new effort to bring to "clear and universal consciousness the experience first presented in singular and irreducible contingency." [56] Again we are brought to the heart of the question: can life and thought be brought together in a genuine philosophy of reflection and a dynamic metaphysics of action. Can a philosophy of reflection have as its natural outcome a personalist spiritualism? [57]

The philosophy of Georges Bastide is an attempt to bridge this gap in a philosophy of spiritual conversion and an axiological metaphysics of action that is, in the final analysis, a spiritual personalism. As he himself notes, it seems that every attempt to grasp the reality of spirit is necessarily drawn in two directions: one towards the rational, another towards the irrational. And each effort can be regarded as a progress towards the goal of self knowledge, for both the idealism of Kant and the irrationalism of Bergson are progressive purifications of a naive realism of the spirit.[58] "Between the dynamic intellectualism of Brunschvicg and the Bergsonian conception of spirit – the distance is minimum (if you take away the vitalistic tendency of Bergson's philosophy) and it seems we discern the spiritual reality from a rather close vantage point." [59] At the same time the *duality* persists.

It is precisely because of this dual aspect of consciousness that the problem remains for further reflection. The conversion to interiority did not resolve the problem of the distance between life and thought, for both Bergson and Brunschvicg tend to emphasize one of the two aspects of spirit – spirit as reason or spirit as life. Therefore, how explain the fact, asks Bas-

[55] Cf. J. Nabert, *Encyclopédie française*, p. 19.05-16.
[56] *Id.*, p. 19.06-1.
[57] Cf. G. Bastide, *La conversion spirituelle*, p. 86.
[58] Cf. G. Bastide, *La condition humaine*, p. 317.
[59] *Id.*

tide, that we can concede as genuine the philosophical method present in either case and yet admit that the basic problem remains unsolved. The answer, as we shall see, seems to lie, for Bastide and others of the philosophy of reflection school, in an axiological metaphysics. For the present, we underline only that in a position of interiority and by a genuine method of reflection, both the philosophies of Bergson and Brunschvicg are orientated toward the reality of spirit as such, for both are philosophies of consciousness, both proceed from a metaphysical experience essentially different from "ontological realism." In the latter case, says Bastide, there is a growing separation between the rational and existential poles, precisely because *the subject* is situated in a position of exteriority, that is, ordered primarily towards *things* as the source of the real rather than towards interiority.[60]

Philosophies of reflection, as philosophies of spiritual conversion, are in a perspective of interiority where the existential and the rational are converging one towards the other. "The intuition of Bergson translates the effort which life makes to become transparent to itself in the clarity of thought; the philosophy of Brunschvicg translates the effort of thought to give itself a life of creativity." [61] The source of both reason and life are the same. Spirit is *elan* just as life is *elan*, but "the latter is not conscious of itself, the former is." [62] Spirit is essentially defined in its own legislating activity, as a function of invention and law of spiritual unity; a "synenergy of spiritual resources," law of progress and not of uniformity, free affirmation of the Good, whose own unity becomes its law and norm.[63]

Each one of these notions must be clarified in part two. Our purpose here has been to present the basic effort of philosophies of reflection to ground the existential and rational aspects of life in one theory of interiority; in a spiritual conversion based on the notion of spirit as free affirmation of the Good. Nabert notes why this approach marks a progress in the reflexive method itself when compared to idealism.[64] The influence of existential thought was essentially to attack the exaggerated intellectualism of the previous reflexive methods and prepare the way for a widened notion of reflection. Spirit must produce itself in effective experiences (philosophy, science, art, etc. . . .) in order to discover its own reality and it is in reflexive analysis that its fecundity is revealed, for it is here that reflection "overtakes the moment when the spiritual act clothes itself in its sign." [65] Reflection is

[60] Cf. J. Nabert, *Encyclopédie française*, p. 19.06-1.
[61] Cf. G. Bastide, *La condition humaine*, p. 318.
[62] Cf. G. Bastide, *La condition humaine*, p. 319.
[63] *Id.*, p. 323.
[64] J. Nabert, *Encyclopédie française*, pp. 19.04-16 and 19.06-01.
[65] J. Nabert, *Encyclopédie française*, p. 19.06-1.

the illumination of the intimate relation of the act with the signification in which it objectivizes itself.

It is from the moment that the connection between act and signification is relaxed, that the function of transcendental subjectivity appears to itself in such a way as to give it access to true values, to essences and to objective significations. It is here that Nabert notes an essential difference between the reflexive method and the phenomenological method.[66] The latter prefers to go to the real life of acts in their birth and first attempt; and by this very fact, it is not attentive, and deliberately so, to the "beyond" or the "outside of" the intention itself. The phenomenological method prefers the meaning as already separated from the original act, while *reflexive analysis*, in appropriating to itself from the works the acts of creative spirit, attempts to grasp the *spiritual interiority* by way of the effective meanings of the works, which are always one, to some degree, with time, space, language and history. The objective meanings, "prisoners of social context, of canons," draw the adherence of consciousness, but also arouse its opposition and its essential reality as spirit.[67] This is in line with Madinier's view [68] (as well as that of Bastide – vd., for example, pp. 324-364 *La Condition humaine*) that self-knowledge is in the act of spirit's own engagement in a spatio-temporal world. This is also why, for philosophies of reflection, consciousness is essentially *tension*, the effort of spirit to give value to itself in giving value to the world of man – but in such a way as not to alienate itself, but on the contrary, to spiritualize itself and constitute itself as person.[69] In the last analysis, reflection is an act which translates itself in the events of the world, but does not understand itself except by its opposition to the world, "in the never ceasing restlessness of the difference between my true self and that which is not my true self." [70]

The goal of philosophical reflection, then, is the illumination (by way of analysis) of the act immanent to the works of art, science and philosophy and the foundation of these acts in the reflexive act itself, that is, in the unconditioned reality of spirit, itself original and underived. For only as a non-contingent reality, it is said, can spirit affirm the Absolute, and thereby see in the Absolute the infinite separation between its original affirmation and its efficaciousness in the world. Kant, in the end, was right in limiting the rational ascent to truth and seeking a further progression towards self-

[66] J. Nabert, *Encyclopédie française*, p. 19.06-1.
[67] *Ibid.*
[68] Cf. G. Madinier, *Conscience*, p. 6 and *passim*.
[69] Cf. G. Bastide, *Méditations*, esp. the eight and ninth meditations.
[70] J. Nabert, *Encyclopédie française*, p. 19.06-2.

realisation in the encounter with the world, with life and with persons in an ethical ascent to the True and the Good.[71]

II. Philosophy of spirit

In the last section we saw that the movement of the philosophies of reflection is an attempt to deepen the philosophical translation of the experience of self-knowledge in such a way as to bring together the singular and universal values. The impersonalism and formalism of critical idealism privileged the construct at the expense of the given, thus isolating spirit and ignoring the existential. The philosophies of reflection, we saw, attempt to better reconcile life and reason.

A similar movement can be recognized in the philosophy of spirit. Here again the idealistic method of reflexive analysis remains essentially intact. But there is an effort to deepen the notion of spirit and to approach more the concrete man in his incarnational and social reality.

The movement of the philosophy of spirit begun by Le Senne and Lavelle in 1934 had for its objective a reassertion of the spirit and human freedom against the double menace of positivistic scientism and the arbitrariness of absolute subjectivism.[72] In the one case there was a tendency to the naturalization of man, thus missing the transcendent nature of spirit and human freedom; in subjectivism there was a misreading of the nature of spirit as regards its incarnational and situational aspects. The new spiritualism aimed at establishing both the dignity of spirit and human liberty while at the same time approaching the concrete and the real through an axiological metaphysics (or in Lavelle's case through a renewed ontology) and a spiritual personalism.

Philosophy of spirit, therefore, aims at establishing a genuine metaphysics by grasping the totality of experience, the origins of all that is, the Absolute. It is an attempt to find once again a source of philosophical fruitfulness in the "Cogito" of Descartes as a metaphysical experience grounding both personality and universality in the relationship of the finite to the infinite.[73] Like the philosophies of reflection, the metaphysical spiritualism of Lavelle et Le Senne employs the reflexive method and through functions of partici-

[71] Cf. G. Bastide, "De la situation de l'homme et des fonctions de la philosophie," in *Les Philosophes français d'aujourd'hui*, textes collected and presented by G. Deledalle et D. Huisman, France, 1963, p. 256.

[72] Cf. R. Le Senne, "De la philosophie de l'esprit," in *L'activité philosophique*, pp. 116-121.

[73] *Id.*, p. 126.

pation attempts to orientate the fundamental antinomies of nature and liberty, knowledge and action, essence and existence toward a concrete solution. In short, it is an attempt to clarify again the problem of man and his destiny.[74]

Both the philosophies of reflection and philosophies of spirit have a similar relationship to idealism and, in this common heritage, to each other. For Le Senne, as for Nabert, contemporary reflections on the life of the spirit are further extensions of idealism.[75] For both, philosophy is eminently a description of consciousness. Both philosophies seek to rejoin experience by a consideration of the interior operations of spirit in act. Both are striving to unite what is most interior and what is most concrete. Like Bastide's philosophy of consciousness (Cf. *La Condition humaine*), the point of departure is consciousness as *genesis* rather than structure. As we have already remarked these philosophies are especially concerned with establishing a just correlation between life and thought. There is an effort to reconcile thought as a movement of life and as a rupture in nature. Like idealism, they strive to recover the unity of spirit.

Perhaps the most characteristic development in the renewal of spiritualism in French philosophy is its *axiological character*.[76] The influence of Kant is especially evident here.[77] In Kant the notion of value loses the ontological character it had in previous metaphysics. It is now especially linked with *will*, which becomes the free source of value. Since there is no absolute knowledge on the speculative level, wisdom is related more explicity to the absolute *Good*. The ideal of the wise man becomes central. Note, for example, the fundamental role Socrates plays in the philosophy of Georges Bastide.[78] It is precisely the "moral intellectualism" and "practical idealism" of Socrates that Bastide finds again in Descartes and Kant and finally incorporates into his own philosophy.[79] It is from Descartes that Bastide tempers the Kantian limitation of knowledge by reasserting the idea of a will enlightened by reason.

Kant, then, is responsible for having given precision to the axiological as-

[74] Cf. E. Morot-Sir, "La philosophie de l'esprit," in *Encyclopédie française*, p. 19.06-11.

[75] Cf. R. Le Senne, *Introduction à la Philosophie* (Coll. "Logos") Paris, P.U.F., 1939, p. 3.

[76] Cf. A. Forest, "De l'idéalisme au spiritualisme," *Giornale metafisica*, 1955 (10), p. 438: "Spiritualism finds itself in accord with this vision (philosophy of value) of philosophy and it finds in it its final justification."

[77] Cf. Chapter I.

[78] Cf. G. Bastide, *Le moment historique de Socrate*, Paris, 1939, p. 87.

[79] Cf. G. Bastide, *Le moment, op. cit.*, p. 192; also: *Les grands thèmes*, p. 140.

sociation of value and liberty. Subsequently we saw this theme in the *idealists* where value is the relationship of the reflexive act to freedom, where the Absolute that is sought is not Being as such, but the Good, that is, that which is over and above essence and existence as Plato intimated. There is, here, the basic movement of Descartes' philosophy now taking the shape of an axiology replacing ontology (Cf. Bastide and Le Senne). At the same time we see the development of a *metaphysics of action*, for it is in *the act of positing itself* that true knowledge is effected.[80] For Kant also, the intelligible world must be, above all, constructed by humanity in its practical moral acts.[81]

Now it is precisely at this point, it seems, that the new spiritualism is able to assert a "via media" for uniting effectively thought and action. For between thought as separation from life and thought as movement of life, there is inserted the *mediation of act*, a principle of spiritual movement towards the Good.[82] It is in the notion of man as *tension* and especially as "task" that the elan of life is preserved and transformed. For the philosophy of spirit, the category of spirit is essentially *value*, not being. It is liberty which is at the crossroads of nature and spirit.[83] Spirit is essentially mediation.[84] Man is more "having to be" than "being."

Thus, just as we had in the philosophies of reflection an experience of the self in the act of giving spiritual meaning to its works, so now in the philosophies of spirit we see the same self-knowledge accomplished in an axiological experience. In Bastide's axiological idealism, authentic reflection is at the same time this revelation of man as value and freedom. For Le Senne, idealism is the best translation of a philosophy of spirit, since it criticizes dogmatic realism and is consequently a quest of spirit.[85] Spiritualism, in turn, sensitive to Bergson's critique, saves idealism from its own tendency to

[80] "It is not a question of knowing things, but realizing ideas." G. Bastide, *La condition humaine*, p. 375.

[81] Cf. J. Lacroix, *Encyclopédie française*, p. 19.04-3.

[82] Cf. G. Bastide, "La nature, la conscience et la Vie de l'esprit," in *Actes* du VII Congrès des sociétés de philosophie de langue française, Paris, P.U.F., 1954, pp. 25-33.

[83] "A mediation of the paradoxes in regards to the object of metaphysics leads us to propose that the object of metaphysics resides: in *freedom*, which presides over the opposition between Being and Nothing; in the constituting *act* of consciousness which manifests this freedom; in *value* which endows the act with authenticity." G. Bastide in *Les philosophes*, p. 256, *op. cit.* Cf. also *Traité*, p. 356 and *La condition humaine*, p. 323.

[84] Cf. G. Bastide, *Méditations*, p. 172; *Traité*, pp. 229-235.

[85] "... idealism seems to us to be the intellectual mediation by which philosophy is able to become a spiritualism, a philosophy of Spirit." R. Le Senne, *Introduction à la philosophie*, p. 87; Cf. also A. Forest, "De l'idéalisme au spiritualisme," p. 433.

objectivism and an implied negation of person and freedom.[86] In a philosophy of spiritualism, then, all the elements of ethics again find a central place, as, for example, in the philosophy of Le Senne, whose idealism is a philosophy of duty as well as a philosophy of freedom. Instead of the pure liberty of idealism (Cf. Brunschvicg, for example), which was more a recognition of the *norm* of spirit than spirit itself,[87] we have in the philosophy of Le Senne and Lavelle, as well as that of Bastide, a spirit that is tension, vocation, struggle for the Good.[88] Spirit is more concretely identified with Love.[89] This spirit is not only invention; it is also consent; [90] it is also "visée de valeur." [91]

The philosophy of value, therefore, in the French school of spiritualism, grounds this spiritualism once again in the metaphysical world by asserting the immanence of the Good to liberty itself, having for finite liberty the role of *End* and determining its function of giving witness to the Good. Reflection thus becomes the revealer of the source of its own objectivity and universality, as well as the sublime vocation of the person. What surpasses man is at the same time what inspires him, and in his liberty becomes manifest the Principle which supports him.[92]

It is interesting to note the similarity between Le Senne and Bastide as regards their very conception of philosophy. For both men axiology is essentially *heuristic*.[93] Morot-Sir, in an interesting article, compares the relationship of phenomenology and existential philosophy to the relationship between idealism and axiological spiritualism. He notes that both existentialism and axiological spiritualism attempted to transform the essential deficiencies of phenomenology and idealism in a new *practical* metaphysics, not unlike, as we have already noted, the double movement within Kant's own philosophy.[94] The result, as Morot-Sir suggests, was not just a juxtaposition of a theoretical and a practical philosophy, but rather a *new metaphysics of action*. In each case (Bastide and Le Senne) there is an attempt to surpass the fundamental insufficiencies of the theoretical and universal in

[86] Cf. Chapter II.

[87] Cf. A. Forest, "De l'idéalisme au spiritualisme," p. 437.

[88] "Man is the one who can take a stand for authentic existence." G. Bastide, *Méditations*, p. 157

[89] Cf. G. Bastide, *Le moment*, p. 208; *Méditations*, pp. 60ss.

[90] Cf. A. Forest, "De l'idéalisme," p. 438.

[91] Cf. G. Bastide, *Méditations*, I, pp. 1-17. These points will be treated in detail in the following sections.

[92] Cf. A. Forest, "De l'idéalisme," p. 439.

[93] Cf. Chapter III, p. 111. Cf. also E. Morot-Sir: "De l'idéalisme à l'axiologie," *Giornale de Metafisica*, 1955 (10), p. 463.

[94] Cf. E. Morot-Sir, "De l'idéalisme," p. 463-464.

the full and concrete universality of moral experience. Even the deficiencies of a pure philosophy of action are supported by a new kind of axiological finality.[95]

Axiological idealism, therefore, marks a new approach to a difficult and perennial philosophical problem, the problem of the relationship between knowledge and action, or, if you will, between nature and freedom, between essence and existence. For idealism is not just a theory exposing a certain approach to the problem of knowledge. For Le Senne and Bastide, it is the very exigence of the spirit seeking itself. For Bastide, as well as for Le Senne, idealism is the only correct philosophical translation of man as spirit, as liberty.[96]

But this idealism must be a moral idealism, "or more exactly, an axiological idealism." [97] It is here that we find centered the central intuition inspiring the philosophy of Bastide. It serves to accentuate his rejection of false idealisms as well as "other kinds of realism." [98] "Axiological idealism" is an assertion of the primacy of Kant's moral philosophy, but within a new and contemporary context. For Bastide it is the context of a philosophy of spiritual conversion and transformation of values that explains the passage from idealism to axiological idealism and spiritual personalism.[99] Practical idealism is, in effect, a critique of systematic, objective idealism, which tends to overlook person and render impossible freedom. Axiological idealism is an effort to resolutely assert the possibility of a speculative voluntarism and a practical intellectualism,[100] for it affirms the necessity of the will in knowledge and of the intelligence in action.

In the end "Metaphysics is Ethics." [101] The philosophy of spirit is by method a philosophy of reflection and in its doctrine a spiritual personalism, an ethics.[102] For it is the moral function which is the practical function "par excellence," [103] the key to the highest realizations of the spirit and the constitution of our being as *person*.[104] Idealism is neither limited to a theory of

[95] Cf., E. Morot-Sir, "De l'idéalisme," p. 465.

[96] Cf. *La conversion spirituelle*, pp. 70-85.

[97] Cf. G. Bastide, *La conversion spirituelle*, p. 70.

[98] Cf. *La condition humaine*, pp. 375-382 and *La conversion spirituelle*, pp. 71-72.

[99] "Spiritual personalism is the normal and unequivocal outcome of moral idealism . . .," G. Bastide, *La conversion spirituelle*, p. 86. For Bastide's relationship to other personalisms see pp. 125-127 of his *Traité*. He identifies himself with the personalisms in the tradition of J. Nabert and G. Madinier.

[100] Cf. G. Bastide, *Les grands thèmes*, p. 140 and *La conversion*, p. 78.

[101] G. Bastide, *Les philosophes*, p. 256.

[102] Cf. G. Bastide, *Traité*, p. 357.

[103] *Id.*, p. 379.

[104] *Id.*, pp. 382-386.

the Absolute nor a theory of human consciousness. It is an authentic "via media," as is the spirit itself, between the purely theoretical and the purely existential. It is the supreme option offered to liberty itself – to sound the depths of man's alienation, to discover in authentic self-knowledge the meaning of freedom, to mark clearly the differences between the spiritual and empirical values, to point the way to the constitution of person, to discover the spirit in the works of promotion of spiritual values or in the processes of dissolution, to distinguish between the "transascending value" and the "transdescending value." [105] The human condition is a tension between being and nothing, a metaphysical drama, an obligation of assuming responsibility for the promotion of spiritual values in the world of man.[106]

Axiological idealism, therefore, attempts to unite in one critique the universal aspects of idealism and ground it in a metaphysics of action within the framework of a philosophy of values. The difficult question of the Absolute and the foundations of moral idealism must be left to the following sections, where we can treat at length the content of the original act of reflection and the problematic of value in its relation to the problem of knowledge and the problem of being. We must ultimately ask the question of the foundations of duty, vocation, liberty and transcendence.[107]

[105] *Id.*, p. 443. Cf. also *Les philosophes*, p. 256. In short, we can say that there are two dynamics of the human situation – one of alienation and one of authentic freedom, one which ascends to the realization of the person and one which descends towards moral decay.

[106] We have in the philosophies of spirit the same effort to escape the notion of spirit as structure. It is an attempt to surpass in moral philosophy the formalism of the categorical imperative by describing the human situation as tension rather than dialectics or structure. For both Le Senne and Bastide it is the effort of the will which can restore at any moment the actuality of consciousness and authentic reflection. As Bastide puts it, spiritual conversion admits of varying degrees and is dependent on an effort of the will as well as the light of reflexion (Cf. G. Bastide, "Esquisse d'une Axiologie de la Personne," *Revue de métaphysique et de morale*, 1944 (2), p. 106).

It is the continuous free taking up again of the factors of personal realization as against the factors of free alienation. This is, as Nabert noted for the philosophies of reflection, through a change in the notion of subject, especially, that transcendental idealism is transferred into an axiological idealism, a spiritual personalism. What is emphasized above all is a change in the subject, a new perspective and attitude worked by spiritual conversion.

[107] Cf. especially G. Bastide, *Méditations*, pp. 117-193.

PART II

AXIOLOGICAL IDEALISM

CHAPTER IV

STATING THE PROBLEM

I. Introduction

In so far as philosophy is a project of man's freedom it is worked out against a horizon that is intimately connected with the philosopher himself. His project can be said to open up the horizon to be studied. His very definition of philosophy determines the itinerary to be followed. The autenticity of his journey will depend on his description of the point of departure, on how faithful he remains to the real.

This fact explains, in part, the living source of disagreement in philosophy. Nevertheless dialogue remains a fruitful source of philosophical progress, precisely because there are also wide areas of agreement on certain basic points. For example, the *Cogito* of Descartes does remain a basic point of departure for philosophy (without attempting to define here what that role is). So does the critical doubt.

The philosophy of Georges Bastide is an axiological idealism. Faithful to the basic necessities of the philosophical intention his philosophy is a doctrine of the human condition arrived at through the mutual intertwining of philosophical object and philosophical method.

For Bastide the concepts which best throw light on the human situation are idealism and value. For the attitude of consciousness which is resolutely idealist is, for Bastide, the perfection of the philosophic activity itself in the subject. It becomes for him the norm for authentic philosophy. The other norm is the notion of value, which, it is said, is the most fruitful notion for overcoming the antinomies of philosophy (especially the antinomies of naturalism and rationalism) and at the same time expresses the human condition in its integrity.

The purpose of this work is to examine the descriptions and philosophical reasonings which bring Bastide to the conclusion that authentic philosophy is axiological and idealist. Our purpose is to examine the origins of the conclusion, to examine the relationship between idealism and axiology and to judge as to the value, in our own mind, of Bastide's philosophy.

How, then, does Bastide justify, elaborate and interpret his axiological idealism? To understand the answer to this question we must begin with Bastide's own description of his central intuition, the nature of the fundamental existential experience preceding it along with the factors leading up to it. The pivotal notion and the central intuition of his philosophy is *spiritual conversion and the consequent transformation of values applied to the human condition.*[1] Only in the spiritual conversion is authentic philosophy realized. It is the source of light and universal intelligibility. In this fundamental reflexive experience the condition of man is not only revealed as liberty – it is itself an experience of liberty.[2] In this fundamental philosophical experience is revealed the necessity of axiology and its authentic use. The fundamental option which constitutes the human situation is revealed here. Spiritual conversion is the authentic moral experience of man in the world.[3]

Our task, therefore, is to describe the fundamental factors leading up to spiritual conversion, for only in this way can it be established that this experience is, in truth, an *authentic human experience* and that it is really a *source* of light for the philosophical doctrine which constitutes the ultimate goal of Bastide's philosophy.

We must further distinguish our problem and our task. For the fundamental experience of spiritual conversion sheds light on two irreducible problems, man and his situation in the world. Not that they are wholly distinct problems, but they are not the same. For the fundamental situation is the presence of *man* in the *world* with the mutual influence of one upon the other. Spiritual conversion is a noetic-noematic reality, that is, it is the revelation of man's axiological situation and at the same time a way of ex-

[1] "In a philosophy of Value, this problem (of spiritual conversion) has seemed to us to be related to the problem of a transformation in values, and it is basing ourselves on this relationship that we have tried to explain this movement of spiritual conversion by changes it brings in the value horizons which it distinguishes." G. Bastide, *La conversion spirituelle,* p. viii.

Cf. also *Les philosophes français d'aujourd'hui, op. cit.,* p. 245: "Many other philosophers have had recourse to this method of axiology; rarely however has this method been used systematically in relation to the problem of man as we would like to use it."

Also: "For our part, we have placed the idea of the spiritual conversion at the heart of our work." G. Bastide, *Traité,* p. 290.

[2] Cf. G. Bastide, *Traité,* p. 140; also *Méditations,* p. 129: "Moreover the reflexive act and freedom are one and the same certitude of consciousness."

[3] Cf. *La condition humaine, op. cit.,* pp. 285, 319. Cf. also: "L'expérience morale," in *Revue de Synthèse,* 1963 (29-31: janvier-septembre), pp. 308, 315, 319 and 320.

isting in the world, a manner of viewing the world and myself, so radically different from the "realist" way of existing that Bastide, like Brunschvicg, can speak of "two consciousnesses" and "two men," depending on whether or not reflection and the regard concerning the world is *authentic* or *inauthentic*.[4] Therefore in the noetic-noematic structure of spiritual conversion the object – the human condition in its axiological dimensions – and the manner of knowing (spiritual conversion, that is, the acquired faith in the ideality of value, the truth of the true judgment) are mutually related and pointing to one another.

But this revelation is a *discovery* and of itself is not given in original experience. It is more the result of a process of purification. It is the end product of an existentially threatening situation and, in the free act of meeting and overcoming, the "merit" or reward, as it were, for the personal act of responsibility as regards the authentic values. Thus, to examine the philosophy of Georges Bastide we must give particular attention to the pre-philosophical situation of man and allow consciousness to bear witness, as he says, to its own life and struggle as it arrives at the spiritual conversion.

For Bastide, the first ontological experience is a negative experience. Only through this experience can man attain the spiritual conversion and philosophy.[5] While it is true that spiritual conversion is based on a reality which is ontologically first (spirit), its revelation is not primarily given in the existential order.

What then is first in the existential order? The answer is twofold: first in the order of philosophical reflection there is the first fact and original affirmation of consciousness: "there is consciousness and I am its witness," [6] in the experiential order the first fact given in experience is the situation of man in the world as tension, as one who is ethically tortured.[7] These are the two starting points for Bastide's philosophy and we must proceed to investigate his own justification, elaboration and integration of those principles into his axiological idealism. In the first fact, the witness of consciousness, Bastide seeks a solid basis for the *rationes cognoscendi*.[8] Philosophy is re-

[4] Cf. G. Bastide, *La condition humaine*, p. 369.

[5] "Il y a conscience et j'en témoigne." G. Bastide, *Méditations*, p. 1.

[6] Cf. G. Bastide, *Méditations*, p. 1.

[7] Cf. G. Bastide, "The Metaphysical Dimensions of Man," *op. cit.*, p. 354.

[8] "We have learned from Descartes that, contrary to the scholastic principle according to which the only authentic movement of thought would be the one which goes from being to knowledge, our reflection ought to be a movement from thought to being. And, on deepening our search for value along this approach we have learned from Kant that a metaphysical axiology ought to replace metaphysical ontology, that is, the reason for being (*raison d'être*) of being, its *ratio essendi* cannot be unveiled

garded as a movement from knowledge to being. The *rationes essendi* (value) can only be discovered beginning with the different kinds of knowing (the first cognitive intention, the movement of naive faith and the imperfect judgment, the experience of alienation and finally the spiritual conversion), that is, the *rationes cognoscendi*.

Bastide's philosophy, therefore, depends for its point of departure on the phenomenological description of the different movements toward spiritual conversion which translate the "often dramatic search" for the *rationes essendi*, that is, the authentic values which move man and the true faith which animates his consciousness. From the outset, nevertheless, we must emphasize that this is not an isolated consciousness, but one immersed in life. "Our problem," says Bastide, "is essentially a problem of life." [9] In this sense the *gnoseological* aim of philosophy (seeking a solid basis for human knowledge) is also a *metaphysical* aim, tending towards the revelation of the ultimate foundations of being. That is why the critical reflection is not only aimed at the discovery of the primary truths bearing the whole edifice of knowledge; it is also a *metaphysical experience* (which is, for Bastide, an eminently moral experience).[10] The primary truth (in the sense of the irreducible first truth) "il y a consience" is intimately linked up with the moral experience of man's dramatic situation in the world. The enveloping and indeterminate unity of both consciousness and the human condition are, as we shall see, intimately connected in one moral experience. It is this primordial and final reality which is present in every act of knowing (authentic and inauthentic) and in every other human activity. In this experience man is present to himself, to others, to the world and to God.[11] The task of philosophy is to manifest and actualize this fundamental reality in the actual constitution of man as person.

II. The original affirmation

It is in knowledge that man realizes and reveals himself, first of all to himself and then to others. The mutual self-revelation of one person to another will be a topic for discussion in the final section of this work. Here we wish to signal out one of the many aspects of knowledge, that aspect which is the most basic intention of knowing in man and which supports and unifies all

except by beginning with the different levels of knowing, that is to say, with the *ratio cognoscendi*. G. Bastide, *Traité*, p. 127.

[9] G. Bastide, *Méditations*, p. 106.

[10] Cf. G. Bastide, *Traité*, I., pp. 385-386.

[11] Cf. G. Bastide, *Traité*, p. 289.

the other possible ways of knowing. Here is the crucial point for every philosophy. Were we can find our basic reasons for agreement or disagreement. Here we find the basic structure of Bastide's philosophy already layed out. In the end our only question can be: does Bastide's description of the primary cognitive intention square with the real in its totality?

Bastide's goal in describing the first and irreducible fact is twofold: he is aiming at establishing by way of description the nature of the human condition and then by way of reflection he hopes to discover the *raison d'être*, the condition of possibility for this reality. "The problem of phylosophy is the problem of man . . . of his reason for being . . . it is the problem of his situation in relation to his reason for being . . ." [12]

The original cognitive intention is the judgment: "il y a conscience et j'en témoigne." [13] Thus, like Descartes Bastide is philosophizing from the "Cogito" as his starting point, as the primary truth (in the sense of being irreducible to any other). Later we shall see that the *Cogito* (as a deepened reflection) functions also as the primary intelligible, the source of light in spiritual conversion.[14]

The appearance of the *Cogito*, of that interiority and spontaneity which constitutes the perennial value of Descartes' philosophy, marks the cornerstone of axiological idealism. But what is Bastide's *interpretation* of this essentially mysterious presence to self which constitutes the foundation of our knowledge?

My consciousness, says Bastide, bears witness to itself. In this bare but undeniable affirmation, consciousness manifests, to some extent, its nature as a power of *self-affirmation* in the act of knowing. But this affirmation, it is to be noted, is not an affirmation of one's being in the spirit of Fichte. For Bastide the problem of philosophy is the problem of man, but not of his being, but of his reason for being (value). "For the being of man escapes us (the ontological question); still, there is a problem of man and it is the unique and necessary problem. It is not the problem of his being, but of his reason for being, not the problem of his notion, but that of his situation in relation to his reason for being, that is, in relation to value." [15] The *Cogito* is inserted in a metaphysics of value in hope of avoiding the unacceptable conclusions of objective idealism and vitalistic romanticism.

Consciousness, then, bears witness to itself. It is the first fact, immediate and undeniable, the point of departure for all knowledge. Consciousness

[12] G. Bastide; "De la situation de l'homme," *op. cit.*, p. 246.
[13] Cf. note § 6 of this chapter.
[14] Cf. G. Bastide, *"Le malin génie," op. cit.*, p. 238ss.
[15] Cf. note § 12 of this chapter.

defines itself in its very act. It is outside all conceptualization. As such, then, the nature of the affirmation is unique. It is not in the order of "things." Nor is it an activity like any other activity – for it is itself the disclosure of all activities. Therefore it cannot be comprehended in terms of anything else but itself.

The object of this original affirmation is consciousness itself.[16] "Il y a conscience et j'en témoigne." When I affirm in all certitude "il y a conscience," says Bastide, I understand simply consciousness' bearing witness to itself as "consciousness of consciousness." But this is not a vain tautology, an introspection, precisely because reflection is not a going outside oneself to affirm oneself as an existing "thing" identical with itself. The affirmation of consciousness is much more.

Furthermore, I am not the "cause" of this affirmation in the sense of being a reality distinct from consciousness. I cannot affirm myself except in this affirmation of consciousness itself.[17] But neither am I a center of creation or emanation of consciousness. I should not even say "I have consciousness" or "I am a consciousness," for these are all inadequate to express the reality of consciousness. The reflexive affirmation is not like other ways of being or having. The affirmation of consciousness is of *another order* than all my determinations.

This irreducibility of consciousness and the witness it bares to itself cannot be denied. It is here, says Bastide, that we begin to realize an *ethical dimension* to consciousness, for consciousness bears witness to itself "ethically apodictically," [18] that is, it asserts itself (over every effort to surpass its witness) as being of another order, as being different. Neither materialism, phenomenalism or rationalism can destroy the unique character of this self-witnessing reality. For whatever I am or whatever I have, my consciousness *of* being this or having that is objective, and the very objectivity of this affirmation keeps me from identifying or attaching the affirmation of consciousness with myself as its author or its possessor. We can only assert "there is consciousness." [19]

But if consciousness affirms itself "apodictically, objectively" does this mean it is something general, abstract or impersonal? Attentive reflection on the matter forces us to say no to this question. Here we note the importance of Bastide's initial position of "idealism" and the affirmation of interiority. For Bastide realism tends to be defined in terms of opposition

[16] G. Bastide, *Méditations*, p. 1.
[17] G. Bastide, *Méditations*, p. 3.
[18] *Id.*, p. 3.
[19] *Id.*, p. 3.

to interiority, that is, as asserting the radical exteriority of the world. There is a tendency in this point of view, says Bastide, "to count everything but ourselves," a new kind of egocentrism which eventually leads to the crisis of nominalism and subjectivism. Subjectivism has its roots in naive realism.[20]

But authentic reflection reveals otherwise. For it is precisely the reflexive affirmation which presents this *twofold* character of an undeniable objectivity which demands and implies *my most intimite interiority*. For the whole point is this – that the *objectivity* of the original affirmation can in no way be likened to exteriority.[21] Therefore, the affirmation "il y a conscience," according to Bastide, is *not* a generalization drawn from my personal, reflexive experience. This would be the "realist" interpretation of a philosophy of representational and conceptual knowledge. But, as was pointed out, it is precisely consciousness that cannot be categorized cosmologically (in terms of what is general and particular for example, simple and complex, active and passive) [22] for these categories cannot be transposed into the realm of interiority.[23]

Nevertheless, there is a "*bearing witness*" in the original affirmation and therefore neither is the original affirmation of consciousness impersonal. *Ego cogito*. Bastide contends the argument of spiritual impersonalism which would deny, logically, the right of reflexive consciousness to affirm itself in the first person. This, says Bastide, is to misunderstand the reflexive *experience* philosophically translated by Descartes in the *Cogito*. With Descartes, maintains Bastide, the *judgment* "cogito, ergo sum" implied a collaboration of the understanding and the will. Thus, even if the objective reality of the ideas which the understanding apperceives seems to justify an impersonalism, the act of the will which doubts, affirms or denies is essentially a personal act, because it is a free act.[24]

It is *I* who know, its is *I* who cannot help but know that "there is consciousness." It is *I* who express and cannot help expressing that "there is consciousness." *I am* this bearing witness of consciousness' self-giving and self-bearing witness.

[20] Cf. *Méditations*, p. 5.

[21] "It is not a question of describing the self complacently in its individualizing characteristics, but rather of discovering oneself as "bearer of the complete sign of the human condition." G. Bastide, *Traité*, p. 90.

[22] Cf. G. Bastide, *La condition humaine*, p. 19.

[23] *Id.* Cf. also *Méditations*, p. 5.

[24] "For in the last analysis, it is in the doubt that the *cogito is* perceived; for the suspension of the judgment in doubt is a willed act as is also the triumphant act of the will affirming my existence as spirit. And the will is freedom; and nothing is more personal than this aspect of my spiritual being." G. Bastide, *La conversion spirituelle*, p. 89.

At this point we have already in the original affirmation the goal of Bastide's philosophy as well as its starting point, for the description of the original affirmation leads to a definition of the *person*. "We call person this witness of consciousness who is in this very affirmation revealed to himself in his own deepest interiority, in the very act wherein he bears witness to the most perfect objectivity." [25] The original affirmation is both a revelation of myself as person (therefore an authentic self-knowledge) [26] and the revelation of what is most perfectly objective.

This original affirmation of consciousness, then, is the first truth and the truth of all truths. As such the witness of consciousness is the "problem of all problems." [27] For the "bearing witness" is none other than the project of truth which is the most fundamental need of man. Bearing witness, when fully grasped for what it is, is man's greatest responsibility – to bear witness to the truth with the totality of my being.[28] *It is not only a fact but a duty.* I must bear witness, and my bearing witness can only be as valuable as my own *awareness* of bearing witness.[29]

It shall become more clear as we go on that Bastide wishes to see the act of reflexion in its totality, that is, as envelopping the total situation of man, both metaphysical and ethical. To be sure the spirit of man is investigation, but it is also a search for salvation. The metaphysical project is not simply situated in space and time, like any other event. Giving witness, in this context, is not simply a factual investigation as to the *explanation* of consciousness in a space-time context. Bergson has made this clear. We can identify the projects of consciousness, for it has a past, but we cannot explain the *act* itself of bearing witness, since it is one with consciousness itself. Every attempt to explain the original act of consciousness in an extrinsic way is bound to fail. For this reason the problem of philosophy or my project and search for truth is not solved, but neither is it illusory or arbitrary, since it is a need, a responsibility of my human condition. Finally, the problem of consciousness is not unsolvable, for "I would not have searched if I had not already found, nor would I ever find anything if I ever thought I could end my search." [30]

[25] G. Bastide, *Méditations*, p. 6.

[26] "... the essential character of this knowledge of self is the objectivity of its direction notwithstanding the interiority of its source." G. Bastide, *Traité*, p. 89.

[27] *Méditations*, p. 6.

[28] "Philosophy is the effective exploration 'with one's whole existence of the fundamental axiological dimensions of consciousness at work, and we know that is precisely this search which truly constitutes the *moral experience* of our personal existence in situation." G. Bastide, *Traité*, p. 357.

[29] *Méditations, op. cit.*, p. 7.

[30] *Méditations, op. cit.*, p. 14.

We shall begin to see that the view of the original affirmation of consciousness in the framework of interiority-objectivity, truth-problem, problem not solved but not unsolvable, follows Descartes' analysis of the finite-infinite, takes on the role of the reflexive judgment in Kant's third *Critique* and assimilates itself to Brunschvicg's notion of progress. For the first certitude, says Bastide, given in the original reflexive affirmation, is not given with the assurance of a possession, but in the certitude of my human condition as a problem, as a vocation of bearing witness, as a duty of giving my attention to what I say and do and believe. In fact every other given is automatically absorbed in my problem, in my person. It is because "to bear witness" is both a *fact* and a *duty* that I understand that the essential human finality is not self-satisfaction (for whatever could be assigned as satisfying me is automatically absorbed in my problem), but self-perfection. "To be a person, that is, a witness of consciousness, is both *to be* and *to have to be* (to become); it is the fact of this duty which gives me the certitude of my necessary condition as *person* and puts me under the obligatory admission that my problem is not yet solved" [31] In other words, for Bastide authentic philosophy is at one and the same time a restlessness to know and to do.

How can we be sure that our definition of man in terms of problem and witness is not a false problem? Precisely, says Bastide, because we have posed the problem, not in terms of concepts, not in a system, but in the undeniable fact of the original affirmation. For the same reason, the problem which man is is unlimited, that is, there is no limit by which we can embrace man's reality in a solution. This is essentially why philosophy itself is the *recognition* of this problem. This is why philosophy is the science of all the other sciences, since whatever else there is beyond the original affirmation of consciousness is itself a *means* of bearing witness. Philosophy itself is never enclosed, but of necessity continual openess to its eternal and infinite problem. In fact, says Bastide, we can say that philosophy is the one inescapable problem. For every activity, every having, every manner of existence no matter how far away from facing up to the problem which philosophy is, remains, nevertheless, a bearing witness to consciousness. Even the denial of the value of philosophy is a bearing witness to philosophy and its problem. Its problem, then, cannot be taken for an illusion.[32]

But neither does the view of philosophy as problem come down to being a kind of nihilism, the simple assertion of man's useless and passionate existence, the mere assertion of his mystery and nothing more. Philosophy is

[31] *Méditations, op. cit.*, p. 8.
[32] *Méditations, op. cit.*, p. 10.

not the attempt to absorb all attempts at knowing and authentic action in the unsolvable problem which man is. For while Bastide rejects the transferral of the subjective certitude of the original affirmation into a dogmatism of realism (the attempt, for example, to absorb the problem of man in the easy solution of a naturalistic empiricism), he rejects with equal vigor the new dogmatism of nihilism, which capitulates in regards to certitude before the relativity of the empirical world. For the sceptic, "whether he speaks or whether he is silent, he remains a conscious witness of himself."[33] We cannot doubt that our problematic lies between realism and dogmatic scepticism.

If philosophy, then, is this *restlessness* of my existence between the dogmatic slumber of rationalism and the ineptness of scepticism, if a life of thought-lessness is ethically forbidden to me, if in other words the problem of philosophy is inescapable to my existence as *person*, then our problematic is orientated towards the question of the authenticity of bearing witness – since the testimony I must give of my existence can be either authentic or inauthentic.

Philosophy then, like consciousness itself, is constituted within the framework of the interval between the presence of a solution that is not given but offered as a promise, between fact and duty. The original affirmation reveals, upon reflection, the basic human condition in its objective and ethical reality. The twofold certitude (the vision of a problem without immediate solution but basically solvable) brings together my most personal interiority in its relation (however distant) with the perfect objectivity of my affirmation.[34]

It is this *metaphysical experience* of reflexive consciousness which orientates Bastide's philosophy towards *axiological* idealism. A further analysis of the *content* and *meaning* of this experience will bring this out.

In the first place, the self-questioning of reflexive consciousness concerning itself has yielded the double certitude of the absolute affirmation "il y a conscience." At the same time, the nature of the subject of affirmation as *person*, that is, as one bearing witness to this objectivity is revealed in the response "and I bear witness." "I bear witness to the truth." That is, it is my project, my responsibility. But there is an infinite distance between my bearing witness and the objectivity of truth, that is the objectivity of consciousness. The solution of my bearing witness in the original affirmation

[33] *Méditations, op. cit.*, p. 10.

[34] "But I see right away between the two a tension wherein is constituted my most personal relationship to myself; at the same time there exists an immense distance with regards to the absolute objectivity of my affirmation." G. Bastide, *Méditations*, pp. 11-12.

to the problem of affirming consciousness is only a solution infinitely distant still from the perfection which calls forth my affirmation. For when we consider it, every problem that arises in man's world and calls forth his care and responsibility in asserting the truth, the infinite and unending truth, is a project immensely disproportionate with my power of bearing witness. As Bastide puts it, either way I look there is *presence* with *absence* at the same time. When the problem is present, the solution is distant; when the solution I bring to the problem – my bearing witness – is present, it is wholly inadequate to the problem which now becomes distant.[35] Yet philosophy remains imperative for man, for his being as person, his freedom is at stake.[36] Man is called to transcendence in immanence; his existence is this paradox of the finite and the infinite; his vocation is perfection.[37]

How express the content and meaning of the basic revelation of consciousness reflecting upon itself? For Bastide, only the language of reflection can bear witness to this vocation. The language of the sciences or the verbalism of rationalism cannot outline the vocation of man as person. Only the language of reflection can situate man in this interval which defines his real situation between the certitude given in the original affirmation and the perspective of his infinite vocation. This is precisely why "philosophies of reflection are more heuristic than dogmatic." [38] For the deepest object of man's search is the truth authentically lived, a bearing witness to the truth. It is the reflexive method which points out this direction.[39]
Why? Precisely because the progress of consciousness' bearing witness depends on the maintained tension between problem and solution. The very existence of man in authenticity, says Bastide, is "to always experience both the distance and the presence of the problem and the solution." [40] For life in the spirit is this constant, ever-renewed search for the authentic spiritual values. It is the spirit's orientation towards the ever more full realization of man as person. It is the progressive incarnation of the spiritual values in humanity. But the goal is given only as a presence that is still an absence. What I have found upon reflection is held and increased only on condition that I do not fail to continue my search. Fidelity to the interiority revealed in the reflexive affirmation and openess to the infinite transcendence which

[35] *Méditations*, p. 12.
[36] Cf. G. Bastide, *Méditations*, p. 13.
[37] *Traité* I., pp, 723-724.
[38] G. Bastide, "Nature, situation et condition humaine," in *Existence et Nature*, Paris, P.U.F. 1962, p. 51.
[39] G. Bastide, *Traité*, I., p. 357.
[40] G. Bastide, *Méditations*, p. 14.

is revealed together with it, requires a regulative rather than a dogmatically orientated philosophical method.

To be sure these statements have yet to find their support in the further development of Bastide's philosophy. Nevertheless, they are brought in here because they already find their principle support in the reflexive affirmation of consciousness, whose elements, for Bastide, are "essentially ethical." [41] To bear witness to consciousness is to seek an authentic existence that is solidly based on this irreducible certitude of the reflexive affirmation. Authentic existence *is* this search. This search defines man's being as person. This search for personal being is a search for authenticity. In brief, the affirmation of consciousness is, at one and the same time: 1. the experience of my *existence* as person; 2. in that which gives it its *value*, 3. in the affirmation of *truth*. Man is this project and need for *personal existence*, for an existence which is *objectively worth while*. Being, knowledge and value are the three necessary and sufficient elements constitutive of this notion of authenticity which defines the essential project of existence. Their mutual relation defines the problematic of philosophy itself.[42] Bastide's *search for a method* (which is intimately connected with the doctrine itself) is determined within this problematic. An examination of the *relation* between values, truth and existence leads him to the conclusion that Value, not being is the primary object of philosophy.[43] The new problematic that arises from this conclusion, namely, how to determine the *authentic values* leads to a deepened reflection and the spiritual conversion and transfiguration of values. We must proceed to examine these further reflections.

III. Search for authenticity

According to Bastide, then, the primitive cognitive experience is essentially ethical. The fundamental revelation in the reflexive affirmation is the situation of man as an existence which seeks, which needs to be authentic and needs to know, in all certitude, what authenticity is. Furthermore the search itself is intimately tied up with man's existence as person. For the primitive cognitive experience is the experience of *my* existence in the act which gives it its value, the affirmation of truth. The original experience is said to be an experience of personal life whose proper act is movement towards fulfillment in authenticity.

Therefore what is given is the reality that *I am* and that *I am to be*. My

[41] G. Bastide, *Méditations*, p. 15.
[42] G. Bastide, *Méditations*, pp. 15-17.
[43] Cf. G. Bastide, "*De la situation de l'homme*, *op. cit.*, p. 245.

existence is experienced as immersed in life. It is experienced as problem and tension. The two poles of this original experience are authenticity (ultimate goal, the coordination of being, truth and the good, that is, God)[44] and my personal obligation to seek to bear witness to the truth by an authentic existence, or better, by the continual search for authenticity. Authenticity is my vocation.

So far it seems that Bastide is faithful to the general movement of an idealist approach to philosophy, which tends to center the philosophical problem around man himself, around consciousness, reflection and self-knowledge, around the basic ethical situation of man.[45] However in Chapter II we shall examine the life situation in which consciousness is necessarily involved. Bastide's philosophy of consciousness is not a philosophy of pure spirit.[46] Still, the question remains whether the *Cogito*, in its content, is enough to serve as an authentic base for a full metaphysics. Even though Bastide's philosophy tends to be only a philosophy of consciousness, we must suspend our judgment to the end in order to see first where his own description of consciousness takes us.

Our first problematic, then, is to see in what relationship the three constituent factors of the original affirmation – being, truth and value – stand with regard to one another. We are still eminently in the area of gnoseological metaphysics. There is a tendency to regard man only in so far as he is a witness of consciousness and to consider consciousness itself as that conscious objectivity revealed in the reflexive affirmation "il y a conscience." We are looking for a definition of authenticity and a definition of man as search for authenticity. This definition will reveal itself upon a confrontation of the three constituent elements revealed in the original affirmation.

1. The problematic of Being

We have seen that authenticity is bound up with my existence and the project of my existence, which is the search for and the affirmation of truth. It is in this effective search for truth that my existence becomes an authentic existence, one of value. But in what does the affirmation of truth consist? In the affirmation of Being? In the affirmation of first truths? Bastide attempts to show that traditional Ontology and subjective idealisms are not authentic ways of bearing witness to consciousness, that is, not authentic ways of existing.

[44] Cf. G. Bastide, *Méditations*, p. 45.

[45] "... the problem of Man and that of philosophical activity constitute one and the same problem ..." G. Bastide, "De la situation de l'homme," *op. cit.*, p. 242.

[46] Cf. G. Bastide, "La nature, la conscience et la vie de l'esprit," *op. cit.*, p. 31.

In the original affirmation of consciousness objectivity is given in *interiority*, that is, in the *relational framework* of the original affirmation: "il y a conscience" (objectivity) and "j'en témoigne" (interiority of the person). Objectivity, therefore, is given in the certitude of my existence as problematic and the orientation of that existence towards a presence which is also an infinite distance. My existence and the affirmation of truth is only a small inadequate solution brought to bear on an infinite problem.

Therefore objectivity is completely different from the "objectivity" which is given in exteriority (for example, in the ontological systems of Leibniz or Hegel). In this sense, says Bastide, objectivity is never given to consciousness.[47] Therefore Bastide rejects Ontology understood as a philosophy of what is supposed to be given in radical exteriority. There can be no philosophy of the thing-in-itself as such. There is no intuition of Being except the "reason for being immanent to the very effort of consciousness itself." [48] It is only in the reflexive affirmation that objectivity is attained. It is not in the things of which we speak. Consciousness is not simply being, that is, the notion of being is not adequate to express the concrete reality of consciousness.

We must note the *sense* of Bastide's critique. He is asking about the possibility of making the objectivity of consciousness equivalent to Being.[49] For Bastide Ontology is impossible because it imagines the solution of the problem which man's existence is – to the dissolution of the reality of consciousness as tension. In the naturalistic point of view, for example, "we count everything but ourselves." In subjectivism there is no objectivity.[50] But consciousness (whose reality constitutes the object of philosophy for Bastide) is of its nature tension between *two* poles – objectivity (given as presence which is also absence) and interiority (problem). Neither naturalism or subjectivism (philosophies of Being for Bastide) retain "the two ends of the chain at the same time," that is, the *interior transcendence* that Bastide

[47] *Méditations*, p. 169.

[48] *Id.*

[49] For Bastide the order of Being refers especially to the ontic order of the reality of nature, of object, of thing in contrast to the order of spirit, freedom, person. (Cf. p. 277 *Le moment historique*; *Traité*, p. 759). It is of the order of reality "que je suis (nature)," or "dont je suis," in contrast to the order of value, the order of "pourquoi," the order of interiority (Cf. "De la situation . . . p. 242, *op. cit.*). In axiology the stable factor is not Being, but the "valeurs finales" of perfection, the imperative of duty immanent to authentic act (cf. p. 760, *Traité*). The order of Being is the totality of being found in the rationalistic ontologies or the vitalistic historicisms or the philosophies of nothingness and opposed to the order of axiology, the order of freedom, person, knowledge. Cf. *Mirages et certitudes*, *op. cit.*, pp. 248-249.

[50] Cf. G. Bastide, *Traité*, p. 357.

wishes to establish in his own philosophy as being the only faithful philosophical translation to the reality of consciousness and to the reality of man's existence. Bastide sees in ontological solutions a certain impatience, a certain lack of philosophical humility on the part of the philosopher rushing, as it were, to the solution of the problem which his existence is, instead of experiencing authentic growth in the company of Being which is absent, but which gives itself to a faithful bearing witness.

Therefore we cannot, according to Bastide, have a philosophy of consciousness ultimately based on the notion of consciousness as ontological reality. Such an approach cannot give adequate expression to this reality in its real conflicts and tensions nor can it express the human condition in its essentially ethical situation.[51] The affirmation of reality (life, consciousness) must be expressed in other terms. Consciousness is openness to its own otherness and cannot be identified to "being in itself" as that which is identical with itself.[52] "No Theodicy can sooth my restlessness by indicating to me the way of authenticity." [53]

At this point we could ask whether the philosophies of consciousness as negativity and non-being could provide a solution, the philosophy of Sartre, for example. No, because we accept the original affirmation wherein we see the *self-affirmation* of consciousness (and therefore its existence) "j'en témoigne." The bearing witness to consciousness is not of the same order as other human activities, such as walking or breathing.

So far, then, we can conclude, says Bastide, that consciousness is not simply "being," because it has yet to be and to bear witness, that is, my existence is given to me as project, as responsibility for the truth. But neither is consciousness nothing, because I am conscious of affirming myself in the act by which my existence is given to me as having a permanent value. Perhaps, then, consciousness is "becoming" and the situation of man is metaphysically one of *duration*?

Bastide rejects the notion of duration as sufficient to express in all its richness the reality of man's situation and the reality of consciousness as objectivity and personal interiority.[54] The reason is clear. We can be conscious of change, but the activity of consciousness in general (the fundamental affirmation by which we are constituted in our reality as interiority) is "without origin" and not subject to change.[55] If we regard the original

[51] Cf. G. Bastide, "The Metaphysical Dimensions of Man," *op. cit.*, p. 355.

[52] Cf. G. Bastide, *Méditations*, pp. 143-144.

[53] G. Bastide referring to the philosophy of rationalism as found in the *Essays on Theodicy of Leibniz*. Cf. *Méditations*, p. 21.

[54] Cf. *Mirages et certitudes* pp. 246 ss. Also *Traité*, p. 148-149.

[55] Cf. Bastide, *La condition humaine*, p. 4.

affirmation of consciousness once again, we see that the real situation of man is dialectical, between two poles that imply stability as well as dynamic movement. As Bastide brings out in his first work *La Condition humaine* stability is a function of consciousness at all stages of its existence.[56] This is brought out by a consideration of the two constituent elements of consciousness – faith (function of adherence) and the judgment (function of coherence).[57] Although the notion of consciousness as genesis is a very important one, it is not capable of expressing faithfully the concrete situation of man as a whole.

Therefore, it seems that consciousness is not any more like becoming than like being or non-being. Or to put it another way, consciousness is being, but it is also non-being and becoming. But in any case to use these categories exclusively would be an *inadequate* witness to the reality.

Finally, Bastide rejects the ontological solution because it seems to him to lead to an impasse when we try to account sufficiently for the other two factors of the reflexive affirmation, namely the cognitive and axiological factors. The passage from being to knowledge seems, for Bastide, to be involved in a representational or subjective idealism.[58] Nor does it seem to Bastide that value can be a derivative of being, that is, that what I am worth can be expressed in terms of what I am (in the ontological framework); we cannot determine the real situation of man and the value of his existence in terms of greater or less participation as efficient causes, or teleologically, as

[56] Bastide considered the psychological aspects of consciousness especially in the first part of this work. On the level of life (the infrastructure of consciousness) consciousness manifests itself as duration conceived without a beginning or end (Cf. Le Senne, *Le devoir,* p. 16), having an active past and accomplishing itself in a constant becoming. But even on the vital level consciousness manifests *two poles* defining the tensional limits of consciousness – "habitude" and spontaneity, aspects brought out by Biran and Bergson. Even on the pre-reflective level there is a certain "primary affective coloration" of a consciousness that is never completely at rest or one with life, always in a state of disadaptation and dynamism. On the other hand, this very disadaptation is a *function,* therefore orientated in a certain direction. There is a presence with an absence (disequilibrium of consciousness) and a future to be obtained (consciousness as problem). There is neither perfect order nor total chaos. While these principles are not yet of the metaphysical order, says Bastide, they point to it. Cf. especially pp. 23-28.

[57] Cf. G. Bastide, *La condition humaine,* p. 125.

[58] For Bastide a theory of knowledge in an ontological framework yields only two possibilities – a representational theory of knowledge or an equation of "being" and "being known." The movement from Being to knowledge in this limited framework would truly be unacceptable. But there are other possibilities which Bastide does not confront. As Dondeyne notes: "... the Thomist doctrine of knowledge is not in the last analysis a representational one." Cf. A. Dondeyne, *Contemporary European Thought and Christian Faith,* Editions Nauwelaerts, Louvain, 1963 (2nd impression), p. 145.

possessing a more or less plenitude of Being and thus approaching to a greater or less degree the plenitude of Being itself.[59] It seems that the primacy of Ontology over axiology leads us into double affirmations of a contradictory nature, the order of necessity (being and finality: "be all that you are" – morality of the status quo) and the order of becoming ("be what you are becoming": pure aspirational morality without foundation). It seems, notes Bastide, that the framework of essence-existence, possible and real remain ambiguous for man if taken as that which is most basic in the constitution of the concrete. It is precisely because essence and existence are not given in conjunction in the original affirmation, says Bastide, that we must seek other notions than these to express the concrete reality of the human situation. To explain the reality of existence by the possibility of essence or the limitation of essence by the exigence of the real seems to leave man in the impossible situation of knowing whether it was existence which lacked inspiration to raise itself higher in the order of essence, or whether it was essence which assigned to existence the perfect limitation of a preestablished order. In either case, notes Bastide, we have the possibility of justifying the *established order* of things – the order of slavery, for example, or the order of the French Revolution.[60] But, he continues, we cannot justify their connection except verbally, for the original affirmation keeps us from bringing them together.[61]

This way of reasoning, then, comes from the basic analysis of the *Cogito* and the definition of person in terms of reflection and self-knowledge. For man's situation is defined as a "to be" and a "have to be" (becoming) at one and the same time. As person man's whole *raison d'être*, according to

[59] Again we should note that for Bastide the essential order is taken in the sense of "être qualité" in a hierarchial order of finality; the existential as "être quantité" in the order of efficiency. But there are other possibilities which we must investigate in our conclusions.

[60] Bastide here criticizes the approach of a philosophy which proceeds from what is supposedly given (ordo ordinatus) to what can be known about the given. For Bastide and for the idealists in general it is rather a question of seeing philosophy as invention and the promotion of an order to be constructed (ordo ordinans). It is, he says, the difference between the realist consciousness and the idealist consciousness and in the moral order between a system which is inherently conservative of the status quo and another which is necessarily continual progress. Cf. *Les grands thèmes moraux, op. cit.* p. 110.

[61] That is, the original unity may be regarded axiologically as the term of the metaphysical *intention* and as the norm *effective* of a progressive unification or it can be regarded ontologically as the source, origin and cause of all that is. But the two ways cannot be brought together for they are opposed one to the other. Cf. *Les grands thèmes*, p. 103. On the ontological order neither dogmatism (the order of salvary) or individualism (order of revolution) have any authentic philosophical justification.

Bastide, is in the *tension* which creates an interval between what I am and what I am to be. In this sense consciousness and the revelation of the original affirmation is the active realization of the disproportion and not the conjunction between essence and existence. The ethical nature of Bastide's metaphysics is becoming more evident. Later we shall see that this is a fruitful source of a certain ambiguity in terminology which, we hope, can be somewhat clarified in our own conclusions.

2. The problematic of truth

So far it has seemed to Bastide that the notions of being, becoming or nothingness are not the notions we are looking for in order to express with fidelity to the real the human situation, especially the fact that that situation is eminently personal. In brief, pure being is not given. Man's "to be" is not, for Bastide, univocal; nor is it analogical. In fact, we can say that for Bastide the question of the analogy of being is beside the point.[62] Man, says Bastide, is not reasonable in so far as he gives one meaning to the verb "to be," but "because he gives to this word several meanings which, "he says, "escape Ontology." [63] And these different meanings do not coincide, "not even partially or by analogy, however modest." In fact, certain meanings are *ethically* exclusive of one another.[64] For man is a combination of being and nothingness that cannot be distinguished in the speculative order.[65]

If, then, our search for authenticity (an existence which is of value based on truth) does not lie open to pure Ontology because of the fact of this mixture of being and nothingness which cannot be separated on the speculative plane (so that being cannot serve as the norm for the true and the good), perhaps it is a pure knowledge that will yield the norm we are looking for, that is, the norm which will be the way of access to the other two (for example, the primacy of value which would situate the two other constituents of our search, being and knowledge) and thus orientate existence towards the gradual unification of the three values. We have already seen that the first fact "il y a conscience et j'en témoigne" is not, for Bastide, a certitude of the ontological order, that is, installing my existence comfortably in being, since, as has been indicated, my existence is a participation in nothingness as well as being. Existence is not a state, but a problem.

[62] That is, once the question has been posed in an axiological and idealist framework.

[63] Cf. G. Bastide, *Méditations*, p. 36.

[64] Cf. also "The Metaphysical Dimensions of Man," *op. cit.*, p. 354.

[65] Bastide's philosophy of being and nothingness must be understood in the context of his moral idealism. Nothingness pertains to the order of exteriority and is engendered by the disorientation of man's acts.

Now it seems that the same is true when we consider the human situation from the epistemological point of view. For it is precisely as relational existence (man as problem, mystery) that man receives his being and therefore a definition of this being will depend on posing the problem correctly, that is, putting in relief the relationship between the problem posed by existence and the solution which is more absent than present.

Two ways seem to be open to knowledge and both have been explored by different philosophies . . . the way of *Logos* and the way of *affectivity*. In fact both seem to be essential in order to express man in all his concreteness. Philosophy, however, has found it difficult to discover the "via media" between rationalism and irrationalism, for "behind the most pure logical judgment there is the context of aesthetic experience . . . and in the most pure aesthetical expression some logical support . . ." [66] The attempts to bring together these two norms (the norm of clarity in the logos, the norm of existential depth in the expression of affectivity) have failed. Consciousness continues to be the *tension* between the truth of the logical order and the truth of the complex global situation taken as a whole.[67]

The convergence of logical and aesthetic truth, says Bastide, is in that quality of our behavior which can be termed "good sense," but this truth is not given to us at the beginning but must be conquered by us. There is, then, *no first truth* given to us at the outset, that is, a point of departure from which all other truths might be deduced. "In reality, we have truth from two sources, and yet we know there cannot be two truths . . . the truth is not given to us at our point of departure." [68]

What, then, is the nature of that "undeniable truth" of the reflexive affirmation that has become our point of departure for philosophy?

Again we must go back to emphasize the content of the *truth* of the original affirmation. The certitude of the reflexive affirmation, says Bastide, is not the certitude of a truth already attained, but rather the certitude of my *obligation* to seek and construct the truth – just as in the ontological order the certitude of my existence was more a certitude of my obligation "to be" against the nothingness also present at the heart of my reality. It was not the certitude of being as such.

And so, for Bastide, the question remains: "what is truth?" The norm or criterion of truth is to be sought elsewhere.[69] The truth of knowledge is of

[66] G. Bastide, *Méditations*, p. 41.

[67] *Id.*, p. 42.

[68] *Id.*

[69] Cf. in this regard the remarks of the first chapter, especially concerning the role of the judgment in the philosophy of Brunschvicg.

its nature a complex reality whose law of composition is outside itself.[70] Essence and existence are given to us from two different sources (logos and aesthetic intuition), but they are not given in the unity of truth. Bastide shows that various solutions to the problem of knowledge and existence are unacceptable for the problem constituting the human condition. The idea of God is not given to us in such a way as to guarantee a solution to our problem in the real order.[71] Nor can transcendental idealism or objective idealism solve the problem of my person which is the problem of man. Spiritual intellectualism and irrationalism are also rejected in their turn. In any case, *the passage from knowledge to being* proves contradictory to the original affirmation.

For like reasons, passage from knowledge to the good results in unacceptable conclusions. Until man is established in the unity of knowledge, how can he be the authentic subject of reference for value judgments? Yet it is the problem of man and the lack of coincidence between the logical and affective elements that make it impossible for us to go from knowledge to the good. We would see arise the same antinomies of individualism or dogmatism if we tried to ground our value judgments on either one of the two ways open to our knowledge, for the unity of the good which we seek is given neither in moral rationalism nor absolute sensualism. In truth, we desire more than we know and we do know what we desire, but neither intellectualism or sensualism can give an account of this truth.

Therefore, just as truth is not given at the outset, neither is the value that we are seeking. It is precisely the conjunction of the two that constitutes the problem of man's existence, for authenticity is that search for the unity of the true and the good which is not given at the outset, which is received as the fundamental obligation and which cannot be achieved except in the unity of both. "Unum verum bonum communicabile sui," is also the ideal of Bastide's axiological idealism, but the question remains as to the norm of truth itself.

3. *The problematic of value*

For Bastide the notion of value is the true object of the metaphysical intention, "metaphysically anterior to and superior to knowledge and being itself." [72] For him this means that "in what concerns me as *person* my know-

[70] For Bastide the function of the judgment is eminently axiological. Cf. *La Condition humaine*, p. 128, 222-234. Also: "Nolite Judicare," *op. cit.*, p. 395ss. The influence of Descartes and Kant becomes all the more evident in Bastide's theory of truth.

[71] Cf. *Méditations*, p. 45.

[72] Cf. *Méditations*, p. 59.

ledge cannot attain certitude and my being cannot be assured of acting unless the Good orientates and animates it." [73] This truth is, for Bastide, the necessary conclusion from the reflections concerning the problematic posed by the first fact. The imperative of authenticity which is immanent to the whole life of consciousness is essentially an *imperative to act*. A being which is absolutely passive "must be considered as nothingness." It is, therefore, "act which causes being, but the principle of action is something different from being." [74] For "all reality is contingent and owes its consistance to the principle which we call the Good (Valeur)." [75] It is only the Good which can render my bearing witness something of value, that is, a manifestation of authentic existence.

The orientation of knowledge, for example, is not haphazard – it is not only orientated toward true knowledge but toward the "bien penser" which in itself is sufficient for the "bien agir," [76] toward the affirmation of truth which is at one and the same time an affirmation of my person and therefore a good act on the way to closing the gap between the solution and the problem of my existence. For Bastide, knowledge is eminently an *act* and the value of truth is due to its being an act.[77] "Value is the *raison d'être* of existence and knowing, and this *raison d'être* must be sought in the source of action itself." [78] My existence is given to me in the framework of a task and is oriented toward a solution. It is not sufficient to "act" in order to be, but it is necessary to act well, in the direction of the orientation of my existence as witness. The *actualization* of my being in its victory over nothingness and the realization of an authentic knowing (one which is an affirmation of my existence as value) is possible only when grounded in the Good. For both

[73] Cf. *Méditations*, p. 59.

[74] *Id.*

[75] *Id.*

[76] For Bastide the two Socratic paradoxes lose their ambiguity and are seen as true in a philosophy of spiritual conversion. It is the "practical intellectualism" and the speculative voluntarism that he sees also in the philosophy of Descartes and takes as the ideal of his own philosophy of action and spiritual conversion. Cf. *Les grands thèmes*, p. 140. Cf. also *Le moment historique de Socrate, op. cit.*, p. 175. As Bastide notes: "Il suffit de connaître le bien pour le faire, car pour le sage, dans la connaissance éthique de soi, connaître et agir ne sont, au fond, qu'une seule chose," p. 23. *Les grands thèmes*, en Socrates was neither a rationalist nor a pragmatist, but a man of the spirit.

[77] But the act which has the consistency of the authentic value which supports it and not just any "act." For Bastide it is impossible to distinguish action and passion except by the consideration of the *Value* which gives the act its authenticity. Cf. *Traité*, p. 357.

[78] Cf. G. Bastide, "Les problèmes majeurs de l'axiologie," *Les études philosophiques*, 1948, pp. 84-85.

certitude and action are caught up in and founded upon the ethical imperative of the original affirmation of consciousness.

It is for this reason that metaphysics is necessarily *a metaphysics of action.*[79] For it is not sufficient "to be" but it is imperative that we *exist authentically.* Therefore, axiology finds its autonomy only in a philosophy of action and a philosophy of action find its authenticity (bien agir) grounded only in axiology. The first principle of philosophy must be: "C'est la valeur qui fait l'être et non l'être qui confère la valeur." [80]

If the Good, then, is the basic reality and condition of possibility for both "being" (authentic existence) and knowledge (the truth of knowledge, that is, knowledge which is an act – where the "bien penser" is a "bien agir") the question rests as to the manner in which the Good is given to us, for how are we to pass from the Value present in the original affirmation to the truth of knowledge and the action of being? Or more to the point – how do we experience the presence of the Good? In general it can be said that we experience it as *given* in the original affirmation. But how is the Good given to us? For Bastide, the real problematic of axiology is the *manner* by which we are to attain the truth of knowledge and the act of being by way of the Good. For what is metaphysically first *quoad se* is *quoad nos* the far off goal of our search. The notion of Value appears as *ambiguous*. In other words, the first conclusion of Bastide's itinerary has brought him as far as *axiology*, but axiology itself is problematic, as we shall see.

For we cannot attribute the original giveness of the Good as being (for this would be to fall back into Ontology), that is, we cannot say that the Good is given in terms of final and efficient causality. Nor can we identify the Good as given to us as the result of knowledge or the result of the act of judgment. To assert the absolute primacy of judgment, says Bastide, would be to fall back into a false idealism. The Value which is given to us is, however, the *principle* of the truth of knowledge and the life of being and is, therefore, above the categories of essence and existence.[81]

We have here a difficult problem for Bastide's philosophy and axiology in general. But our interest at this point is to follow as faithfully as possible the movement of this thought and later on, only, draw our conclusions. If the Value which is revealed to us is itself the principle of being, of knowledge, then, says Bastide, we must admit that what is given to us, at least *quoad se* is pure value." [82] Its presence is not experienced as "knowledge"

[80] G. Bastide, "Les problèmes majeurs," *op. cit.*, p. 85.
[81] G. Bastide, *Méditations*, p. 60.
[82] *Id.*

or "act," but as "a call to truth and existence." Therefore the experience of the Good is "*in a kind of movement*" calling us to an authentic existence,[83] by which "the purely axiological transcendence of the principle manifests itself in the act of enlightening and creating us," in the act of "confering on us knowledge and being," in the act of "impregnating with its own vivifying and rectifying action the activity by which we know what we know and are what we are only because we are authentically what we are in and by Value itself." [84]

This difficult and basic passage must be commented on further. What does it mean? In general, it means that the principle of our authenticity is Authenticity itself (God) and that *real* certitude and *real* living is only given when it is the product of authenticity itself which is immanent to all true certitude and all true life. That is, not every kind of knowing is a promotion of my person, not every kind of "acting" is an increase and deepening of my existence. When we experience ourselves in our personal existence, when, that is, we *really* know that we know (authentic knowledge orientated toward the solution of my problematic existence) and when we really live our own life (and not the life of the self constituted by external, non-interiorized experience) *then we experience not only ourselves, but the principle of our personal existence.* Here the call to authentic existence and the act of authentic existence are one and the same movement.[85] The need for authenticity *is* the presence of Value and the experience of this need is the experience of the presence of God.

It is in this deepened reflection on the problematic of Value that Bastide becomes aware of a *new form* in which reflexive thought can come to grasp this *need for authenticity* which is the presence of the Good, which is the presence of God. The new aspect in which this presence is revealed is named Love, that is, Love is the name we can meaningfully give that movement which translates in us this presence, "by which everything takes on value and wherein everything issues in an authentic existence." [86] Says Bastide, "I find in myself, in my own meditation on myself the certitude that the way of existence is only open to him who answers in love this call of Love itself, as our eye answers to the light and as everything on this earth answers the heat of the sun's rays." [87]

Here we must note well that the deepening of our reflection on the mean-

[83] *Id.*
[84] G. Bastide, *Méditations*, p. 60.
[85] *Id.*
[86] G. Bastide, *Méditations*, pp. 60-61.
[87] *Id.*, p. 61.

ing of our human condition as revealed in the original affirmation is at the same time *a deepening of our problematic*. For now it has become clear that the human condition as vocation to authentic existence is a vocation to a corresponding movement, value giving, which can also be named love, that love "without which nothing is of value." For the metaphysical experience is deepened only in the deepened realization of the original *experience* of the *distance* that *separates*. The primary experience which is the base for all the rest of our experiences, the primary and indubitable given which we can never exhaust in our knowledge or ever escape in any of our activities (no matter how far from the center of our being that activity be) is not, for Bastide, the experience of existence, but the experience of the *call to existence*; it is not simply the experience of myself-in-the-world with others, but existence (myself in the world with others, to be sure) in its relation of its being called by the ground of its *authentic* being. It can be given only in an act of authentic existence. The primordial, constant and final experience revealed in a deepened reflection is the experience of God's love. And this experience is not a fact, nor a possession of ourselves in any act of knowledge, it is a call to realize ourselves by approaching more and more the presence we experience at an infinite distance, the presence which takes on the name of Love. Our authentic existence goes beyond the effort to grow in the understanding of being. It is accomplished only in growing to love the ground of our authentic being which is at one and the same time a love of others and a love of God.

The discovery of the philosopher in his authentic vocation (love of wisdom) is, then, basically problematic, not only from the point of view of knowledge (which we lack) but also from the point of view of existence (which we lack) or, in our present context, we could say that this lack is a lack of love. For love, we can say, is the condition of possibility for true knowledge and true existence. Yet the philosopher has only discovered the key to existence; the way, the road that stretches out towards the Good in the very act of self-fulfillment is not yet clear. The problematic of axiology becomes the problematic of the *philosophical method*.

For if the notion of value as we have seen Bastide describe it is really the notion which must nourish philosophical thought, then we have to further determine the method for distinguishing the authenticity of love itself. For the presence of the Good which is given to us in the movement and experience of personal existence is in itself (*quoad se*) pure authenticity; but *quoad nos* it is yet undetermined.[88] That is, what is given in the original affirmation

[88] G. Bastide, *Méditations*, p. 62.

are the two relational terms constituting the human condition, but as yet no road is marked out. The question therefore remains: how can I begin to answer the question posed by the problematic of my existence, the problematic posed by Love itself? For *to me* Love is essentially ambiguous.[89]

In what does this ambiguity consist? We have seen that the basic certitude concerning our situation is the necessity of authentic existence. But where are the true values? By what method can I hope to distinguish the source itself of true knowledge and authentic activity? For if value is of the very essence of act, are they the empirical values, the object of desire? Or are they the spiritual values, the object of a dialectic of promotion? Are they absolute or relative, many or one, immanent or transcendent? How are they known? With reference to man? How pass from axiology to a metaphysics of being, to an assertion of reality? It seems that the vision opened up in the original affirmation has suddenly closed and left us at a loss for a possible solution. We seem to be back where we started – with the three constituents of our philosophical search: being, knowledge and value. Each one demands a hearing. Each one is necessary to support the other: existence needs the clarification of knowledge as well as the ultimate support of value in order to be *authentic* existence; the authenticity of knowing demands the act of existence and its value; and value itself must be rooted in truth and existence to be itself of value.

Our problematic may have taken us up to a philosophy of action and an axiological metaphysics, but most of all it has layed bare the human condition as even more problematic than the original affirmation itself. For what good would it do to have certitude as regards my vocation to authenticity (the real unity of the good and the true in act), if no method manifests itself by which the authentic values may be distinguished from the inau-

[89] Bastide also points out the ambivalence of emotional movements of consciousness on the vital level of reality, due to the fact that it is nourished from two different sources. One source is the disadaptation factor of consciousness itself. The other source is the readaptation factor, with all the uncertainty of its outcome. It is on the emotional level that our higher affections and values become obscured. By his very nature man is a restless being (Cf. Le Senne, *La découverte de Dieu*, Paris, Aubier, 1955, p. 165). He can neither afford perfect rest or enjoy perfect activity. Tension is the very *raison d'être* of consciousness. The real problem of life is not the release of tension, but its maintenance in a just equilibrium. We love adventure, but hate the failure our actions can bring, or the loss of tranquility that activity seems to impose. We fear disadaptation, but we also love it. We need to follow and love some ideal, but we hate not being a part of the world where these ideals seem to be lacking. The love of what we love is rendered ambiguous at every turn. This essential bipolarity of value constitutes the essence of the new problematic and renders axiology insufficient to itself.

Cf. *La condition humaine*, pp. 34-35; also *Méditations*, p. 63.

thentic values? For while the human condition is an imperative of authenticity, it is also the possibility of inauthenticity. Eventually we must seek the root of this possibility. For perhaps there we can find the meaning of true love, as far as man himself is concerned.[90]

4. From Axiology to knowledge and reality

The reality of our new problematic, the problem of axiology itself, will become apparent when we reconsider the problem of knowledge and the problem of being from the point of view which Bastide has taken as regards the metaphysical primacy of value in philosophy. Let us considerer first the problem of knowledge.

Bastide is well aware that no philosophy of value can escape the problem of belief. There is no philosophical consciousness without Faith.[91] Philosophy itself depends, in a way, on an original act of faith, namely, that the original task of philosophy itself is a possibility, that consciousness can eventually become aware of itself in an act of reflection, "that the genesis of a spirit transforming itself and growing to maturity" can be eventually known.[92] For Bastide, philosophical faith is not removed to the existential, pre-metaphysical aspect of the philosophical intention, since, for him, the act of philosophy is a willed act as well as a self-clarifying one. As we shall see later the will is the principle organ of belief as well as the nerve of the judgment.[93]

The activity of consciousness is, for Bastide, one unique function of judgment. This function, in turn, reveals upon reflection certain *forms* of activity. Philosophical faith ("qui sousentend le jugement") [94] is immanent to every judgment ("par lequel une conscience se pose comme telle") and therefore, says Bastide, to every conscious act. It is the *dynamic factor* of consciousness as opposed to the structuring factor (judgment as such) which analyzes and synthesizes. Faith represents the complex movement of adhesion which accompanies the intellectual aspect of every act of consciousness.

The intervention of faith in the judgment is manifold: it directs the attention to a particular matter, gives the general orientation to the philosophical projects of the intellect, and creates the sensitivity for the evidence that will determine the mind's assent.[95] Therefore the conscious act is determined by

[90] Cf. *Méditations*, pp. 66-67.
[91] G. Bastide, *La conversion spirituelle*, p. 1.
[92] *La condition humaine*, p. 9.
[93] Cf. G. Bastide, "*Le malin génie*," *op. cit.* p. 239.
[94] Cf. *Traité*, p. 128.
[95] G. Bastide, *La conversion spirituelle*, p. 4.

the light of the intellect as well as by the force of faith, just as the navigator's course is determined both by the light of the sun and the force of the wind. Parallel to the judgment, which we shall discuss later, faith has three functions: a gnoseological function, an ontological function and an axiological function. As regards the *gnoseological* aspect, faith (croire que) underscores the system of intelligibility structured in the analysis-synthesis activity of the judgment. The work of disassociation for example in the elaboration of the judgment is effected in a manner commanded by the interests of the judging consciousness. The *ontological* aspect of faith (croire en) has to do with the witness of confidence present in some way to every conscious act (whether naive, critical or religious). This confidence is in a being (myself, others, God) whose presence and nature alone can validate and guarantee in the last resort the validity of my action. But most fundamental of all is the *axiological* aspect (croire à) of faith in every conscious act. For in the conscious act the deeper interests (affective) that move consciousness, that orientate the direction of *attention* and the *field* of exploration (wherein every judgment that does not isolate these factors becomes a value judgment) play the most important role.[96]

The importance of the notion of philosophical faith in an axiological idealism has already become apparent. "To speak of faith is to speak of values." [97] Value is defined by Bastide in terms of a philosophical faith.[98] Faith is defined as the movement of consciousness towards value. The notion of philosophical faith, alone, can integrate the notion of truth and the world of values. Otherwise, as Bastide notes, we would have to abandon the universal and objective aspects of a philosophy of value. If we separate truth from value, then values become "appreciations," simple facts.[99]

Therefore, in an axiological idealism, where consciousness is defined as above all "direction towards authenticity," [100] where the primacy is given to the notion of value, where the mode of faith in consciousness is "croire à," there is given both the dynamism immanent to axiology plus the transcendence of the value which is the object of axiology, but a value which is pregnant with a gnoseological content and able therefore to give rise to the

[96] Georges Bastide, *La conversion spirituelle*, pp. 4-6.

[97] G. Bastide, "La nature, la conscience et la vie de l'esprit," *op. cit.*, p. 29.

[98] *Id.*

[99] Cf. G. Bastide, *Traité*, I., p. 209. For this reason Bastide rejects the individualism of R. Polin, *La création des valeurs*, Paris, P.U.F., 1944. As Lavelle notes Polin's approach refuses to take into account the metaphysical supports which alone can ground an axiology. Cf. *Traité des Valeurs*, I., p. 145-146. (Paris, P.U.F.; 1951).

[100] "If man reflects, it is in order to be authentic." G. Bastide, *Méditations*, p. 144.

truth.[101] The "croire à," says Bastide, includes a *reciprocal specification* of love by the truth and of truth by love. For the *value* which is the object of *love* becomes "ce à quoi on croit," and the "truth" becomes worthy of love as a value. It is precisely in axiology, says Bastide, that truth is able to be integrated in the world of values.

Nevertheless, at this point in our reflections the notion of faith and axiology and truth remains highly problematic. For we have seen that the knowledge of myself as *person* (therefore not ontic knowledge) is *not* given, but is the object of my search. Therefore, it is not only a question of "what is true" but most of all a question of the "rectitude of truth," that is, the *path along which* the truth of myself as *person* is to be discovered and achieved. In this context it was said that value has ontological primacy, for the "rectitude of truth is value," [102] and it is axiology which orientates the authentic search for truth. But axiology itself is problematic.

For in axiology the problem of knowledge is a problem of belief. It is belief which is the notion which is able to translate at one and the same time the movement proper to the emotional side of man and the adherence of the spirit in its search. But this confidence is at the same time a *fundamental uncertainty.*[103] For in the passage from value to truth, the "obscurity" of love imprints a certain precariousness "which truth supports with difficulty." [104] If this were our final say on the matter than we would have to admit that axiology rested on a "certain sensibility to value," "with supreme jurisdiction," which sensibility might not be pure emotion, but "a kind of perception of first truths," which truths constitute the field in which one believes (croire à), being at the same time regulative of what "one ought to believe by reason of the axiological supremacy which the situation confers on them." [105] In other words if there are these truths of the heart of which Pascal speaks, then the reasons for belief might well be said to excell the reasons of reason itself. But would this be to solve the problem or to pose it? Who would be the first one to pronounce these first certitudes of the heart? We have already indicated that as far as man is concerned, love itself is problematic. How can it be a first principle? There is no divine instinct.[106]

We must regard man himself, therefore. Man is desire and will.[107] The problem is to be attacked here. The problem is not desire and will as in-

[101] *Id.*, p. 68.
[102] Cf. G. Bastide, *Méditations*, p. 59.
[103] G. Bastide, *Méditations*, p. 69.
[104] *Id.*
[105] *Id.*
[106] *Id.*, p. 70.
[107] *Id.*, p. 72.

stinctive movements (which they are) but *as related to consciousness*. For *human* desire and will are only such in and by the conscious grasp of these movements and the *problem of truth* is related precisely to the conscious act. "The knowledge of instinct is not of the same order as instinct itself." [108]

Here we come to the heart of our problem. For Bastide is faced with his own conclusion as to the necessity of axiology as having ontological primacy over being and truth. Furthermore he rejects as the basis of knowledge blind instinct or moral sentiment theory. He refuses to reduce truth to any one value, since in its own right the truth value has its own demands and presides over all the other values, demanding an account of them. There can be no authenticity without truth. But truth must be a value.[109]

Finally, a discussion on pragmatism reveals the same dead end. It seems that at every turn truth revindicates itself and the problem rests: How pass from value to truth? For we desire to establish our values in truth – but we experience the imperative to give witness to only objective truth. My belief is suspect when determined by feeling. My merely subjective opinions cannot pretend to objectivity.

In conclusion we have seen that value is the object of belief (ce à quoi on croit). Faith is necessary for conscious life. The problem is the relation between truth and value. My subjective credulity is not a sufficient norm of credibility. But if metaphysics is axiology, the faith aspect of consciousness rests an essential element. But if dogmatic axiology, moral instinct or pragmatism are insufficient to explain the human condition, then, it would seem, their faith is not a true faith. The problematic of metaphysics as axiology continues to give rise to this new problematic concerning the authenticity of the values themselves. We are forced to reflect more deeply. In reality Bastide is moving towards his own philosophy of spiritual conversion.

The problematic of axiology and reality is not without similar difficulties. For once having stated the primacy of value in the philosophical order, how are we to pass from value (axiology) to reality (ontological aspect). For authenticity calls us with the threefold exigence of an *existence* of *value* in all *truth*. Our existence, that is, to be authentic, must have both the transparency of knowledge and the consistancy of value. Thus each constituent of authentic existence needs the support of the other two. In this section we are faced with the problem of how value itself is to ground its own validity in all truth and *concreteness*. Ultimately it is the question of the positive *unity* of the person that Bastide is trying to explain and promote.

[108] G. Bastide, *Méditations*, p. 72.
[109] Cf. G. Bastide, *Méditations*, p. 73.

How does our problem pose itself when we try to go from the primacy of value to the ontological order? So far we have seen that axiology, in its development, is essentially regulative rather than dogmatic, concerned more with the maturity of consciousness rather than philosophical system. In this sense value was said to be situated above essence and existence. By its very nature, faith (croire à) is an existential act of being transcended by the value which is the object of the faith intention. For the "croire à" is essentially a *practical faith* whose product is action. It is not a theoretical faith whose object is one of speculative contemplation.[110] In this light, it would seem only too tempting to take this value as our starting point while still asserting dogmatically the speculative nature of the valued *reality* itself. But is this possible?

Bastide correctly judges that it is not. As we shall see, he abandons all hope of "knowing reality" in the "naturalistic or dogmatic sense of the word, that is, by the notions of a more or less cosmological metaphysics." [111] The transcendence of the Good is such that it cannot be fitted to any ontological categories and it is, therefore, bereft of any causality.[112]

But neither does Bastide feel that reality can find a suitable account of itself in the notion of a demiurge who would have fashioned the world based on the *model* which the Good offered. In fact, Bastide believes that it is precisely in the consideration of this notion of model that we can finally conclude to the illigitimacy of all passage from the axiological to the ontological order... in the classical sense of the word. For the notion of model, he says, *seems* to work this passage because it has in its notion both ontological and axiological possibilities. That is, it is a *mixed* notion and as such might appear to have this mediating effect. But it is precisely as a *mixed* notion that we see that it cannot be the *means* of passing to the limit concept (a passage which, for Bastide, is acceptable for the pure concept and which, in truth, is the extent of the notion of value as it has been discovered so far). For the error of all eclecticism is based precisely on this misuse of the mixed concept.[113] For the notion of model can only translate a subdetermination of a reality already determined. Its nature is properly *adjectival* and it can only translate a transitive action from a *given* reality to a projected one. As an absolute, it would either be *the substance* of ontology, the *Perfection,*

[110] "... there is no necessary relation between the order of rational explanation and the value of the practical motivations determining the goals of our actions." G. Bastide, *Traité,* I., p. 37.

[111] Cf. G. Bastide, *Traité,* I., p. 25.

[112] Cf. *Méditations,* p. 76.

[113] Cf. *Méditations,* p. 77.

that is, it would be Being itself . . . or else it would be above Being, but *without reference* to any determination whatsoever, absolutely undetermined and therefore not even a model.[114] In which case the notion of *Value* either falls into the philosophy of justification (the problem resolved) or a materialism of values (value brought down to the determination of the real).[115]

Bastide's intention here, in his critique, is to preserve the heuristic characteristic of the notion of value and thus avoid what he believes to be the contradiction of the ontologies, all the while preserving a *metaphysics of action*.[116] In other words; for Bastide, as we have seen, philosophy is identified with the *search* for the Good and the *progressive approach* to the ideal (authenticity, unity of the true and the good). As such he rejects Ontology in the framework of its being a rationalistic explanation of reality, for "a metaphysical explanation of reality (in the rationalistic sense) would imply the search had reached its term and had ceased to exist as such, thereby eliminating the search for the Good; the activity of the search for the Good implies a *constant transcendence* of the Good itself, so that we cannot install ourselves at the source of Value in order to view from this vantage point the movements of generation and corruption." [117]

Thus the very notion of philosophy as *axiological idealism* prohibits the physical realism implied in a genetic explanation of reality. The only conclusion possible is that "we cannot deduce Being from the Good," "any more than we could deduce the Good from Being." [118] For we cannot *believe* in that justice which we desire to restore in an unjust world, while, at the same time and in the same movement of thought, we are thinking about an Absolute Justice which we would be believing in an attempt to explain its work.[119] For Bastide, in moral idealism it is pure value which is the object of the *practical intention* which necessarily situates thought over and above the notion of Being; in Ontology the same notion as principle of reality, says Bastide, is necessarily aimed at the notion of Being.[120] The problem of evil becomes, he says, one of the primary obstacles to such a philosophical approach.

The causality of the demiurge (causalité poétique), then, must be rejected

[114] *Id.*

[115] Cf. G. Bastide, *Traité*, p. 357.

[116] Cf. G. Bastide, *Traité*, I., p. 357.

[117] G. Bastide, *Méditations*, p. 78.

[118] G. Bastide, *Méditations*, p. 78.

[119] *Id.*

[120] "These two ways are precisely the ones experienced by Greek philosophy with the ethical idealism of Plato and the ontological realism of Aristotle." G. Bastide, *Les grands thèmes, op. cit.*, p. 103.

as a suitable explanation for a possible passage from the axiological to the ontological order. But what about the notion of finality? It also has an "axiological function" over reality. In pragmatism, for example, (and here we take a rather naive notion of finality) the notion of success is pliable in any direction desired, that is, in any "knowledge" of the world we might acquire. Here we see, says Bastide, the anthropomorphic relativity and consequent illigitimacy of this use of the concept of finality.

On a more serious level, however, we have the proposal of *critical idealism* (which itself warns against the facile use of limit concepts) endeavoring to attain the real by bringing together a system of knowledge (the connections of phenomena one with another in a relative system of knowledge) and value as known in the *experience of duty,* whose absolute character would, supposedly, be sufficient to convert our relative knowledge on the phenomenal level to a knowledge of reality itself. This union is rejected by Bastide, and rightly so, for it involves two *different* and (for Bastide) *opposed* orders. Their artificial union does not give us access to the real. For either the relativity of our knowledge will have its influence in the practical values (as in pragmatism, utilitarianism) or else the absolute nature of the practical values will be transferred to our knowledge and we will end up with a notion of finality corresponding to a noumenal, underlying reality immanent to nature (or to history or both together). In which case we are left with the problem of knowing *how value itself is of value,* that is, how its purity is retained when it becomes the genetic principle immanent to the determined order of things.[121]

Nor does an evolutionary durational concept of a "finality without end" help us make this passage from axiology to the order of nature and the forms which nature takes (whose reasons cannot be explained by the life force alone). In fact, such a world view is equally open to the pessimistic interpretation of the absurd *vouloir vivre* of Schopenhauer or the optimistic triumph of the elan of life in Bergson. But the theory itself cannot give reasons for one or the other.

Historicism likewise fails to explain the incarnation of values which axiology must seek to explain . . . as if the "sense" of history were the ground for assisting at the coming to light of a world bearing as its support an Absolute Value. But every attempt to *determine* the reality of this value leaves us with the same dilemma, namely, as to the ultimate, transcendent value (pure and above the succession of historical change). Nor could we determine whether all the movements were really in a linear direction or

[121] Cf. G. Bastide, *Méditations,* p. 80.

whether there were other possibilities, for example, of movements in opposite directions of progress and decay, directions of two totally different orders. Optimism and pessimism rest interchangeable in such a philosophical approach. There is no pure value distinguishable.[122]

So far, then, our problem remains. If we have seen the necessity of the primacy of Value, says Bastide, that primacy itself rests fundamentally problematic, both as regards the problem of knowledge and here as regards the question of the real order itself. This problematic is essentially what was given in the original affirmation, *the problem of the interval* between existence and the affirmation of the ideal of authenticity which was evidently absent (while being present) from the reality which affirmed it. No number of intermediaries so far has seemed sufficient to preserve the transcendence of the ideal, while at the same time asserting its creative efficiency. Our problem remains one of bringing together immanence and transcendence without the two extremes represented globally, so to speak, by the two tendencies of stoicism and platonism which find their recurrence in the history of philosophy. No notion of nature as life or history seems to be able to cover the ground and close the gap between the two. Each attempt seems to dissolve the purity of value in its various ontological incarnations. Is it therefore necessary to abandon the absolute altogether as many wish to do today? [123] But then what becomes of human freedom and the person? What becomes of the original affirmation as witness?

The posing of this problem anew is not without interest. It is our task to determine the validity of the answer given to this fundamental philosophical problem by the axiological idealism of Georges Bastide.

[122] Cf. G. Bastide, *Méditations*, p. 81.
[123] Cf. A. Dondeyne, *op. cit.*, p. 170.

CHAPTER V

SEARCH FOR A METHOD: THE HUMAN CONDITION IN INAUTHENTICITY AND ALIENATION

Experience and reflection in experience are the poles of all philosophical endeavor. Philosophical reflection is both a recognition and a deepening in understanding of what is already in some way present. More specifically, philosophy is a search for the foundations of being and knowing. From an epistemological point of view philosophy seeks the primary (irreducible) truth which will bear the edifice of knowledge. Ontologically, philosophy seeks the ultimate horizon, the primary truth which is the principle of other derived truths in the philosophical structure. As such philosophy is looking for that principle which is the source of light for all other truths, the mysterious reality which is already present before we begin our search and which is always absent no matter how much our search progresses.

We have seen so far the basic movement of the thought of Georges Bastide. From an examination and description of the first fact, he has layed the basis for his own interpretation of the project proposed at the outset, the project of philosophy as a consideration of the human situation as revealed in the act of self-knowledge.[1] The affirmation and description of the first fact is a revelation of man's vocation to authenticity. A further examination of our problem indicated that for Bastide philosophy is essentially an effort to discover the fundamental ground of the human condition as a *search* for authenticity.[2] The imperative of authenticity is immanent to the entire conscious life. It is essentially an imperative *to act* and that which secures the act in its authentic reality is Value, which, he says, we can call Love itself. For "it is fitting to designate as Love the movement which

[1] Cf. G. Bastide, "De la situation de l'homme," *op. cit.*, p. 242.

[2] The intimate relation between doctrine and method is especially to be noted: "... in a kind of normative reciprocity: we philosophize in order to know ourselves well, but it is necessary to know oneself well in order to philosophize well. That is to say, the problem of Man and that of philosophical activity constitute one and the same problem." G. Bastide, "De la situation de l'homme...," *op. cit.*, p. 242.

translates in us this presence by which everything takes on value and wherein everything issues in an authentic existence." [3] However, as we have seen, we have yet to discover the philosophical *method* for distinguishing *within the human condition* the real meaning of authentic love, the real source *for man* of the authenticity of value itself. As we proceed further in our philosophical search, then, we are aiming for the ultimate foundation (raison d'être) of the human condition, not only as a search for authenticity, but as a *possibility for inauthenticity as well.* For our first examination of the primitive cognitive experience has discovered a certain ambivalence in the human condition itself. A basic complementary relationship between different poles of value seems to be the actual condition of man from an axiological point of view. But the notion of an axiological metaphysics stands in need of a further determination before the essential ambiguity of the human situation can be clarified. For since philosophy is a project of man's freedom already rooted in a history, we must ask the *second* question concerning the *roots of the original affirmation itself.* That is, we must discover the *relationship* between reflection and experience, for there are no innate ideas. Whether the idea be regarded as a result of abstraction or as "the immanent law of the spirit in act," the idea is a *realization* of the spirit and presupposes some reality along with its act, the reality by which the spirit and the primary cognitive intention is an openess to the world and others in a structured, organized body.

The all important question, therefore, is the relationship between the free initiative of the spirit positing itself in the original affirmation and this primary experience we are about to reflect upon. It is the basic philosophical problem of identifying with fidelity to the concrete the structure of the basic cognitive intention. For the original and basic affirmation (in all its fulness and not merely as presence to self, that is, in its epistemological and ontological or axiological aspects) which we are seeking is the original source and final discovery of philosophy itself, namely, the fundamental ground of all certainty and the primary significant reality which brings together *man and his human condition.*

In this chapter, then, under the title of the human condition, we propose to consider Bastide's evaluation of the prephilosophic experience and his phenomenological description of that experience. It will be important for us to determine whether this experience is to be regarded in a negative, pejorative sense, or whether it is to be part of the synthesis of the full Cogito, that is, of the basic philosophical experience.

[3] G. Bastide, *Méditations,* p. 60.

I. Alienation

„Man is fallen in the world and he has filled it with his debris." [4] These words indicate Bastide's conclusions concerning the basic original world situation which is primitively experienced by man. The man who awakens to reflection and the philosophical life affirms himself in the original affirmation of reflection as problem, as witness to authenticity, as one called to search himself for authentic existence. But the certitude of the original affirmation is made in the context of the world and the world has already long been filled with the debris placed there by man himself. In pre-philosophic experience man is given to himself in a state of free alienation.[5]

The real origin of the axiological problematic which brought our first reflections to unsatisfactory conclusions is to be found here. As a matter of fact, if man can experience the ideal of Love in the original affirmation, this love is not given in its purity, but only "heuristically," [6] as the object of human faith and the imperative of authenticity, an imperative that is grounded in an alienation and a *need* for redemption. But despite the imperative which is given in the original affirmation, man himself is incapable at this point of taking one step towards his goal. He has no guarantee of the authentic values. No road of action has opened up before him with the certitude that this is truly the way to exist authentically.

Bastide ascertains the original condition of man in several carefully constructed ways. In two original works, one treating the psychological and metaphysical aspects of consciousness (*La Condition humaine*), the other a biographical study of Socrates under the aspect of the origins of reflection and philosophy (*Le moment historique de Socrate*) he traces the movement of thought from alienation to spiritual conversion; afterwards in a historical study (*Les grands Thèmes moraux de la Civilisation occidentale*) and a social study (*Les Mirages et Certitudes de la Civilisation*) he comes to the basic conclusion that the philosophical life of reflection and the authentic existence of man as a person depends intrinsically on the original, dramatic nature of the human condition as alienation. It is *because* man is alienated that philosophy and the experience which grounds it is possible.[7]

1. Alienation of mind (pre-reflective level)

On the psychological plane man is alienated because conscious life has its origins in a naive optimism whose movement is progress and non-

[4] G. Bastide, *Traité*, p. 131.
[5] Cf. G. Bastide, "L'expérience morale," *op. cit.*, p. 314.
[6] Cf. G. Bastide, *Méditations*, p. 62.
[7] Cf. G. Bastide, *De la condition humaine*, p. 269.

progress at the same time.[8] The development of conscious life is progress in so far as man continually and successfully adapts himself to the demands of new situations, especially in the gradual formation and purification of the judgment itself.[9] However, this same movement, being a naive optimism, and being essentially a position of exteriority (a non-critical relationship to the world of experience, which, for Bastide, takes on a negative significance in an ethical context) is not a movement in the direction of authenticity, in the direction of man's self-fulfillment as person. Rather, by its very nature, the development of reason along a linear representational level leads to the crisis of nominalism in the intellectual life. This state represents a kind of negative limit to conscious life and to man's ultimate goal of authentic existence.[10] In reality it is a growing away from existence.

How does man grow away from existence on the conscious level? Precisely by accepting as the ultimate source of personal stability and self-identification the accord he has established between himself and his world on the basis of a qualitative identity which he has imposed on reality through the categories, especially the most general of all categories, the notion of being.[11] But consciousness is not only stability, but becoming; and consciousness in the juridical function must bring together not only simultaneity, but also the aspect of succession (becoming).

It is at this point, says Bastide, that we find the origin of the notion of *substance* and an interpretation of spirit in the framework of substantialism.[12] The world view of consciousness at this level is based on a faith in the qualitative nature of things and a system of coherence constructed by consciousness through the instrumentality of such notions as identity, substance, matter and form. It is here, for example, that Bastide places the phychological origin of moral theories of happiness based on the desirable and the self-satisfying, as well as their connection with philosophies of efficient and final causality. Man becomes essentially *passive* and egocentric, as one who supports the actions of things rather than engaging in action himself.[13]

On this representational level thought uses the syntheses already given to it, to which it attaches spontaneously and un-critically both value and objective reality. There is a tendency to grasp man mechanistically, to view

[8] *Ibid.*, p. 157.
[9] *Ibid.*, p. 82.
[10] Cf. G. Bastide, *De la condition humaine*, p. 158.
[11] *Ibid.*, p. 133.
[12] *Ibid.*, pp. 134-135.
[13] *Ibid.*, p. 137.

God dogmatically under the categories of efficient and final causality and to see consciousness noetically, without taking into account its vocational reality.

This alienation of mind as consciousness moves towards reflection is also an alienation of human existence. To understand the full import of this statement we have only to recall the close relationship in Bastide's philosophical viewpoint between philosophy, reflection and existence. For Bastide, the unique problem of philosophy (which he concludes to after an examination of the history of conscious life, cf. *La Condition humaine*) is the problem of self-knowledge to which all other problems are from now on related.[14] Man, the object of philosophy,[15] is a being "whose whole essence is to seek himself." [16] That is, for Bastide man's whole essence is to be engaged in the dramatically situated search for self-knowledge. The essential movement of his idealism is from knowledge to existence. The notion of person and the act of existence are seen in terms of bearing witness to consciousness, that is, in terms of *reflection.* It is in this context that Bastide can speak of authentic and inauthentic reflection and relate both directly to the condition of man as such. For philosophy is impossible without authentic existence and authentic existence is impossible without authentic reflection, that is, without authentic philosophy.[17]

A more precise description of this alienation of the mind in its imperfect efforts at reflection is discribed by Bastide under the notion of the four excesses (*vertiges*) of consciousness as it seeks the philosophical life and authentic existence. These are represented in general in the history of philosophy by the excessive centralization of an aspect of the real. The most frequent and global abuse of reflection, says Bastide, is the naive acceptance of reflection as the "turning back upon oneself" in order to "see" oneself as if in a mirror.[18] This effort is nothing more than the work of our imagination which fails to attain our existence as *person,* as spirit, and instead arrives at a conception of man as "personage." What is realized is not an authentic knowledge of self, but only an imaginative view of the different caricatures of the self, resulting from the four excesses of the reasoning power.

The original movement of naive faith, as will be brought out in a following section, is precisely an original, but alienating engagement of conscious-

[14] Cf. G. Bastide, *De la condition humaine,* p. 137.
[15] *Ibid.,* p. 9.
[16] *Ibid.,* p. 365.
[17] Cf. G. Bastide, *Traité,* p. 141; also p. 140.
[18] Cf. G. Bastide, *Traité,* p. 141.

ness in the world seeking a solution to its problem in the diversity of empirical exteriority.[19] It is this world of empirical values that gives rise to the different modes of alienation on the reflexive level.[20]

Both dogmatic rationalism and dogmatic empiricism attempt to establish on the speculative level this "vision of reality" which, in fact, could be realized only by "a pride without limitation and an immagination without control." [21] What is really effected in such a movement of thought is not the vision of God or reality but the vision of oneself (personage) as the center of all things. As a result the basic foundation of philosophy itself (self-knowledge) is destroyed by the complete relativity of truth and values.[22] The real source of philosophical error, then, is grounded on the natural tendency of the human spirit to see before or in himself the speculative resolution of the problem of existence or a least the problem on the way to a speculative solution.

In all this, Bastide, a philosopher of action, is condemning the "spectator" attitude towards existence.[23] Introspection or extraversion are both condemned as being inauthentic attitudes of reflecting consciousness. The attitude of "wanting to see" is seen by him as diametrically opposed *to that kind* of reflection which is a "bearing witness to consciousness" in the order of action and not that of the passive registration of facts (the fact of one's introspective self or the fact of things in exteriority, in either case the result is of the nature of "image").[24]

Faithful to idealism, Bastide believes that "the imagination and reflection cannot go together." The "pure presence of consciousness itself" (authentic reflection) [25] is not seeing oneself in the act of reflection, but the act of reflection itself revealing and constituting personal existence. It is one with the experience of freedom.[26]

This "doubling back of the imagination" then, is the source for the

[19] *Ibid.*, p. 620 of T. II.

[20] On the level of a will seeking only the fulfillment of its desires, on the level of thought imbued with a naive faith and on the level of act giving rise to a world of culture which is alienating instead of liberating.

[21] G. Bastide, *Méditations*, p. 84.

[22] Cf. G. Bastide, *Méditations*, p. 84.

[23] There is however a definite ambiguity here since in some way the spectator attitude says something essential about philosophy itself which "inevitably involves standing back from the sphere of immediate experience." Cf. F. Copleston, *Contemporary Philosophy*, London 1963 (4th impression), pp. 128-129. The problem as we shall see lies with the very definition of reflection and of philosophy itself.

[24] Cf. G. Bastide, *Traité*, p. 141.

[25] *Ibid.*, p. 141.

[26] *Ibid.*, p. 140.

alienation of thought. And this alienation of thought is at one and the same time an alienation of man in search for authenticity, since authenticity, for Bastide, is essentially realized in the act of reflection. But what is given in this inauthentic act of reflection, says Bastide, is in truth the opposite of being, knowledge and value. "Everytime I fall into this illusion, it is my method and my doctrine of life which finds itself falsified in the solidarity which binds them together." [27] Without having first determined his own nature as person in authentic self-knowledge, the alienated man regards the world as if it existed to bestow its values on man and not as the place wherein man is to realize himself and give value to the world. As if the world "owed us a living" instead of our being full of care for the world; as if the "value" of the world was grounded by our desires and the satisfaction it brings to desire; as if the world was "necessary" for me in the sense that without the satisfaction of my desires I could no longer live. An "image" of the world and an "image" of man – both giving the lie to the true human condition. It is here that man's relationship to the world is falsified (as being a world of his own idols) and man's relation to himself is falsified (because he regards himself as perishing without the satisfaction of his desires). Man ceases to exist as man, that is, as "witness to consciousness." The horizon of man's self-centered world has falsified man himself. Whether the world view of satisfaction is replaced by one of success or one of ontological or logical truth, it makes no difference as regards the fact of man's self-alienation.

Thus it is the *attitude of consciousness* (and the values which become the objects of naive faith) that constitute this alienation. Nothing is wrong with the world. For the world is merely the place of the various possible human realizations. The condition of alienation or authenticity is wholly rooted in the attitude of reflexive consciousness and the employment of freedom.

Since, therefore, the question of alienation is put in terms of consciousness and its attitude toward values, it is, in the last analysis, a question of faith. The faith of the alienated man is a naive faith.[28] Here again, we are concerned more with the direction and adherence of consciousness rather than the content of the pre-reflexive state.[29] Bastide is concerned with the pre-critical situation of consciousness (an examination of which is, for Bastide, the key to finding the essential man which is the object of his philosophy), the fundamental disposition which conditions the whole field of our exploration. To put it another way, the pre-reflexive situation of

[27] G. Bastide, *Méditations*, p. 87.
[28] Cf. G. Bastide, *La conversion spirituelle, op. cit.*, p. 11.
[29] *Ibid.*, pp. 7-8.

man is uniquely related to the reasons for being, believing and willing which as yet have no reflexive guarantee.[30]

The state of naive faith is *native* to man as such, but it does not follow that it is his natural state, as Rousseau presumed.[31] Bastide follows the radical dualism of Brunschvicg. It is not the dualism of being and being known, but the dualism of a philosophy of consciousness, "the duality of being and thought being irreducible and primitive." [32] It is not only the duality of the different modalities of consciousness (the diverging and converging directions of life and thought [33]) but the duality of *two consciousnesses* moving in different directions within the poles of value that constitute the human situation.[34] The discovery of interiority by the philosophies of reflection has to do with a new kind of existence, a new man.[35] In fact, it is the human condition created by the presence of this essential duality that Bastide is trying to elaborate in his philosophy.[36]

It is in this context we are to understand the duality that comes constantly into play as regards every aspect of existence (act, knowledge, judgment, reflection, faith, value, etc.) in Bastides' axiological idealism. What interests us here is to determine whether the naive faith of consciousness is *merely* pre-philosophical and therefore to be incorporated into our final synthesis, or whether it is a state to be finally and constantly overcome because it is an "unconscious betrayal in regards to the true value." [37] We have already indicated that for Bastide the evolution of consciousness is just that – a betrayal of the authentic values. Whether on the gnoseological plane or on the ontological or axiological level, the critique of Bastide is brought against the arrangement and systematization of values according to a consciousness imbued with naive faith (realism, objective and subjective idealism, romantic individualism, empirical pragmatism). In any case it is in the state of naive faith that man takes on an egocentric, anthropomorphic point of view when he comes to judge reality and its value.

In general naive faith is bound up with empirical exteriority. It confuses, says Bastide, the "liberty" of arbitrariness with true liberty and the "duty"

[30] Cf. G. Bastide, *La conversion spirituelle*, p. 12.
[31] *Ibid.*, p. 8.
[32] L. Brunscvicg, *La modalité de jugement, op. cit.*, p. 98.
[33] Cf. G. Bastide, *De la condition humaine*, p. 369.
[34] Cf. note § 4, Chapter I, Part. II.
[35] Cf. G. Bastide, *De la condition humaine*, p. 372.
[36] "It is from the point of departure of these two levels of consciousness that we can now determine the human condition within the framework of the essential great philosophical problems." *Ibid.*, p. 375.
[37] Cf. G. Bastide, *La conversion spirituelle*, p. 10.

of passive obedience with the authentic responsibility for the human condition.[38] It is signified for example by the will to power combined with the fear of inevitable failure. It calls infinite that which is indefinite and perfection the satisfaction of desire.[39] As long as it rests in the empirical framework, the problem of possession and the will to power dissolve the consciousness of man in an ever widening circle whose only issue is totalitarianism.[40] It is this position of exteriority that becomes the source of dissolution as regards the authentic values; animated by the will to power, with its fundamental ambiguities of fear and aggressiveness, the strategy is a self-defeating one, for the search for the totality of power is at the same time the dividing up of the knowledge in community which alone can provide the will with the unity it seeks under the guise of power. What our will to appropriate divides, our knowledge cannot unite except in the poverty of the most abstract and general concepts.

Here we have a simple example of the critique Bastide brings against all "realism" of consciousness signified in the term naive faith. The main thing that Bastide is saying is that man cannot know himself in the same terms or in the same attitude of consciousness by which he knows nature. Nor can man ascertain the authentic *raisons d'être* until he is situated in this authentic self-knowledge. As long as it is the attitude of naive faith which is immanent to the judgments of consciousness, then man exists inauthentically in alienation. He lives in a state of ethical contradiction where what is said does not coincide which what is believed or what is done. Instead of finding that responsibility which alone can save him, the regime of native faith justifies the condition of alienation.

2. *The alienation of liberty*

For Bastide metaphysics "is nothing more than a search for authentic existence." [41] Authenticity of existence consists in the assurance in certitude of the value giving power of our acts. Just as the philosophical life is the mutual relationship of progress in maturity in the philosopher as well as the philosophy, so the authentic existence of men is that mutual relationship between the authenticity of their works and the power authentic culture brings in the liberation of man himself.[42] This relationship is ex-

[38] *Ibid.*, p. 52.
[39] Cf. G. Bastide, *La conversion spirituelle*, p. 46.
[40] *Ibid.*, p. 84.
[41] G. Bastide, *Traité*, p. 140.
[42] Cf. Note § 19 of this chapter.

pressed philosophically in that union between "le métaphysique" and "la métaphysique" which is the ultimate goal of philosophy.

But this coincidence of philosophical doctrine and method with concrete reality, this harmony between action and authentic existence becomes precarious, as we have seen, from the very doubt and ambiguity found as to the nature of the very search for authenticity, or as to the precise constitution of authentic action and authentic value. If consciousness does not give an adequate testimony, by that very fact its own reality becomes vitiated in regards to its search for authentic existence. In other words, only the consciousness of the actual exercise of authentic existence (bearing witness) is authentic existence.[43] The very meaning of the search for authenticity is defined by this coincidence.[44]

It is in this context that we can understand Bastide's description of the human condition before spiritual conversion as the alienation of liberty itself. This alienation consists in an attitude of consciousness grounded in naive faith, an attitude more anxious "to explain than understand." For, says Bastide, it is alienation to seek to contemplate our existence as freedom instead of discovering authenticity where alone it is to be found, namely, in the *exercise* of freedom itself.[45]

Here again we see the radical nature of Bastide's philosophy of action. For him there can be no metaphysics outside authentic moral activity itself. The act of reflection (and the act of the will which accompanies it) is essentially a moral act, as shall become clearer in the following sections. Here we note that what is not at its origin moral (experience or act) cannot give rise to authentic philosophy or authentic existence. The experience of self-knowledge implies the authentic exercise of freedom. The alienation of man is found wherever this exercise of freedom is not authentic.

Therefore, the alienation of human freedom parallels the alienation of mind. The four fundamental "vertiges" are paralleled by the four "excesses" of liberty.[46] The alienated man seeks to rejoice in a so-called "free-

[43] Cf. Note § 17 of this chapter.

[44] Cf. G. Bastide, *Traité*, I., p. 208.

[45] Cf. G. Bastide, *Traité*, I., p. 141.

[46] As we shall see more clearly in the following sections the axiological situation of man is composed (using a topographical image) of two opposed axes (retrospective values and values of prospection, noetic and existential values) of value forces and directions. The proper coordination of these different value areas determines Bastide's description of authentic and unauthentic existence. For the non-reflecting consciousness, the immagination can carry man in one of four different directions, in so far as one value is stressed over and above or to the exclusion of the other three. This gives rise to the four excesses ("vertiges"): *retrospection* (the imaginative projection into the past in order to posit an indefinite original source of

dom" based on the precarious images he has projected in his immagination. For example, there is the alienation which results from a concept of freedom whose norm is more nature than the consciousness of man in authentic knowledge. The tendency to interpret "natural right" in cosmological categories instead of in terms of persons and spirit springs from this alienation .The problem of freedom is related more to a natural morality than to a morality of aspiration.

Or there is the opposite exaggeration of a liberty "in itself", knowing no contradiction or alterity. Here we find the tendency to reduce the notion of "right" to that of "force" and to substitute for the notion of will that of power, where "my power becomes your will."

On the noetic level there is the liberty of formalism where we imagine we can escape being-in-the-world, taking refuge in a noumenal source where liberty becomes ultimately lost in unintelligibility and purely formal in its pure essence. But an eternal essence, individual and affirmative, cannot be given except in God, that is to say, outside of all choice.[47]

Finally, there is the tendency to irrationalism and an "absolute contingency as inconceivable as a total necessity." [48]

Each one of these exaggerations situates man outside his real situation, "alibi" as Bastide puts it. For as we have seen in the original affirmation, the authentic human condition is to "face up to the moral act we have to accomplish and the unity of value we have to promote." [49] The alienation of man is a flight from responsibility in a liberty which is supposed to be spontaneous and infaillible, one which might have its own excuse to escape the call to continual effort and progress in moral invention. Or it may be a flight in a blind liberty evolving in the world apart from my most personal responsibility concerning my own existence; or flight in a liberty which is too formal and too mysterious to make any sense in a real world.

unity and resolution of the problem posed by philosophy; *prospection* (the immaginative anticipation of the co-existence of all possibles simultaneously realized, the concept of a final Totality serving as the teleological pole of reality on its way to an automatic self-realization); *noetic* excess (the immagination of a world of self-sufficient essences eternally immutable and free from the order of life and change, offering a contemplation without the effort of the free choice of man coming to grips in a fallen world); *existential* excess (exaggeration of the irrational to the extent of undermining the true nature of the rational and its role in authentic existence). "It is to these fundamental excesses of consciousness that the four excesses of freedom are related." G. Bastide, *Traité*, p. 143. Cf. also *Méditations*, pp. 123 ss. and *Mirages*, pp. 245 ss.

[47] G. Bastide, *Traité*, p. 145.

[48] *Id.*

[49] *Traité*, II., p. 449.

The alienation of freedom, like the alienation of mind, finds man in the one and same egocentric position regarding himself and the world.

3. *Alienation in society*

Civilization, says Bastide, exists ultimately in the minds and hearts of men and in the spiritual works that come from a conscious reflection concerning what is authentically human.[50] Man is ultimately in search for the reasons for being, reasons for living one way rather than another. In the regime of alienation there is a basic conflict between the individual and his society. For the two factors of human sociality – nature and spirit – are two necessary but irreducible notions pertaining to two distinct axiological orders. There is no natural harmony of vocation when it comes to man. Thus, for example, "tolerance" and "solidarity" remain ambiguous in a pragmatic, positivistic context. For the accord between man and nature is not a simple one, and the ultimate reasons for uniting the two cannot be found in the empirical order, exterior to man himself.[51]

Man needs both a morality of situation (nature) and a morality of aspiration, needing the latter most of all. Not that there are two moralities, says Bastide, but two sources (nature and spirit). In the regime of alienation man is in society more in the attitude of assimilation than creation, observation rather than reflection. The social "order" and the function of Law are, in a regime of alienation, only superficial expressions of authentic order and true law. The "ontologies of order" might well reverse the pragmatic order by submitting the lower to the higher value, but their principles hardly permit them to keep from falling into the other extreme of the best possible world supported by a transcendent view of authority.[52]

[50] Cf. G. Bastide, *Mirages et certitudes de la civilisation, op. cit.*, pp. 24-25.

[51] This conclusion is the result of Bastide's own investigations, from the viewpoint of the social problem and the problem of culture, concerning pragmatism, ontologism, vitalistic historicism and scientism. Cf. Part. I of *Mirages, op. cit.*

[52] Bastide also makes some remarks in this direction in the *Grands thèmes, op. cit.*, where he remarks the fictitious unity of Rome's pragmatism (the superficial equilibrium obtained through the function of Law, but a law based on the precarious stability between man and his works, a stability that could even be called, says Bastide, "human nature." As a matter of fact the law did not sink to the very roots of man's being as a responsible person. It was more founded on what man was *in fact* by his traditions and circumstances and this law become identified with morality. But such a morality lacked a moral foundation for absorbing radical change. The Church did not escape the same pitfall – in so far as she saw herself justifying and consolidating dogma, almost as if this were her essential role. Eventually reason found itself hampered in its own search for personal unity, weighed down as it was by a certain ambiguity present in the relationship then existing between faith, reason and authority. On the philosophical level, says Bastide, it seemed as if the ontological

The moral problem, even on the social level, comes back to the fundamental ideal of authenticity revealed in the original affirmation. The norm for attaining the ideal does not come from without, says Bastide, but from man himself. That is, there is no "pure order" whereby we could determine the natural laws pertaining to man's self-realization as person. Why? Precisely because the order of things has been touched by man's freedom and there is no way, says Bastide, of distinguishing the "natural" order of things. In the last analysis, the social order cannot find its justification in God or in experience.

Contemporary philosophies of becoming attempt to save man from this alienation by defining life in terms of his search and creative effort. The totality becomes life instead of order. But the alienated man does not find his individuality any more clearly defined and again, it seems, he has the ambiguous choice between anarchy and totalitarianism. For history becomes for man either fatality or value, but in either case these values cannot give the ultimate reason for action that he is looking for. *Morality* seems absorbed once again in *Nature*. Duty seems swallowed up by necessity. Libelty is virtual contingency. The antinomies in the social order, notes Bastide, are not unlike those which were revealed on the psychological level, for "dogmatism and vitalism are two mythologies of the different basic life tendencies." [53]

It is precisely the inability to have a morality of person in either empirical or rationalistic dogmatism that constitutes man's alienation in one regime or the other. The three poles of value in every idea, says Bastide, are *nature, culture* and *morality*, the power of life, the acquisition of knowledge and the communion of consciousnesses. These correspond to the threefold need of man revealed in the original affirmation: man is a power to exist, a need to understand and a will to be authentic.[54] Authenticity seems tied up with a just equilibrium between the three constituent and necessary aspects of authenticity. Exalting one at the expense of the other, we have already remarked, results in man's alienation. There can be no monism of nature, culture or morality any more than there can be a pure ontology or a pure gnoseology or a pure axiology. Nor can the three be brought together in a system (ontology, empiricism), because they are of different orders. It is not, therefore, a question of hierarchy.

Just as the problematic of the relation between being, knowledge and

function was pulling against the axiological function. Cf. G. Bastide, *Les grands thèmes, op. cit.*, pp. 44-59; 94-103. Cf. also *Mirages*, p. 72, also pp. 61-86.

[53] Cf. G. Bastide, *Mirages*, p. 124.

[54] Cf. G. Bastide, *Traité*, II., p. 620.

value seemed to run up against a mysterious ambivalence, so now on the level of nature, culture and morality a certain essential instability is seen to appear. Culture can take the sense of nature or it can take the sense of spirit. Nor is culture always impregnated with morality. It is so different with nature – it is not orientated necessarily towards morality, that is, it is not a natural law for man's actions.

For it is culture which separates and unites nature and morality and it is in the free insertion of culture into nature that unites nature and morality – but the point of insertion, says Bastide, is the act of man himself. But the rectitude of that act is not guaranteed, precisely because it pertains to man's freedom. If the act is not authentic, instead of giving to culture its mediating function, man is said to "short circuit" culture in nature.[55] There is no pure nature. There is no pure spirit. Man, as an incarnate reality at work in the world, is by that very fact ordering that world in one of two essential directions. His works become objects of knowlelge, a knowledge which is clarified by the work or (if the work is inauthentic, that is, without its truth and moral value), it contributes to the passional aspect of human reality.[50]

The alienation of man consists in being separated from himself (having a knowledge which is not truly his own) and from his existence (his acts being not truly his own, since they are not known). It is the notion of culture which can mediate philosophically the human condition of man, who "having never lived in another world, finds himself a stranger in the world," [57] but the notion itself (as also the need to act) remains fundamentally ambiguous.

In concluding this section (admittedly all too short to do justice to the detailed critique of philosophy that Bastide brings to bear upon this subject of man's alienation) [58] we can say Bastide's purpose is to show, in all his various critiques, the disequilibrium of man as he stands at the crossroads of his existence and affirms the call to be authentic. "Man is born free and yet everywhere he is in chains," as Rousseau put it in the opening words to his *Social Contract*. Man retains the deepest sense of this alienation despite the conviction of his freedom.

The original affirmation of consciousness is pronounced in this essential ambiguity of the human condition – the relative autonomy of man is mixed with an equal experience of being strange to himself and to his own free-

[55] Cf. G. Bastide, *Mirages, op. cit.*, p. 205.

[56] Cf. G. Bastide, *Mirages*, p. 205.

[57] G. Bastide, "De la situation de l'homme," *op. cit.*, p. 249.

[58] Besides the places and books already cited special attention should be given to the second volume of the *Traité* where Bastide treats in detail the subject of man's alienation and the dialectic of dissolution. Cf. particularly Book I.

dom. Man can affirm the goal of authenticity – but he does not yet know what to do, how to do it, if he can do it or if he will do it.

The original state of man, therefore, is one of alienation.[59] "Each one begins from an original state of alienation in the confusion of contradictory desires and inclinations." [60] The capricious freedom is genetically prior to authentic freedom and as a result, the world is filled with the debris of mankind. "The first exercise of freedom, like the first intentions of the mind, are more alienating than liberating, ... we always begin by doing wrong or by letting be done what later on we have to win back, repair and transfigure ..." [61]

Bastide, then, sees a necessary link between the original state of alienation and the possibility of freely assuming responsibility for the human situation. Just as in the intellectual order there was this intrinsic link between naive faith and authentic reflection, so also in the order of the will. "The spirit ... is first of all knowledge of evil, assumption of responsibility; it is the spirit which sees injustice and which demands from man that he impute it solely to his own freedom, in order to take charge of its redemption. Every philosophy, which does not begin here, will always be a philosophy which falls short of itself, discharging itself from all responsibility as well as from all nobility ..." [62]

It is in this context of original alienation that Bastide speaks of the philosophical tradition which connects the idea of an alienated spirit and an ontological fall of man. "The deep roots of alienation are at least of the moral order, if not of the theological order." [63] If we experience so profoundly our real alienation, insists Bastide, then it cannot be attributed to chance or to blind necessity but only to the injustice of man himself. For Bastide, the historicity of consciousness contains its reference to the eternity of spirit. "History is dramatic because of the original presence of evil." [64]

II. Ontological anxiety

1. Introduction

Philosophic doubt is the beginning of the philosophical life of reflection. For Bastide this basic moment on the way to authentic reflection is born out of an experience essentially moral in character. It is not basically, says

[59] Cf. G. Bastide, *Traité*, I, pp. 177-178.
[60] *Traité*, p. 178.
[61] *Id.*
[62] *Id.*, p. 228.
[63] G. Bastide, *Traité*, II, p. 475.
[64] G. Bastide, "Le malin génie," *op. cit.*, p. 245.

Bastide, because of curiosity that we are aroused to the philosophical search for wisdom, but more often than not it is by the "lived experience of a kind of fundamental doubt" that the philosophical life is born in man.[65]

The true nature of this doubt must be placed in a *fundamental restlessness* basic to the consciousness of every man, that is, it is an aspect of human existence as such. So fundamental is it, says Bastide, that we can say that this "scruple" is more rooted in existence than the naive faith which manifests itself as a primary state in the progressive development of consciousness. In other words, the *law of unity* is more a part of man than the natural tendency to avoid the real problems posed by our dispersion in a world of multiple values and distractions. The need for truth and perfection eventually is more demanding than the need for the satisfaction of our desires. The task of objectivity is more imperative than the tendency to subjective individualism. The ideal of constructing a world of universal validity is more pressing than introspective self-complacency. The ideal of authenticity calls us from deeper levels of our being than the natural tendency to self-justification and self-mystification. In short, the way of interiority is more a part of our authentic existence than the way of the false objectivity of empirical exteriority or the false interiority of a decadent narcissism.

The moral experience of the original reflexive affirmation is one with consciousness itself and, in a certain way, defines the human situation as such.[67] Spiritual experience is "metaphysically anterior" to empirical experience,[68] for "moral value ... calls forth a general mobilization of experience in every meaning of the term." [69] The "primum movens," therefore, of the authentic life is the lived experience of this quality of restlessness which imposes itself over and above the natural tendency of action, not as a regrettable accidental addition tending to paralyze action, but rather situating action for the first time on the metaphysical level of man's existence and directing it heuristically towards authenticity.

Therefore, our interest here is expressly philosophical, examining the nature of this aspect of human existence as it pertains to the metaphysical intention as such (without however denying the psychological, phenomenological, sociological aspects of this experience). As a metaphysical experience, the phenomenon of the "conscience malheureuse" introduces man to

[65] Cf. J. Wahl, *Le malheur de la conscience dans la philosophie de Hegel*, Paris, 1951 edition, p. 8.

[66] Cf. G. Bastide, *La conversion spirituelle*, p. 21.

[67] Cf. G. Bastide, "L'experience morale," *op. cit.*, p. 308.

[68] Cf. G. Bastide, "La conversion spirituelle," in *Encyclopédie française, op. cit.*, p. 19.06-4.

[69] G. Bastide, "L'expérience morale," *op. cit.*, pp. 308-309.

his own being as being related to an order of transcendent values. It presents man to himself in his situation of being in some way absent from the solution to the problem of his existence and estranged in some way from the world of nature in which he communicates. "Having never known any other world, man begins to think that this world is probably not the true world ... and in the very moment of trying to accept our existence by affirming "that's the way life is," we cannot help thinking that this life "is no life at all." [70] Consciousness is at some time or other "malheureuse."

What, then, is the nature of this experience? For Bastide, it is more than the negative reality it was for Nietzsche, a symptom of disorder in the evolution of man, a vital fatigue consecrated in certain decadent civilizations and institutions, the norm of weakness and slavery. Nor can we situate Bastide's description of this aspect of man's existence in the Hegelian phenomenology of mind, where it signifies the restless, experiental search of mind after its own content and the truth about objects.[71] The problem might well be the same, but the explanation is different. For Bastide, the "conscience malheureuse" must be seen in the context of the Cartesian doubt and generosity on the way to spiritual conversion and the affirmation of the *Cogito*. The radical failure of the realist consciousness to ground a metaphysics, the resulting crisis of consciousness due to the failure of the functions of representation to provide the fundamental unity necessary for personal life, the critical doubt arising out of the sensitive but enlightened and forceful will to face the crisis, the reward of this generosity in the discovery of the life of the spirit and the birth of consciousness concerning this life – these are the horizons within which the "conscience malheureuse" is situated in Bastide's philosophy. It is an essential moment in the movement toward spiritual conversion and the subsequent transfiguration of values.

Consciousness is both an exigence to unity and a tension of multiplicity. It is precisely because consciousness is openess and not a unique closed reality, not an absolute that it can become "malheureuse." Consciousness is open to its own otherness. Otherness is as much a part of its life as the need for unity. No wonder, then, that in its initial awakening to reflection, it becomes "malheureuse," for it is only in the openness to the other than ourselves that we experience the conflict between the attitude of naive consciousness (and its intentionality toward the empirical values) and the fundamental need for unity in an authentic existence. It is precisely the interiorization of this conflict (as opposed to the attitude of flight from this essen-

[70] G. Bastide, *La conversion spirituelle*, p. 21.
[71] Cf. J. Wahl, *op. cit.*, p. 8.

tial problem of our existence) that constitutes hte unhappiness of consciousness.[72]

Man becomes essentially unhappy because of his own cooperation in the constitution of that attitude of realism which is creative of that multiplicity and dispersion of conscious life which is intrinsically at variance with the need for unity in personal existence. Man becomes unhappy because of his naive attitude of passive reception to the empirical values instead of an active construction and promotion of the deeper and more fundamental spiritual values.

Therefore, it is precisely the "delicate" consciousness which becomes unhappy, that is, consciousness in the act of refusing to flee from the question and problem posed by existence in the world. This sensitiveness is not a weakness. Just the opposite – it is the interdiction of facility. The *act of doubting*, of withholding consent, then, is the proper act of the delicate consciousness. It is not hesitation, but the recognition and actualization of an immense need for authenticity and intelligibility. In brief, the "conscience malheureuse" contains the real reasons for spiritual conversion and the eventual transfiguration of values.

The "conscience malheureuse," then, is a positive notion, linked to the sensitivity of consciousness. It is also linked to consciousness' *generosity*. For what makes the experience of the unhappiness of consciousness a *maturation* of the life of the spirit is the *resolution* to face up to the rupture as experienced in the original affirmation, the disjunction in existence between what is given (my existence as problem) and the call towards the transcendent ideal of authenticity (Value). To this dislocation of man's spirit corresponds also the separation of knowledge and existence, as we have

[72] Here we can recall once again the nature of the conscious reality on the psychological level. Cf. *De la condition humaine*, p. 73. For Bastide, there are two fundamental characteristics of human consciousness: one is the power of man for deep engagement in action with the ability to bring a *unity of effort* to action characterized by a strong individuality; on the other hand, the same consciousness presents a second, almost (seemingly) opposed characteristic, namely, a *sympathy*, that is an openness to otherness, a suspension of action on the vital level in the contemplation of different points of view and the unification of these in the function of representation. These two characteristics of concentration and openness (the coordination of rich and complex functions brought to bear in the unity of action, together with the power of sympathy based on the differentiation of functions) form the "sensitive consciousness." This "sensitivity" of consciousness is not a sign of weakness, but rather one of richnes and strength, force of action and strength to understand. As such the sensitive consciousness is at once a power of unity in the face of dislocation and a power of openness ready to be enriched by the various aspects of reality.

seen. The "conscience malheureuse" and the "conscience douteuse" and "généreuse" are intimately connected.

2. Ontological anxiety

The fundamental experience of the "conscience malheureuse" is geared toward the act of becoming aware of our alienation. Therefore a more detailed description of this experience follows the general lines of this alienation. But it also can be described according to the triple axis constitutive of the faith aspect of conscious life. For the "conscience malheureuse" is precisely the result of the "loss of faith" [73] which is necessary for conscious life itself. Even naive faith is necessary for conscious life – until it has been replaced by the acquired faith of the spiritual conversion. The precarious interval between the loss of naive faith and the new faith in the ideality of value constitutive of the idealist consciousness constitutes the "conscience malheureuse." On the ontological level of faith this experience is one of *failure* as regards the order of being; on the gnoseological plane it is the experience of error; on the axiolgical level the experience of *fault*.[74]

The experience of failure is essentially the experience of the inutility of our efforts whenever they are centered on empirical values (means) as ends in themselves. As we have already noted in our discussion of alienation, the dialectic of naive faith is by its very nature a *dialectic of dissolution*. That is, the search for satisfaction in the possession of empirical goods, attained by the will to power, is at variance with itself. For man cannot resolve a problem of possession, for example, by opening up another problem in its place: "we cannot possess except by acquiring, but we cannot acquire anything except by possession." [75] The life of man becomes a self-alienation as long as that life is rooted in the ideal of self-satisfaction. For the empirical man the failure of death is the supreme and ultimate symbol of failure.

However, it is precisely in the experience of failure that we *lose faith* in the direction of consciousness inspired by naive faith. It is in this experience, then, that the possibility of a new kind of faith is opened up to man. "To become aware of failure is already a victory, provided that this awareness is accompanied with new horizons capable of further illuminating our existence in search of authenticity." But until these new horizons are actualized, the existence of man is radically unhappy.[76] For what naive

[73] Cf. *La conversion spirituelle*, p. 2.
[74] Cf. G. Bastide, *La conversion spirituelle*, p. 23.
[75] *Ibid.*, p. 84 .
[76] Cf. *La conversion spirituelle*, p. 26.

faith believed to be a solid foundation becomes a bottomless abyss, an experience of pure existence surrounded by nothingness. Man is left without an answer as to the ontological foundations of his existence.[77]

"In the same movement where the scrupulous consciousness, delicate but strong, unhappy but clear, experiences failure, naive faith experiences error." [78] The experience of the essential instability of existence empirically situated brings into question the value of knowledge itself. By error Bastide does not intend an erroneous judgment due to a lack of vigilance on the part of the intellect. Rather it is a radical dissolution of a *global orientation* of knowledge "as believing itself destined to assure the empirical success of our being, that is, as situated in an empirico-pragmatic perspective as regards its destination." [79] In other words, the heretofore justification of reason related to a naive view of my existence is now radically called into question.[80]

Included in this eventual breakdown of a naive use of reason would be the corresponding justification of subjective solipsism as well as the reasonings of nominalism or empirical positivism.[81] The resulting state of doubt is evidently "malheureuse." For an adequation between knowledge and reality has temporarily, says Bastide, become impossible. The extension of knowledge seems only to widen the circle of abstraction and place man farther from life itself. The effort at comprehension as regards the concrete seems doomed to failure.

The moral aspect of "the conscience malheureuse" is the experience of fault. It is intimately connected with the experience of failure and the experience of error. The persevering attachment to the exterior values of a naive faith bring into question the validity of *the will itself*. The perseverance of a state of alienation previously called into question our *power to be authentically* and our ability *to know*. Now the value of freedom itself is called into question. In other words, in each case it is the *essential man* and not just the validity of certain acts that is at stake. As a consequence it can be said that philosophy itself is being questioned.[82] At the basis of this drama of man is the inevitable failure of radical empiricism, the threatening triumph of the multiple over the one. The deepest root of

[77] G. Bastide, *Traité*, p. 130.
[78] G. Bastide, *La conversion spirituelle*, pp. 27-28.
[79] G. Bastide, *La conversion spirituelle*, p. 28.
[80] *Ibid.*
[81] *Ibid.*, pp. 29-32.
[82] "It is first of all indispensable to never forget that the consciousness of spiritual conversion presupposes genetically the realist consciousness." G. Bastide, *De la condition humaine*, p. 370.

the unhappiness of consciousness is seen here. For it is precisely this *multiplicity,* in the essential openness to the other, that seems to be the place of man's alienation. It can only be in the *effort* of interiorizing the incoherent multiplicity to which we are open that there is any hope of salvation for man in the discovery of that *unity* demanded by the call to authenticity in the original affirmation. It is this seemingly hopeless situation that renders man's situation profoundly "malheureuse."

3. Philosophic doubt and philosophical resolution

We have already noted that, for Bastide, the fundamental experience of the "conscience malheureuse" is seen especially in its positive function (and not just in its pathological reality) in connection with the notion of reflection. In the philosophical context the experience of anxiety rests transparent and reflexively master of itself. The experience of anxiety, in other words, becomes the *reflexive awareness* of the *significance* of this anxiety. The original experience gives way to an objective evaluation of failure, error and fault. It is the opening up of a road to authenticity.[83]

However, in our first analysis of the "conscience malheureuse" we saw that in its global nature it is much more than a calling into question the validity of certain particular actions. The experience of anxiety on the metaphysical level is a questioning of human existence as such, and especially the value of the will, which is the ultimate center of the conflict. All of which indicates that reflection in its essence aims "at the moral problem, not by way of the objects of our desires, but by way of the value of our will." [84] True and total reflection is regarded by Bastide as an "engagement," coming to grips with the moral problem and the value of willed activity. This engagement is signified by the generosity of consciousness. The search for authentic existence is seen to be, in part, the "discovery of freedom from the very first act of thought," [85] together with the proper use of this power. The metaphysical function of reflection is to join moral consciousness to the source of value.

It is the sensitivity of consciousness as both a need for unity and an openness to multiplicity that leads to the *philosophic doubt.*[86] The ex-

[83] Cf. G. Bastide, *La conversion spirituelle,* p. 34.

[84] G. Bastide, *Traité,* p. 105.

[85] G. Rodis-Lewis, *La morale de Descartes, op. cit.,* p. 80.

[86] Both the critical doubt and the scruple have their common source in that aspect of conscious life which is openness and effort towards unity, that is, in the "sensitive consciousness." Cf. Note § 72. The word doubt here should be taken in a sense that is not strict. The philosophic scruple is itself the cause of the basic restlessness of consciousness and the condition of the transformation of the vital consciousness into one of generosity and moral life. Cf. *Traité,* p. 383.

perience of the conscientious scruple in its metaphysical dimensions is translated in the supposition of the Evil Spirit by Descartes, where the doubt is regarded by Bastide as "much more" than a methodic purification of the objects of our knowledge.[87] In its full significance and in the moral context in which Bastide situates the doubt, it must be regarded as extending to the very significance and value of the instrument of knowledge as such, in the direction of the Kantian critique.[88]

This is especially true since the hypothesis of the Evil Spirit calls into question the *will* which is the real object of his action.[89] It is the will which is accused of radical perversion as an instrument of belief. That is, the objective judgments of existence are suspect, or "the will judging in exteriority" as Bastide notes.[90] The doubt is the refusal of the "bad conscience" turned to exteriority in the naive position of the realist consciousness.

Bastide interprets the Kantian experience of duty along similar lines, especially as it appears in the second *Critique,* with less of the rigorous character it might seem to have in the more formal description of the categorical imperative.[91] In the second *Critique,* says Bastide, it is engaged in action and "is one with moral reflection itself." As such its imperative is directed against what is essentially inauthentic in existence.[92]

In this context the philosophic scruple is ultimately an experience "of the authenticity of our *freedom.*" [93] Here liberty is seen as much more than the indifference of equilibrium, a simple hesitation before an option. In relation to the scruple of the sensitive consciousness (which equals the concrete experience of obligation for Bastide) liberty is seen as a *need,* an exigency rather than something which is known as a "given." Here the experience of freedom takes on the sense of *personal authenticity,* that is, "the unity of consciousness in the ethical conjunction of power, knowledge and will, in a word perfection." It is this fundamental experience of scruple (taken in the context of the "conscience malheureuse" and the "conscience délicate") that gives access to the experience of duty and subsequently, to authentic freedom. In this sense can it be said, says Bastide, that the "conscience malheureuse" contains the real reasons for spiritual conversion and

[87] Cf. G. Bastide, *De la condition humaine,* p. 275.

[88] *Ibid.,* p. 273.

[89] "The hypothesis of the evil spirit, therefore, consists in accusing the will of a radical perversion in so far as it is a factor of belief." G. Bastide. *De la condition humaine,* p. 274.

[91] Cf. G. Bastide, "L'expérience morale," *op. cit.,* p. 312.

[92] G. Bastide, "L'expérience morale," p. 312.

[93] Cf. G. Bastide, "L'expérience morale," p. 312.

the transfiguration of values.[94] The scruple becomes the original core of consciousness' progress towards the maturity of reflection. It seems that we are on the way to a solution as regards the problematic of the original affirmation.

How is this movement of the philosophical scruple in the context of the "conscience malheureuse" the beginning of a solution of our problematic? The original affirmation revealed the duty of bearing witness to consciousness in the constitution of my being as person. But this imperative is not fulfilled automatically, as the fact of man's alienation bears out. What was revealed, says Bastide, is the fact that alienation was essentially a *self-alienation,* that is, the work of man's own will. The problematic is now taking shape as a dramatic engagement between a *generous will* seeking authenticity and a perverted will (symbolized by Descartes' Evil Spirit as the personification of all the powers of alienation), between a naive faith (essentially determining a realist attitude of consciousness with a world view in exteriority and thus opposed to the authentic reflexive method) and the experience of a "conscience malheureuse" which undermines the naivité of the realist consciousness in the experience of failure, error and fault. The *will to know* is accompanied by a strongly entrenched doubt demanding light. Existence, indeed, is both a will to live and a need to know.[95]

The doubt, then, or the critical function of consciousness, is revealed in its essential and permanent role in the cycle of authentic reflection.

The last moment in the cycle of consciousness' progress towards full maturity is the resolution of the generous will. Up till now the gradual clarification of the original problematic has begun to reveal itself as a problem of freedom as well is the problem of the faith of consciousness. The resolution of the will to face as its own responsibility the state of its problematic and inauthentic existence, instead of continuing its self-justification and self-mystification, is what Bastide means by the generosity of consciousness. It is the generosity of an action (instead of the passive attitude characteristic of the alienated consciousness), the generosity of a will giving itself and no longer seeking the mere satisfaction of its desires. It is a movement of the will seeking to repair the dislocation of thought and action in the opposing philosophies of rationalism and irrationalism.

The supposition of the Evil Spirit by Descartes is an example of such a will, says Bastide.[96] It represented the hypothesis of an absolute nothing-

[94] Cf. G. Bastide, "L'expérience morale," pp. 312-313.
[95] Cf. G. Bastide, *De la condition humaine*, p. 347.
[96] Cf. G. Bastide, "Le malin génie," *op. cit.*, p. 237.

ness, the supposition of the pure negativity of thought, a metaphysical deception where nothing is consistant as represented in thought. Its purpose was to bring the "conscience malheureuse" to an "infinite distress" wherein is born the triumphant intuition of the *Cogito*. The very engagement with an Evil Spirit already presupposed a force stronger than the supposed power of absolute negation, the certitude of the act of thought itself. To think the Evil Spirit, that is, to doubt, is itself an act of the spirit. But this certitude was born of a willed act, an act of generosity, an act wherein is revealed not only the spirit I am, but also the absolute power of the will. In this sense is thought said to be the bearer of the idea of God as the infinite and absolute reality. The generosity of consciousness, coupled with the presence of God, surmounts the doubt and brings to light the shadows cast by the reflexive doubt.

In brief, if consciousness were not sensitive it would not come to realize the misery of its condition and begin to doubt. If it had not doubted, it would not have realized the generosity of its response to that doubt. If consciousness had not been generous, it would not have been open to the infinite horizons of the spiritual conversion and the "Cogito, ergo sum."

CHAPTER VI

SPIRITUAL CONVERSION AND THE TRANSFIGURATION OF VALUES

I. Spiritual Conversion

We have so far proceeded from our original affirmation, through the problematic which it posed (the problem of authentic existence), to an analysis of the human condition – all in an effort to clarify man's situation in the world and discover a method for the authentic employment of an axiological metaphysics. An analysis of the human condition revealed the structure of inauthenticity as genetically linked to the maturation of consciousness as it receives an essentially new orientation. That is, a consideration of the "conscience malheureuse" revealed that inauthenticity and the conscious awareness of this condition, when resolutely faced by a generous will, effected a dramatic and wholly new attitude of consciousness. It is this change that is signified by the term "spiritual conversion" and we must now proceed to point out the full ramifications of this movement in Bastide's philosophy.

We are at the point of discovering the *relationship* between "what has been" (pre-philosophical level) and the present problem of existence as it broke into awareness with the original affirmation, declaring "what is" ("there is consciousness") and "what ought to be" (I am its witness). Ultimately, says Bastide, it is the problem of man – his immanence and transcendence. The situation of man is essentially and ultimately dramatic and ethical and therefore it will not be surprising to find that the central intuition is the drama of a spiritual conversion.

For Bastide, the spiritual conversion is a "heroic movement," a triumph of the will over the forces of alienation, a "generous wager" bringing man out of the depths of philosophical despair in the revelation of personal existence in the spirit.[1] The spiritual conversion is a revelation of man to

[1] Cf. G. Bastide, *Traité*, p. 133 of T.I.

himself as spirit.[2] Spiritual conversion is consciousness having reached the maturity of reflection. It is the revelation of my most intimate self as being person. In brief, the spiritual conversion is "the most clear evidence of all, that is, the experience of freedom." [3] For, "reflection and freedom are one and the same certitude of consciousness." [4] The true nature of the human condition and the real possibilities of the human situation will become clear if we proceed to consider the nature and the effects of the spiritual conversion.

Spiritual conversion is not a real genesis in temporal stages. Nor is it a definitive state to be obtained once and for all. "Conversion defines more a *rectitude of direction* and a way of search rather than the certitude of a possession and state." [5] Man is in the world and intentionally related to the world. But he is also presence to himself. Man's presence to the world and presence to himself has a twofold orientation, one authentic and one inauthentic. On the primitive level of conscious life man's inauthentic presence to the world and to himself arises from an attitude of consciousness that has been called "realist," because of its being a position of exteriority. For Bastide, as we have seen, the original and native (but not natural) orientation of man (his conscious faith and liberty) is directed toward the world empirically, for example, the logical, existential and axiological functions of consciousness are orientated superficially, but not radically in their mature and fully developed possibilities.

We have indicated in some way just what this inauthentic orientation means. The functions of conscious life are directed, says Bastide, towards the *objects* of representation as the only norms for truth, reality and value.[6] Up to a certain level of existence in the world (that is, in a certain social milieu and stage of human development) the "judgment" of consciousness about the world and about man is naively orientated in its natural function to seek unity and adherence to life on the "representational" level, that is, on the basis of spiritual intentions (animism) or, in more advanced stages,

[2] *Ibid.*, p. 133; cf. also G. Bastide, *De la condition humaine*, p. 284.

[3] Cf. G. Bastide, *Traité*, p. 140.

[4] G. Bastide, *Méditations*, p. 129.

[5] G. Bastide, *Les grands thèmes*, p. 91.

[6] The primitive function of judgment does not distinguish between value judgments and existential judgments. For in the early stages of consciousness' development "the object has no reality except by its value and no value except with reference to a subject." The judgment is, in this context, a confrontation of subject-object, such that the subject has no reality expect by its tension and no consciousness of its tension except by reference to the object. Cf. G. Bastide, *De la condition humaine*, p. 79.

on the basis of the "qualitative nature of things." [7] The representational consciousness is exercising its function of bearing witness, but from a position of exteriority.[8] Consciousness tends towards its own alienation by an overemphasis on the stable aspect of life to the neglect of the dynamic aspect.[9]

This basic *attitude* of consciousness has its influence on every aspect of man's life (his relation to the world and to others) and this relationship (inauthentic) has adverse effects on man's being as person. It is precisely the estrangement of naive faith in the experience of failure, error and sin that brings consciousness to its deepest paroxysm and prepares the way for spiritual conversion, provided that consciousness remains sensitive to its state and does not yield to the false justifications and mystification of the several dogmatisms. When the will is generous in face of alienation, the experience of the "conscience malheureuse" is one of *purification* and in the infinite doubt of the Evil Spirit the true self is revealed in its spirituality.

Spiritual conversion, then, is the philosophical translation for the appearance of the spirit to itself in the act of reflection (cf. the "pensée pensante" of Descartes). Spirit is nothing more "than the vision of consciousness present to itself in the perspective of interiority which is that of the converted consciousness." [10] Spirit is essentially pure self transparency.[11] This pure presence of consciousness to itself (which is also the definition of reflection for Bastide [12]) implies no change in being or nature (for spirit and life, he says, are not ontologically distinct [13]). It is nothing more than life reflecting on itself.[14] Bastide, then, is concerned with the

[7] The first part of Bastide's *De la condition humaine* is devoted to a psychological consideration of the development of consciousness as it moves towards reflection and spiritual conversion. Bastide's purpose is to discover the essential and fundamental needs of all conscious life, since these already point to the metaphysical order in some way. Id. p. 34. All along the way of the reflexive method the *objective disciplines* (which consider man "outside himself") are necessary, since they afford reflection the elements of a "constant confrontation" in the "constant check of verification." There is a "felicitous synchronism," says Bastide, "between the objective critiques of the primtive, infant and pathological mentalities (Lévy Bruhl, Jean Piaget, Pierre Janet) and the reflexive analyses of the idealists, together with the historical perspectives of Brunschvicg himself. Cf. G. Bastide, De la Condition humaine, pp. 6-7.

[8] Cf. Note §9, part. II, chapter II.

[9] Cf. G. Bastide, *De la condition humaine,* pp. 133-134.

[10] *De la condition humaine,* G. Bastide, p. 284.

[11] Cf. G. Bastide *De la condition humaine,* p. 284.

[12] Cf. G. Bastide, *Traité,* p. 141.

[13] Cf. G. Bastide, *Traité,* p. 141.

[14] While the terminology of idealism is at times strange to a realist point of view, it is necessary to see it always in the light of its original project of placing the

act in which consciousness is revealed to itself in spirit, and this *act* is itself the definition of spirit. For Descartes also the content of the idea of the soul is eminently the *Cogito*.

Bastide insists himself on returning to the *Cogito* of Descartes in order to deepen our understanding of the spiritual conversion. For Descartes the *Cogito* is eminently light, that is, the aspect of rationality is stressed. After Descartes Malbranche insists rather on the "sum," the sentiment of existence. With Biran also the *Cogito* is criticized for its formal content: it is more the spirit as resistance to matter which is the first fact of consciousness.[15] The experience of the personal *ego* is an experience of tension. We have, then, a twoford tendency in the various interpretations of the *Cogito* – one tending to rationalism, another towards irrationalism.

Bastide insists on starting from the *Cogito* as judgment and then following out the noetic aspect of the *Cogito*. Are we, he asks, necessarily condemned to an impersonal "cogitatur" because of the immanence of the "pensée pensante"? Are we unable to proceed to the affirmation of the thinking being in its personal reality? Bastide does not accept existence as the immediately given in the Cogito – since we cannot escape the logical order given in the understanding. But is there another way of positing the personal subject and escaping impersonal idealism or logical substantialism?

Bastide, we already know, insists that there is. It is in the recognition of the nature of spirit given in the spiritual conversion – for the spirit is not only revealed as legislating activity (Kant) but it is also a power for moral invention in the daily encounters with the obstacles, frustrations and unforeseen circumstances wherein consciousness is engaged with itself and with other consciousnesses striving for the "essential man." Following Kant there is the hesitation between rationalism (e.g. Hamelin, Lachelier) and irrationalism (e.g. Schopenhauer) concerning the nature of spirit, which indicates that Kant himself had not wholly defined this revelation of the spirit in its reality (which Bastide seeks in his exposition of spiritual conversion [16]). But this much, says Bastide, we have received for certain

spontaneity of thought in a non-objectivist context, in a philosophy of action. The incorporation of the life elan of Bergson into the idealist context is not without foundation.

Cf. A. Dondeyne, "Idealisme of realisme?" *Tijdschrift voor Philosophie,* 1941 (November), p. 614.

[15] Cf. A. Cresson, *Maine de Biran,* Paris, 1950, pp. 123 and 128.

[16] It is a question here of making precise the notion of spirit. Bastide accepts Kant's critique against ontological substantialism. But Bastide believes that Kant missed the full creative nature of spirit by reason of the formalism of his method, which passed from the given to the metaphysical conditions in the direction of an absolute purity.

from Kant, namely, that spirit cannot be revealed in the realist attitude of consciousness. It can be grasped only in its very life.[17]

It is here that Bastide points out the positive orientation of Bergson's method.[18] While not admitting Bergson's intuition, Bastide still insists that spirit can grasp itself only at the heart of spiritual activity itself, genetically in the very movements which constitute the reflexive cycle. In fact, Bastide sees a complementary relation between Bergson's notion of spirit in terms of life and Brunschvicg's conception of pure thought.[19]

Spiritual conversion, then, is concerned with the *act* in which consciousness is revealed in its spiritual dynamism as it "bends inwards" to the interiority of being.[20] Spiritual conversion is the act by which the individual consciousness arrives at the clear transparency of the interior horizons.[21] It is the grasping of thought in its irreducible opposition to absolute nothingness. As such, it is not a solution to our problem. For there is no solution. Rather, spiritual conversion works a *change in the subject,* not an ontological change, but a change in the orientation of the faith of consciousness and the use of our freedom.

In the realist attitude of consciousness there is a growing separation (alienation) between thought and existence. I no longer believe or do what I think. The natural demand for unity is frustrated more and more. The various facts of multiplicity no longer find a corresponding abstract synthesis. There is a general proliferation of the ego.[22] Spiritual conversion is precisely that "turning towards the light" where the orientation of conscious life and action are no longer in divergent directions, but now con-

Anxious to complete his revolution Kant ended up by giving a *structure* to "human consciousness in general" in the a priori forms. As such, says Bastide, transcendental idealism, in so far as it attempts to translate this structural conception of spirit, was an unstable equilibrium between subjectivism and absolute idealism. *The problem* is to reconcile the concrete, individual and dynamic aspects of personal subject with the *universal and objective* character of human existence. Eventually Bastide finds the orientation of his solution in the *practical* philosophy of Kant. In the postulates of practical reason and in a practical faith the spirit is attained on a new level, especially if the tendency to formalism is avoided by an approach to spirit in its "hand to hand" engagement with the problem of its existence not only as immanence but as transcendence as well, i.e. the notion of spirit as tension in an axiological metaphysics of action. Cf. G. Bastide, *De la condition humaine,* pp. 293-303.

[17] Cf. G. Bastide, *De la condition humaine,* p. 302.

[18] *Ibid.,* p. 313.

[19] *Ibid.,* p. 317.

[20] Cf. G. Bastide, *De la condition humaine,* p. 284.

[21] Cf. Note § 13 of this chapter.

[22] Bastide gives a very enlightening exposition, from a psychological point of view, of the various forms of psychological alienation in *De la condition humaine,* pp. 177-194.

verging towards authenticity itself.[23] Exactly how this takes place will become clear in the following section on the transfiguration of values. For the time being it is sufficient to have realized that, for Bastide, spiritual conversion is not a grasping of the act of thought in the act of legislating (that is we do not "see" ourselves reflecting or contemplate our freedom). We reflect (promotion of the idea). We act in authentic freedom. And in the authenticity of these acts we know ourselves. It is the light of spiritual conversion which makes possible the authenticity of our acts and in this sense it is said to bring together life and thought. Spiritual conversion is not a source of knowledge in the sense of *explaining* my reality or in the sense of revealing how I must act in a particular case. It is rather an *understanding* of the fact that I do not know my self in this sense,[24] that I must act and invent in order to construct my person which is not given to me in "knowledge," that I must conquer or be conquered, but that at least a way is *open* to an activity which is authentic and value – giving and that this way will manifest itself to the converted consciousness in the hand to hand engagement with life itself.[25]

The spiritual conversion, in other words, reveals the nature of spirit as *tension* (as was already intimated in the original affirmation). The difference is that, in the spiritual conversion, it is seen for the first time as *the problem,* that is, it is recognized as the *responsibility* of man whether life and thought are in diverging or converging fields, whether the use of liberty is alienating or promotive of my person. The spiritual conversion is the point of return from the free alienation of man by himself. Man's position between the two poles of conscious life is still precarious, but as a matter of fact he has changed his position. He stands facing the light and the shadows are behind him.[26]

In this context Bastide says that the spiritual conversion is the revelation of spirit, or "consciousness of consciousness" [27] that is, it is the metaphysical experience of life reflecting upon itself. It is a realization of this need for unity which constitutes the spirit itself.[28] It is this *awareness* that constitutes the self-mastery of the spirit over itself which constitutes the spiritual conversion. For unity was not to be found in things (multiplicity) but in the spirit. It is this ideal and place of unity in the spirit which is the

[23] Cf. G. Bastide, *De la condition humaine,* p. 319.
[24] Cf. G. Bastide, *De la condition humaine,* p. 366.
[25] *Ibid.,* p. 321.
[26] Cf. G. Bastide, *De la condition humaine,* p. 319.
[27] *Ibid.*
[28] *Ibid.,* p. 320.

result of the spiritual conversion.[29] For Bastide, the empirical world, in comparison with the spirit, is nothingness.[30]

The awareness that comes with the spiritual conversion, therefore, brings the recognition of the impossibility of spirit defining itself. It can only live its need for unity as the conscious and immanent law directing from within authentic activity. Spiritual conversion brings the clear awareness that there is no solution to my problem. It brings the tranquil abandonment of the restless search for the stable, in the dogmatic sense. The spirit knows now that its work is to imprint on all its endeavors the mark of unity which is its own law. It is in this sense that Bastide insists that "the spirit does not know itself as subject of a law but as the very function of legislation, as the law of laws, or better, as the principle of every norm." [31] The *law of the spirit,* understood in this sense, neither fixes the spirit itself in the state of "a thing" nor closes – in its activity as an endless beginning without end. Rather does it translate "the indefinite inventive function of the spirit." The works of the spirit do not point towards an "order" as much as they point towards progress. This "unity," then, is neither the unity of the general abstraction or the unity of totality, but "synenergy," [32] an effective collaboration of ressources, a law of progress and not a law of stability or uniformity.

Spiritual conversion, then, has orientated our problem anew. For now we begin to understand the nature of this unity (Valeur) calling us in the original affirmation. Not only is the problematic clearer, but the *subject* who is to bear witness is himself liberated in the very discovery that his bearing witness is the liberty of the concrete action of a spirit conscious of itself and that the authentic norms for the authentic values are spirit, unity and liberty, that is to say, spirit itself.

II. Spiritual conversion and the transfiguration of values

The spiritual conversion is a turning toward the interiority of the spirit in the discovery of spirit itself. But this discovery of which Bastide speaks is not the discovery of spirit which could fit into a realist philosophy, whether naturalist or ontological. Spirit is not of the same order, not even of the ontological order in Bastide's understanding of the term. Every at-

[29] *Ibid.*
[30] Cf. G. Bastide, "La conversion spirituelle," *op. cit.*, p. 19.06-4.
[31] Cf. G. Bastide, *De la condition humaine*, p. 321.
[32] *De la condition humaine*, p. 322.

tempt to unify nature and spirit fails to grasp the essence and orientation of spirit itself.[33]

The real importance of the spiritual conversion, therefore, lies in the clear awareness that there has been a change of *order*. Not to see this, claims Bastide, is to fail irreparably as regards philosophy.[34] Spiritual conversion discovers a "verticle dimension which is, in the deepest interiority of the self, openness to the light of the highest transcendence." [35] Philosophy is both "way" and "light" and it is the latter which gives sense and value to every act.[36]

At first glance, it might seem that there is nothing radically new here, but we have yet to see the full implications Bastide draws out of this central point of his philosophy. Bastide asserts his theory of the *two orders* in an *axiological dualism*. For Bastide, as for Brunschvicg, there is an essential duality in the epistemological and ontological orders. "To be" is neither univocal or analogical. "To be true" is likewise of an essentially dual order, finding its authentic fulness in only one.[37] Bastide aims at giving expression to the human situation in terms of a consciousness that is ethical as well as theoretical, a metaphysics that will incorporate in an essential way the fundamental problematic of our actions.[38]

Axiological dualism in a philosophy of spiritual conversion gives this framework to what Bastide has regarded as the human condition, namely, this essential and irreducible duality. The bast intelligent instrument for expressing this dualism is the notion of *orders* which he takes from Pascal.[39] For Bastide the Pascalian notion of the two orders "was a prophetic foreshadowing of the Kantian primacy of practical reason and the various value philosophies more or less directly descended from it." [40]

What, then, is the content of this notion central to Bastide's philosophy? We can say in general it is twofold: spirit and spiritual values.

[33] Cf. G. Bastide, "Le malin génie," *op. cit.*, p. 240.

[34] Cf. G. Bastide, "Le malin génie," *op. cit.*, p. 240.

[35] G. Bastide, *Traité*, p. 133.

[36] Cf. G. Bastide, "De la condition temporelle de l'homme," *Les études philosophiques*, 1962 (17), p. 80.

[37] Cf. G. Bastide, "The Metaphysical Dimensions of Man," *op. cit.*, p. 351.

[38] *Id.*

[39] "Three spheres of reality here detach themselves from one another: the sphere of 'corps,' that of 'esprits' and that of 'charité.' Between them lies a 'différence de genre'; ... each sphere has its own kind of value ... Associated with each is a particular cognitive prerequisite and a particular 'vue,' a view corresponding to the specific object."

R. Guardina, "Man and his situation in the world," in *Pascal for our Time*, translated by B. Thompson, Herder (New York), 1966, p. 72.

[40] G. Bastide, "The Metaphysical Dimensions ..." *op. cit.*, p. 354.

Spiritual conversion is the discovery of spirit as being one with the act of reflection.[41] The content of the revelation of the new perspective of interiority is especially *act* (which equals reflection, that is, liberty). The first discovery, then, of the spiritual conversion is that the norm for truth is the interior perspective of spirit and not the position of exteriority of naive realism. In other words, it is the idealist consciousness (which is the same thing as the converted consciousness [42]) and not the realist consciousness. The norm for truth is the unity of the person.[43] In spiritual conversion "the light of this need for unity makes clear the very notion of truth." [44]

In fact, the misery of our alienated condition was perceived only in the light of this unity which is one with the call to perfection. The light of the spiritual conversion (spirit) is the very power to see the misery of our condition in alienation in the light of the ideal of perfection. The sign of unity, then, has given us the norm for distinguishing the true values. And this norm is realized only in the *act* of *reflection,* that is, only by the reflexive method.[45]

The second and more important aspect of the notion of order is that it is open to an *axiological* content. For Bastide, the function of philosophy is to explore the *vertical* axiological dimensions of consciousness, where the method of immanence (the reflexive method), when rigorously applied by a sensitive and generous consciousness, leads to the discovery of the *interior transcendence,* completely different from the realist transcendence in exteriority. Like spirit, the *spiritual values,* which are revealed in the spiritual conversion and the discovery of spirit, are grasped, not as "objects understood," but in the "subject understanding." [46] That is, philosophy is not a Theodicy, like the philosophy of Leibniz, but a "rigorous position of orders of values." [47]

Thus the notion of *orders* gives a schema for situating heterogeneous realities (two orders of values, truth, knowledge etc.) and for placing *different directions* of conscious realization (for example, introspective subjectivity or interior reflection).[48] In short, the notion of orders affirms the *discontinuous* hierarchy of values, the irreducible character of the spiritual values and the impossibility of passing metaphysically, epistemologically or

[41] Cf. G. Bastide, "La nature, la conscience," *op. cit.*, p. 27.
[42] Cf. G. Bastide, *De la condition humaine*, p. 376.
[43] Cf. G. Bastide, *Traité*, p. 166.
[44] Cf. G. Bastide, "La condition spirituelle," *op. cit.*, p. 19.06-5.
[45] Cf. G. Bastide, *La conversion spirituelle*, p. 66.
[46] Cf. G. Bastide, *Traité*, p. 357.
[47] *Id.*, p. 358.
[48] Cf. G. Bastide, *Méditations*, pp. 104-106.

practically from the inferior to the higher degree of this axiological structure.[49]

Thus in spiritual conversion we have a *transfiguration* of the metaphysical horizon in the new direction of consciousness.[50] Spiritual conversion is the demarcation of two opposite, inverse movements open to conscious life, one alone being the true and authentic mode of action.[51] For Bastide, the immanent ideal of the unity and perfection of spirit posed in spiritual conversion is the "locus" of all authentic activity.

Spiritual conversion, then, results in a *mode of activity* of consciousness which Bastide calls the *transfiguration of values*.[52] The term "transfiguration of values" translates philosophically the *ethical change of horizon* resulting from conversion.[53] It consists "in a sudden change in the coloration and appearance of everything." [54] The source of change is wholly in the subject and it "implies no material change in the things themselves." That is why it is "essentially of the axiological order." [55] For the transfiguration affects only the *relation* of the subject to the object, where the *faith* of consciousness is brought into play in an integral way. As such, it can be understood only in the context of the *two orders* (spiritual and empirical) outlined above. It has little in common with other theories of transformation of values which suppose a continuous empirical horizon.[56]

As a result of spiritual conversion, the world of experience passes from the world of empirical experience to the world of spiritual experience, that is, of reflection. What was spiritually accidental and empirically essential for native faith radically reverses itself in the *new and acquired faith* of spiritual conversion.[57] The transfiguration defines a radical change in the subject of reference in regards to values: "... man in so far as *open* upon infinite transcendence (replaces) the empirical and egocentric man of naive faith." [58]

To further explain the difference in the two orders of values resulting from spiritual conversion, Bastide has recourse to Spinoza's norm: the empirical values are those which are lessened by division and whose pursuit

[49] Cf. G. Bastide, "The Metaphysical Dimensions of Man," *op. cit.*, p. 355.
[50] G. Bastide, "La Conversion spirituelle," *op. cit.*, p. 19.06-6.
[51] Cf. G. Bastide, *La conversion spirituelle*, p. 46.
[52] *Ibid.*, p. 6.
[53] *Ibid.*, pp. 54-55.
[54] Cf. G. Bastide, *Traité*, p. 134.
[55] *Ibid.*, p. 135; see also *La conversion spirituelle*, p. 55.
[56] Cf. G. Bastide, *La conversion spirituelle*, *op. cit.*, p. 19.06-6.
[57] *Ibid.*, p. 19.06-7.
[58] G. Bastide, *Traité*, p. 135.

engenders the city of misery and hate; the spiritual values are those which are increased by communion and which constitute the "verum bonum communicabile sui." [59] The notion of "disinterestedness" comes into play here. For it pertains to the critical function of the converted consciousness to disregard in a spirit of detachment what the realist consciousness assepts as the "given," and instead accept only those values of intrinsic worth, that is, the values constituted by the spirit itself.[60] The spiritual man is indifferent to empirical values in the same sense in which the empiricist is indifferent to spiritual ones.

In concluding this section, we might do well to consider at this point the notion of value in Bastide's philosophy. Value is defined by Bastide in terms of reasons for being (*raisons d'être*). Man, as a being who thinks, cannot know another being or even his own reality, says Bastide, except in terms of its *raison d'être*. "A being having no reason for being would be nothing as far as our knowledge is concerned." [61] This is why all philosophy must begin with man and not with the world or with the Absolute. And this is further qualified to mean that we must begin with reflection and the authentic knowledge of the self.[62]

Axiological metaphysics replaces ontological metaphysics "in this sense, that value, that is the "*raison d'être* of being" (ratio essendi) cannot be known except by taking as our starting point the different modes of knowing, that is, the *ratio cognoscendi*.[63] Philosophy is a search for these reasons for being, that is, the values which move the person in the search and the faith which animates it. For value, as we saw, is defined in terms of faith as that which one believes (ce à quoi l'on croit). More specifically, value is that which moves to act and as such it is more than a sufficient reason and less than an efficient cause, "being that which the subject believes and acts upon." [64]

The problematic of axiology was to distinguish the authentic values. For the justifying ground of a being who acts in the light of an autonomous will is value, that is, what one believes in. A further examination of metaphysics by way of the reflexive method and spiritual conversion became the awareness that there are two orders of values – one order related to exteriority and subjectivity, the other to interiority and objectivity.

[59] *Ibid.*, p. 136. See as well pp. 190-191 and *La conversion spirituelle*, pp. 650-66.
[60] Cf. G. Bastide, *Traité*, p. 136; also *De la condition humaine*, pp. 329-331.
[61] G. Bastide, "De la situation de l'homme," *op. cit.*, p. 245.
[62] G. Bastide, "The Metaphysical Dimensions of Man," *op. cit.*, p. 353.
[63] G. Bastide, *Traité*, p. 127.
[64] G. Bastide, "The Metaphysical Dimensions," p. 360. We are in the practical order of the postulates of the practical reason.

The most important aspect of every value judgment is the subject of reference, notes Bastide, for values can change precisely with reference to the subject. Such a change, we have seen, is effected by the spiritual conversion. Spiritual conversion changes the ethical horizon by substituting for the indefinite of desire the infinite of perfection and the *unity* of value. This produces a radical change in the subject who becomes "a new man" with a new consciousness and a new kind of willing.[65] But since the change in the subject implies a change in the value judgment, we have a real transfiguration of values corresponding to the new attitude effected by the spiritual conversion. In the attitude of openness to the infinite and to the idea of perfection, the values in relation to such a subject of reference are no longer the values of empirical satisfaction, but spiritual perfection.[66] For this reason, it is only the spiritual man who can truly become the "measure of all things" and be really engaged in a practical humanism.[67]

In relation to the human condition and the situation of man as defined in our original problematic, we can now define more clearly the reality of that situation in terms of value and in terms of the transfiguration of values. For our original problem was constituted by the situation of man's existence (problem) and the authenticity (solution) which was present only as a yet distant ideal. Man's situation *is* a situation of value, says Bastide. But what exactly is the content of this axiological situation?

Up to now we have seen that man is situated in a field of values constituted by certain intervals and directions. This is topographically represented by Bastide by a *horizontal plane* composed of four values (those values which, we saw, constituted the major poles of existence: the logical, existential, retrospective and prospective (past, future) values).[68] But this field of values which constitutes man's situation and provides the normal and necessary tension of conscious life, is able to be ordered *as a whole* in *one of two directions,* represented by a vertical to the horizontal. One of these vertical directions ("transdescendance") is that of consciousness moved in naive faith and operating a dialectic of dissolution; the other ("transascendance") is the consciousness of spiritual conversion (idealist consciousness) operating a dialectic of promotion.

In the first case (that of naive faith) a solution to the problematic was sought in the empirical or dogmatic order; in the latter the solution to the problem of existence is sought authentically in the unity of spiritual interi-

[65] *Id.*, p. 365.
[66] Cf. *La conversion spirituelle*, p. 66.
[67] *Ibid.*, p. 69.
[68] Cf. G. Bastide, *Méditations*, p. 104.

ority. In the former, existence is in a divergent direction; in the latter it converges on its goal which is authenticity. The *orders* of values are seen in two different lights. The *self-same values* participate in two vertical, axiological directions. Empirical values are those correlative to naive faith; spiritual values are those correlative to the acquired faith of spiritual conversion.[69] Thus each of the four central poles of values constituting the human situation can have a spiritual or empirical orientation.

For this reason the assertion of a spiritual conversion and transfiguration of values is not a repudiation of the "empirically" given as such, but only in so far as *values,* that is, objects of a deceived naive faith. The spiritual values are the only values. In this framework the spiritual conversion and the subsequent transfiguration of values is only a displacement of values, that is, they are seen in the same light, but the source of that light is known only through spiritual conversion.[70]

[69] Cf. G. Bastide, *Méditations,* p. 106.
[70] *Id.,* p. 108.

CHAPTER VII

AXIOLOGICAL IDEALISM & SPIRITUAL PERSONALISM

I. Introduction

The function of philosophy, according to Bastide, is to open up the meaning of the problem which man's existence is. "The being of man escapes us and nevertheless there is a problem of man; it is the unique and necessary problem, not the problem of his being, but of his reason for being; not that of his notion, but of his situation in relation to his reason for being that is, in relation to Value." [1]

Philosophy, then, is said to derive its fruitfulness in its search for the *raisons d'être* and not from any ontological search for "being." For being, says Bastide, is only known in terms of its *raison d'être*. Philosophy, he insists, must be axiology applied to the problem of man.[2] He sees his own particular contribution to philosophy as the systematic use of the axiological method applied to man.

But what does this mean – to grasp the problem of man axiologically? Negatively, it consists in bringing the critical doubt to bear upon any formulation of the problem of man in terms of his nature. The integral, practical humanism which Bastide seeks cannot express man or his existence in ontological categories, the word ontological being understood, as we have seen, more in a naturalistic sense. Positively, says Bastide, it seems that the notion of the *human condition* can be the faithful transmitter of the concrete reality of the essential man.[3] But what is the human condition?

So far it has become clear that for Bastide the human condition is eminently *man knowing himself* in the act of reflection through a spiritual conversion and transfiguration of values. The condition of man is the *tension* of consciousness between two essentially different orders of values

[1] G. Bastide, "De la situation de l'homme," *op. cit.*, p. 246.
[2] *Ibid.*, p. 245.
[3] Cf. G. Bastide, "Nature, situation et conditions humaines," *op. cit.*, p. 59.

and the experience of man as the *freedom* to choose between these two directions of consciousness. The condition of man is precisely this dramatic situation between noetic universality and axiological transcendence in a world of positive and negative values. It is no wonder, then, that for Bastide the central intuition of authentic philosophy is the revelation in reflection of two orders of reality that are neither homogeneous or continuous or analogical, but which constitute an *axiological field* within which man passes, not in a linear, hierarchical movement, but vertically and through a spiritual conversion.

Therefore, philosophy, in this viewpoint, is necessarily a metaphysics of the *act* of consciousness constituting the axiological field of the human condition wherein the liberty of man finds its authentic realization and man is constituted as person. Since the problem of philosophy is *act*, says Bastide, it is only through a consideration of Value that this act receives its metaphysical foundation and its authenticity.[4] It is in this context that the philosophy of Georges Bastide is an axiology. The notion of the double *order* discovered in *reflection* is given an axiological content, thereby enabling philosophy to situate without contradiction heterogeneous realities (nature and spirit), providing at the same time the metaphysical framework for two distinct directions of thought.

Finally, in this very movement the philosophical *method* is defined, that is, Bastide's way to the truth. Having established Value as the fundamental source of authentic philosophy, there arose the question as regards the *way* in which axiology itself was to be employed. For example, it would be wrong to use a philosophy of value to explain the particular ways of being (manières d'être) instead of Being itself, falling back into a disguised materialism. The *method* of axiological metaphysics can only be reflexive analysis (philosophies of reflection).[5] By the reflexive method he means an exploration with "the whole soul" (Plato) of the central axiological dimensions of consciousness at work. This search *is* the *authentic moral experience* of person in situation.[6] In the authentic use of the reflexive method (in spiritual conversion, that is, in the idealist consciousness) man discovers an *interior transcendence* that is completely different from any corresponding transcendence in a realist philosophy of God.

In particular, then, the function of philosophy, according to Bastide, is to explore the vertical axiological dimension of consciousness and the immanence-transcendence relationship that is at the heart of the problem

[4] Cf. G. Bastide, *Traité*, p. 357.
[5] Cf. G. Bastide, *Traité*, p. 357.
[6] *Ibid.*, p. 357.

of man. For the interior unity attained in the spiritual conversion and the idea of perfection discovered therein, did not do away with transcendence, that is, the infinite axiological distance which separates man and authenticity. But the problem of man and the knowledge of man and the revelation of the speritual conversion is nothing more than *the idea of man himself in this relationship to perfection.*[7] But this idea is not revealed as an ontological power, but its revelation is axiological, heuristic, a practical postulate in the sense of a loving imperative to search for authenticity as the unique human vocation. It is in this framework that Bastide says that the *doctrine* of axiological idealism is *not* an explanation of values,[8] but a rigorous positing of the *orders* of value. In other words, philosophical method plays a central role, as we might expect in an idealist point of view.

Therefore, the *doctrine* of philosophy, according to Bastide, aims at showing clearly the options open to human liberty within the human condition. It aims at marking off clearly the way of authenticity and inauthenticity, showing which values pertain to which orders. The fundamental philosophical option (and therefore the option of existence itself) is to choose between axiology and ontology.

The doctrine of axiological metaphysics becomes *Ethics.*[9] Metaphysics becomes Ethics in the knowledge of the idea, which is the idea of the Value of all values, the idea of perfection.[10] For the reflexive experience is above all the revelation of man to himself as an interior transcendence, that is, "man has no other idea of himself than that which he has of himself in relationship to perfection." But the idea of perfection is not related to man as an ontological transcendence of efficient causality, nor is it a pantheistic immanence. Rather is it this call to authenticity axiologically interpreted.

Thus moral philosophy is essentially linked to axiology and the reflexive method in Bastide's philosophy. It is in the act of spiritual conversion that the idea of the infinite (Descartes) and the idea of duty (Kant) become certitudes generative of moral life in the spirit.

In the final analysis we are brought back to the personalism of the original affirmation. The function of philosophy is one with what Bastide calls the construction of the person. The role of philosophy, we have seen, is to clearly separate the regime of liberty and the regime of alienation, the regime of action and the regime of passion, the regime of the promotion

[7] *Ibid.*, II, p. 724.

[8] G. Bastide, *Traité*, I, p. 357.

[9] Cf. G. Bastide, "De la situation de l'homme," *op. cit.*, p. 256.

[10] It is especially here that the *Ethics* of Spinoza are a source of inspiration for Bastide, as they were also for Brunschvicg.

of spiritual values and the regime of dissolution and disfiguration of the same values. Philosophy introduces us *effectively* (for it is of the order of practical reason) into the new faith which causes us to acquire possession of our existence in its authentic center and its true vocation. But this is what Bastide means by personal being – the subject questioning itself reflectively concerning its own *raison d'être* and bringing this reflection to the *practical* answers which are the normal completion of the reflexive cycle itself.[11] The final sense of authenticity comes down to the practical bearing witness to consciousness in the testimony of spiritual works.[12] It remains for us to consider axiological idealism in its natural outcome in a spiritual personalism.

II. Axiological Idealism

Axiological idealism, then, is the philosophical translation for the doctrine of Bastide's philosophy. His philosophy is an *idealism* because idealism is the philosophical translation for the attitude of consciousness resulting from spiritual conversion and the transfiguration of values. For Bastide, it is this attitude which makes authentic philosophy possible. It is the attitude of reflection.

But this attitude of reflection is the acquiring of a *new faith* "in the ideality of value." Therefore idealism is axiological.[13]

Nevertheless philosophy, it must be admitted, aims at the real and the concrete. But, insist the idealists, the "real" of the naive consciousness is of the order of the imagination, not of the order of perfect reflection. Idealism is of the real, concrete order precisely because it is immanent to the consciousness which discovers the order of spirit, the interior source of unity and the transcendent vocation to Perfection. It is in and by the idealist consciousness that the true values are discovered under the norm of that unity which is the "value of values," the "unifying unity" which is the philosophical name of God.[14] As such, idealism is at one and the same time a dramatic realization of the failures of realism, a becoming conscious of the fact that "the quantitative and qualitative determinations of being are relative to us and that what 'bad faith' dislocated by a misguided search for power, the disinterested activities of science, art and morality can rejoin in the establishing of a web of comprehensive relations." [15]

[11] Cf. G. Bastide, *Traité*, p. 384.
[12] *Ibid.*, p. 125.
[13] Cf. G. Bastide, *La conversion spirituelle*, p. 70.
[14] Cf. G. Bastide, *Traité*, p. 289.
[15] G. Bastide, *Traité*, p. 137.

Furthermore, as an axiology idealism is not a philosophy of value "en soi." It is rather a power of giving value, not a doctrine explaining values. It is a *life* of promoting the spiritual values against the dissoluting force of nothingness which is also the power of man. It is above all an effective engagement of the spirit in the act of moral invention.

Moral invention is the act of positing new values by a subject conscious both of the value and the newness of the value which is being posited, for "matter invents nothing, instinct invents nothing, chance invents nothing and the unconscious man invents nothing . . ." [16] There is no moral invention without consciousness, a consciousness which, for Bastide, is decidely idealist.[17] The imperative of authenticity revealed in the original affirmation – "to say what one thinks in believing what one says in order to do what one believes" – makes each one who accepts his vocation a porter of value and the promoter of a regime of spiritual values in the unforeseen situations of daily life.

Axiological idealism, therefore, seeks its original source in the philosophy of Plato and the practical philosophy of Kant.[18] For it is an assertion of the Good over essence and existence, of the practical reason over pure reason. Spiritual conversion affects "not only our faculty of knowledge, but above all the faculty of will, in such a way that it is (in the last analysis) on the moral ideal that the validity of our knowledge depends." [19]

Therefore, axiological idealism is the philosophy of the *moral ideal*. It is not the ideal of subjective phenomenalism or absolute idealism. For the former rests "on this side" (en deça) of the true moral ideal while the latter passes illigitimately "au delà" of the authentic spiritual experience wherein the moral ideal is revealed. As we have already explained, the authentic moral experience is intrinsically related to the experience of the "conscience malheureuse," but it does not rest there as in a final and all embracing experience. The moral ideal is not that of closed existentialism or historical vitalism. It is rather a "living reality" constantly calling man to perfection.[20]

Idealism, then, is not a system of Being but a doctrine of Value.[21] Or better it is the idealist consciousness in its power of giving value, that is, of constructing, not a world of being but the reasons for being in the very act

[16] *Id.*, p. 207.
[17] Cf. G. Bastide, *Traité*, p. 208.
[18] Cf. G. Bastide, *La conversion spirituelle*, p. 73.
[19] G. Bastide, *La conversion spirituelle*, p. 73.
[20] Cf. G. Bastide, *De la condition humaine*, p. 387.
[21] G. Bastide, *De la condition humaine*, p. 383.

of spiritual life by which value defends being against the power of nothingness.[22] It is a philosophy of the idea – not the idea of false idealisms, subjectivisms of the concept, but the idea of authentic idealism, a "living reality" discovered in the spiritual act of invention and promotion of spiritual value.[23] The idea here is one with act, for it is the law generating the object itself. It is known only in its realization on the practical level. In short, it is the truth elevated to a living expression which speaks to us (for example, the life of Socrates in so far as it speaks to us today because we find him in ourselves). It is the law which is generating in man both philosophy and morality.[24]

Expressed in another fashion, axiological idealism is the faith of the converted consciousness in an infinite power of giving value, that is, in the spirit itself causing this faith to be actively present. This certitude of the value of spirit is acquired in the experience of the transfiguration of values rising out of the philosophical doubt. From this point of view we can say that the *ideal* revealed in the spiritual experience of the victory of the spirit over the powers of the empirical world finds an echo in our being as a whole and is existentially lived, so that it becomes the norm *commanding effectively* both knowledge and action. It traces out heuristically what we are to become, what lies ahead of us as our vocation and self-realization. But it is also generative of the concrete actions of morality.[25]

It is precisely because the ideal is given to us as a *value* and in an authentic attitude of consciousness that it is, by its very nature, not "ready-made" but subject to a constant search and re-evaluation. Value "dominates both knowledge and existence together."

Bastide analyses further the doctrine of moral idealism along the axis of acquired faith and its threefold object. In opposition to realism, moral idealism is *critical* and *relative*. It is critical because the constant acting in the spirit requires a constant effort of defense against the attitude of realism, a constant purification in self-knowledge and a constant vivifying and value-giving activity in the various situations arising in daily life. It is relative because the qualitative and quantitative determinations of the world are relative both to each other and to us. The idea, whose object is value, approaches more and more the concrete action. But the idea is not a given (in abstraction, for example), but an ideal to be sought and constructed, the object of the idealist faith (croire à). This faith extends as well to the

[22] Cf. G. Bastide, *De la condition humaine*, pp. 383-384.
[23] Cf. G. Bastide, *Traité*, p. 155.
[24] Cf. G. Bastide, *De la condition humaine*, pp. 387-391.
[25] Cf. G. Bastide, *La conversion spirituelle*, p. 74.

system of intelligibility of the idealist consciousness (croire que). Finally, it is faith in the spirit (croire en) and its value-giving power. In this context axiological idealism is an intellectualism as well as a spiritualism.[26]

Finally, axiological idealism must be understood in the framework of a philosophy of action. For it is, above all, not a theory of knowledge, but the "faith of a consciousness in act." [27] As we have seen, a basic duality determines two dialectics open to free choice. These two dialectics, moving in opposite directions, are irreducible to one another. There is "depassement" and "engagement" from one problem to another (dialectic), but only in a movement already orientated by value "which is the only means we have for philosophizing about action." [28]

It is becoming clearer now how the three constituents of the original affirmation are made to fit together in an axiological idealism. The call to action in truth and authenticity finds its philosophical explanation here. For the need to act is orientated along the way of spiritual conversion and the transfiguration of values in the discovery of the authentic values and the norm for truth which is the unity of spirit.

III. Spiritual Personalism

Spiritual conversion is the discovery of spirit. Put in another way, the reality or content resulting from the initiative of the movement of spiritual conversion in the discovery of spirit is the discovery of that which grounds the authentic self, the spiritual and the Absolute. For it is the personal "ego sum" which is seized as being irreducible to anything in the empirical order; and it is the self as something of the absolute order which resists the infinite power to deceive of the supposed Evil Spirit. It is the experience of the "infinite" aspect of my freedom.

The experience of the spiritual conversion, then, is not the experience of the empirical self at all. It is not a return to solipsism, but to my *spiritual being,* to the clarity of an *idea* comprising the whole self in its most intimate and most transcendent vocation.[29] Thus, the revelation of the "Cogito, ergo sum" is taken by Bastide as the very foundation of a philosophy of personalism. The subject given in the original experience of the *Cogito* is not simply a "left-over" from the category of substance. It is my personal being, says Bastide, resisting the infinite power threatening it. The subject

[26] G. Bastide, *La conversion spirituelle,* p. 78.
[27] *Id.,* p. 81.
[28] *Ibid.*
[29] Cf. G. Bastide, *Traité,* p. 133.

is discovered as given and being constituted in the free act of resolution of the "conscience généreuse." [30] Man cannot *know himself* except in the act of *being himself authentically*. And it is only in the act of spiritual converson that man *is* himself authentically.

Spiritual conversion, then, is essentially bound up with the act of reflection – for reflection without spiritual conversion would be a false reflection (realism) and spiritual conversion without reflection would be a false conversion ("bad faith").[31] But this "fundamental experience" is essentially an ethical experience, "where the high idea of humanity is discovered and without which it would rest unknown and never guessed at." But the definition of *person* in our original affirmation was already in terms of reflection in act, that is, as a bearing witness to consciousness.[32]

It is in this context that Bastide maintains that *spiritual personalism* is the "normal and unequivocal result of axiological idealism." [33] Here we find the incarnation of the notion of spirit about which so much has already been said. Four concepts are essential to our discussion of spiritual personalism: duty, autonomy, responsibility and understanding. For it is in reflection that the transcendence of Value is *freely* welcomed by every man in his person. And it is only in the intimate conjunction of duty and freedom that the transcendent Value becomes incarnate in the world.[34] Furthermore, freedom is the key notion for understanding the true relation of values and duty to the ideal of perfection.

1. Duty

We have seen in our discussions of moral idealism that the knowledge of the new faith acquired in spiritual conversion is a certitude of the *practical order*. For it is the Good which is *present* in the consciousness of spiritual conversion and the presence of this value is a light as regards the way of authenticity. The first *good action* is the generous act of the will in the spiritual conversion itself. It is prior even to the truth which is regarded as the "production" of the witness of the consciousness already converted.[35]

The criterion for the good action is the spiritual conversion itself. It is its

[30] *Ibid.*, p. 134.

[31] Cf. G. Bastide, *De la condition humaine*, p. 277.

[32] Cf. G. Bastide, *Méditations*, p. 6.

[33] G. Bastide, *La conversion spirituelle*, p. 86.

[34] G. Bastide, "La conversion spirituelle," in *Encyclopédie française, op. cit.*, p. 19.06-8.

[35] Cf. G. Bastide, *Méditations*, p. 112. The primary certitude for Bastide is the practical certitude of the human conditioin in the act of spiritual conversion, the practical certitude of the new faith and its precarious position in regards to freedom.

own certitude. The passage from one order to another in the spiritual conversion is not a theory but a "pratique." [36] It is of its nature unifying, because it is of the spiritual order.

On the other hand, in the regime of alienation actions are "passions" in so far as they are more "laisser faire" than actual action; they are aimed more at the empirical values as ends and therefore necessarily part of a regime of dissolution. It is "only in the spiritual order that prospection is action and not passion." [37] Yet in every inauthentic action there is a corresponding increase in the disequilibrium which the human condition can support only so long. As Bastide puts it, the exaltation of one value over another is not without a corresponding protest on the part of the neglected value.

Yet there is an imperative to authenticity and good action. Between what I am and what I have yet to be there is an evident distance and subsequent to this an evident duty to bridge the gap which separates my existence from authenticity. This separation of essence and existence, this need to give to my existence that I am something of the essence I am not (or to my essence something of the existence that is still lacking) – this is the law of duty, the law of my bearing witness in authenticity, the law of the constitution of my person.

The law of duty, then, is the result of the human condition as such. That is why, for Bastide, it is already essentially revealed in the original affirmation, already grounding the philosophical search and the ethical nature of that search. Duty, then, is central to his own axiological idealism and the metaphysics of action. The original affirmation brought with it the need to act authentically and the need to discover a method for determining the authentic values. Once again, we see that the search is everywhere inspired by this basic need, this all embracing duty. The notion of duty, in Bastide's philosophy, therefore, is necessarily linked to the presence-absence description of the Value present in the original affirmation of consciousness. For it is this presence in absence that founds the exigence for unity and the fulness of value, that is, the unity of authenticity. It is the duty to act.

But the notion of duty becomes much more clear in the light of the "conscience malheureuse" and the spiritual conversion. For the appearance and the presence of the Good and with it the immense possibility of man to inaugurate the good in the spiritualization of his actions is only as strong

[36] Cf. G. Bastide, *Traité*, p. 191.
[37] G. Bastide, *Méditations*, p. 113.

as the realization of the amount of failure, error and sin man himself has brought into the world. The real meaning of duty (in its rational reality and not simply as impulse of nature or social pressure) is revealed only in reflection, the spiritual conversion and the transfiguration of values.[38] Man has first to see for himself, personally, the wreck of value possibilities before he himself can perceive in a practical way the duty of seeking perfection by the value-giving effects of his own spiritual activity. He has to experience the futility of an empirical society or see the damage of nominalism, for example, before an immense, salutary "scruple" becomes the road to his own spiritual conversion.

Duty, then, is necessarily related to moral need as its moving force here and now, but its true object is always the unity and totality of value.[39] Duty is first and foremost an affirmation of the axiological primacy of that which is still only a far-off goal of man's vocation, really present however as the sure promise of the power of the spirit over all the powers of dissolution. Thus, Bastide calls duty a "transcendent immanence" which moves against the tendency to fall back into materiality and empirical exteriority.[40] In this sense, duty is a metaphysical condition in the "personalization of our being in authenticity of life." [41]

For man duty is incarnated in the human condition as the separation of the four poles of value which, as we have seen, can be said to define the human situation. As far as man is concerned, then, duty has four roots: the past, the future, the existential and the rational. Man is at the crossroads of this painful separation in the very moment in which he is called to realize himself authentically by ascending the vertical dimensions where alone self-fulfillment can become a reality.[42] The nature of duty is eminently axiological and idealist. It is idealist because it is only in spiritual conversion that it is revealed in its true nature as a loving imperative creating a practical impossibility of not accomplishing certain acts or of accomplishing others that are to be left undone.[43]

"Therefore it is necessary to say that the vocation to unity arising out of multiplicity itself translates the imperative of our engagement . . ." [44] For man it is the disjunction of the major values and the difficulty of their

[38] G. Bastide, "La conversion spirituelle," in *Encyclopédie française, op. cit.*, p. 19.06-7.
[39] Cf. G. Bastide, *Méditations*, pp. 119-120.
[40] *Id.*, p. 196.
[41] *Id.*
[42] Cf. G. Bastide, *Traité*, p. 192.
[43] *Ibid.*, p. 662.
[44] *Méditations*, p. 120.

composition which demonstrates the infinite separation from authenticity revealed in the original affirmation. At the same time, it is the presence of the absolute value in the need for unity and its absence in the goal of perfection that is really being revealed in the duty assumed by the responsible man.

The certitude of this duty is the self-awareness of the person himself and therefore it participates in all the undeniable sureness of the original affirmation. The existence of man and the poles of value constituting his situation leave no doubt, says Bastide, as regards the reality of duty and the hope of the goal it marks out. As sure as man is that his existence is yet to be won, so sure can he be that the duty to accomplish this work exists. It is both a present moving force and a goal yet to be attained.

Duty, then, *engages* man in the work which is marked out in the human situation. The *right* to be person gained in the spiritual conversion is correlative to the duty to be personally responsible in the effective instauration of the spiritual values.[45] Duty is the *way* to the goal, but is such only by reason of the spiritual conversion and the *action* which makes it possible.[46]

It is, then, the intervals of consciousness itself that make of human existence a quest for authenticity, which quest is known in duty as the obligation of a conquest and a promotion. Duty is "that form of action by which, in order to promote myself in authenticity of life towards the unity of value which saves me from radical nothingness, I conquer myself, I have yet to conquer myself in regards to my own powers of dissolution and alienation." [47] Man as person is a "devoir vivant" whose only mesure is that which is above all measure.

2. *Autonomy*

To speak of duty is to speak of autonomy. In Kant's *Foundations of the Metaphysics of Morals* the presence of duty as a categorical imperative leads to the notion of the autonomy of the will. For duty, as imperative, commands us to act in such a way so that the will is able to consider itself as being itself the legislating power of the universal law to which it submits. Duty is the *ratio cognoscendi* for the transcendental reality of liberty, which in turn is the *ratio essendi* of morality.

For Bastide, too, the reflexive connection of duty conceived as universal law and freedom conceived as autonomy is the basic fact of morality. But the revelation of this fact is not grounded in the distinction between the

[45] *Méditations*, p. 121.
[46] Cf. G. Bastide, *Mirages et Certitudes, op. cit.*, p. 242.
[47] G. Bastide, *Méditations*, p. 122.

noumenal and phenomenal orders, but in the notion of spiritual conversion and the transfiguration of values – in Bastide's own idealism, therefore.[48]

We have seen that the situation of man is essentially "value-giving." That is, the situation of man as revealed in spiritual conversion constitutes a system of axiological relations made up of a certain number of cardinal values (retrospective, prospective, rational and existential) able to be divided into one or two orders marked off by the movement of spiritual conversion. The two dialectics constitute the very law of consciousness as value and the awareness of the two orders is itself the experience of liberty.[49]

Duty is originally expressed as a law of unity centered in this axiological situation. It might also be expressed as the law of interiorization concerning the multiplicity given to consciousness in the world of values. For the world is encountered first in a naive way and secondly in the profound doubt arising from the experience of my own alienation by a world of values imposed from without and not yet interiorized in reflection. But the transfiguration of values is by way of the constructing power of the spirit elaborating its own values in an *action* opposed to the *passion* of the first engagement with the world in a naive attitude of consciousness. It is only in the value-giving *action* of the converted consciousness that what was simply given exteriorly (and not interiorized) is now made anew as my own work and as an adequate expression of *my person*. Thus, the retrospective "doubt," says Bastide, finds its real meaning in the prospective "I ought" of the converted consciousness. In turn the spiritual conversion and the revelation of the "I ought" is the foundation for *knowing myself* as a spiritual power of creative activity. That is, there is moral invention.

A second couple of values, we saw, is also distinguished in the spiritual conversion: the existential and rational values of the *Cogito* (pure thought) and the *sum* (pure existence). "Il y a conscience et j'en témoigne." There is a thought and an existence which is "disponible." [50] There as the rational values and the existential values.

In regards to the naive consciousness these four poles of value are not clearly marked off by a sufficient reflection and as such are often pressed to extremes (the four "vertiges" of thought and the corresponding four "excesses" of liberty). Consciousness as *liberty* has two principle uses (authentic and inauthentic); it is itself the source of a life of facticity (empirical level) or a source for life in the spirit (devoir-autonomy). For in the

[48] Cf. G. Bastide, *Traité*, p. 151.
[49] Cf. G. Bastide, *Traité*, I., p. 40; II., pp. 442-444; *Méditations*, p. 134.
[50] Cf. G. Bastide, "De la situation de l'homme," *op. cit.*, pp. 274-248.

original affirmation consciousness is given as *fact* and *duty*, but the liberty of free choice can separate the two. Reflection, consciousness of duty and a life in the spirit depend on the *right* exercise of liberty.[51] The possibility of choice is grounded in the experience of alienation.[52]

Furthermore, the act of reflection (spiritual conversion and the transfiguration of values) has revealed the full nature of existence as *problem* rather than the synchronized unity immagined by the non-reflecting consciousness. The unity of existence is the object of our moral effort. This situation revealed in reflection (namely what I am is not what I ought to be, but there is a transcendental unity marking out the unique possible way of being eventually more and more one with myself, the possibility of uniting more and more knowledge and existence) *is also the experience of liberty.* "Reflection and liberty are one and the same certitude of consciousness." [53]

As such liberty escapes, says Bastide, the opposition of the intelligible and the irrational because it is the *act* by which we bear witness to consciousness. The act consists in the composition of the cardinal values in the spiritual dialectic of promotion.[54] Like the original reflexive affirmation it cannot be denied, but it can be ordered in one of two basic directions. Like the movement of spiritual conversion (with which freedom becomes identified [55]) authentic freedom is always born of a previous alienation. Man is free by the transcendental condition of his reality to dispose of his own existence by a "yes" or "no" in regards to the vertical ascension in the world of spiritual values, or the opposite descent of the regime of naive faith in the world of empirical values and the dialectic of dissolution. That is, two dialectics distinguished in the reflexive movement of spiritual conversion are open to man's choice. He stands at the crossroads of Being (which he inaugurates by the authenticity of his actions) and non-Being (which he inaugurates in the inauthenticity of his actions).

The relationship between spiritual conversion and the exercise of autonomous freedom in Bastide's philosophy becomes clear. For man cannot exercise his possibility to choose autonomously until he sees clearly his situation and is able to distinguish the possibilities for becoming more and more autonomous. The clarification of the two orders is really the work of freedom itself and in this sense *philosophy* is regarded as a pedagogue of liberation, since it is one with the *act* of spiritual conversion.[56]

[51] G. Bastide, *Méditations*, p. 135.
[52] Cf. G. Bastide, *Traité*, p. 450.
[53] G. Bastide, *Méditations*, p. 129.
[54] Cf. G. Bastide, *Méditations*, p. 130.
[55] *Ibid.*, p. 133.
[56] Cf. G. Bastide, *Traité*, p. 140.

Like duty, the autonomy of man is central to the situation of man. The authentic exercise of liberty implies an orientation of consciousness towards the work of unity and axiological equilibrium in an effort of moral invention, that is, an effort aimed at the just composition of values. For Bastide, the wisdom of philosophy is precisely the continuous creation of a dynamic equilibrium of value.[57] But this work of freedom cannot be undertaken apart from the clear knowledge of the mutual relations of the values themselves, which is only revealed or deepened in reflection.

"The connection of autonomy with duty places autonomy at the crossroads of the structure of man where passion is transformed into action, or better, in Kant's words, where the "pathological" is transformed into the "practical." Bastide is interested in talking about *practical* freedom (autonomie de fait), one not only connected with the *presence* of duty to consciousness, but also to the effective *exercise* of duty in the direction of freedom. As such it is a limit never fully attained in fact and a function which varies with obedience to duty. Autonomy is an "idéal à incarnation variable," [58] that is, it must be constantly won by man in the ever-renewed will to obey the law of existence marked out by duty. There are degrees of freedom (Descartes) and degrees of the legislating power of the will according to its submission to the law of duty (Kant). Again, "we are absolutely free to be more or less autonomous." [59]

Therefore, the different alienations of man can be regarded as coming from liberty, absolutely speaking, and in this sense the work of giving value to a fallen world is regarded as the work of autonomy. For it is only in the axiological field of the spiritual values that the authentic exercise of autonomous freedom is possible. Freedom, as a basic structuring of the person, can only be realized in the transcendent vertical dimension of the axiological field constituting the human situation.[60] The most important law of moral philosophy, says Bastide, is the law of the practical primacy of spiritual imperatives over empirical indicatives.[61] The destiny of man is not to satisfy himself but to perfect himself.

It is, then, in axiology that the formalism of the duty-autonomy relationship is avoided. The "distance" between the moral law and the moral act is not to be conceived in naturalistic categories. Rather is duty to be conceived in the framework of a provocative reflection, that is, a call to the

[57] Cf. G. Bastide, "De la situation de l'homme," p. 252.
[58] G. Bastide, *Traité*, p. 151.
[59] *Id.*, p. 152.
[60] Cf. G. Bastide, "The Metaphysical Dimensions of Man," *op. cit.*, p. 363.
[61] *Id.*

vocation of perfection in the affirmation that nothing is valid except by moral invention or re-invention. Bastide hopes to overcome the theory-practice antinomy by seeing the law immanent in the act by the work of invention, an invention that is always in the concrete order: "Every precept was first lived by authentic persons whose exemplary value made it a law." [62] That is, the total and perfect incarnation of the idea precedes the law. The "distance" between law and act signifies only the distance between the letter and the spirit of the law. That is why, says Bastide, it is *proper* to the moral ideal to be an "incarnation variable." The *axiological* immanence of the moral law to the act which inspires it is not equal to the immanence of the "ontologies" (formalism, conformism, fatalism), for it depends on each one to interiorize more or less in order to incarnate more or less the moral ideal proposed by the moral law.[63] Each *person* must transform in a personal act the *given* by giving it value according to the moral law in order to make a willed construct an expression of autonomy.

Thus, the imperative is not an *a priori* of a virgin nature, for the *matter* of morality is not a "given nature" indifferent to morality, but the real human condition of evil (alienation) which man himself has freely brought about or let be brought about.[64] The moral law is grounded in the human condition as immanence-transcendence of the moral law itself which gives consciousness its *vocation* in the *historical* conquest of autonomy. Duty is the only way we have for knowing this transcendental mystery of our freedom and it is only as *value* that the notion of autonomy is given as transcendent to the human condition and immanent to every conquest of morality.[65] Liberty is the immanent principle, the fundamental condition and the final goal of human action.[66]

There is neither pure nature or pure morality. The imperative exercises itself "psychologically coercitively" [67] on a man whose alienated situation has been revealed in spiritual conversion and the transformation of values. The moral person is constituted in all autonomy on the base, not of a pure nature indifferent to morality, but on the painful recognition of failure, error and sin which becomes the very heart of the generosity of a new effort to overcome the facility of the routine passions and assume responsibility for the difficult mastery of self.

[62] G. Bastide, *Traité*, p. 159.
[63] Cf. G. Bastide, *Traité*, p. 160.
[64] Cf. G. Bastide, "Morale et Liberté," in *Les études philosophiques*, 1959 (1), p. 45. See also *Traité*, p. 161.
[65] Cf. G. Bastide, *Traité*, p. 161 and "Morale et Liberté," *op. cit.*, p. 46.
[66] Cf. G. Bastide, Mirages et certitudes, p. 246.
[67] Cf. G. Bastide, *Traité*, p. 161.

3. Responsibility and spiritual personalism

Duty and freedom define the moral person. But the liberty of duty and the duty of liberty are revealed only in reflection. Here we have the complete picture as to the place of reflection in the constitution and promotion of the person. Bastide, it will be recalled, sees the act of reflection as the proper object of philosophy, the problem of self-knowledge being the "unique philosophical problem on which all the others depend." To be sure, it is the problem of man, but the man "whose whole essence is to seek himself." [68] That is why a metaphysics of reflection is an analytical exploration of consciousness, especially in the conditions for the exercise of liberty, "for it is in the constituting activity of consciousness that liberty manifests itself." For this reason, too, metaphysics is a metaphysics of action and an axiology, since it is in the notion of value that we find the norm for authentic activity.

The problematic of reflection, therefore, is the problematic of the person.[69] For the proper task of the philosophies of reflection is to live and translate as far as one can the life of the spirit, that is, to be very attentive and faithful to the interiority demanded by the spirit and very generously open to the vocation of its infinite transcendence. The philosophies of reflection are expressely concerned with the maturity of conscious life. But it is precisely the notion of person that can bring together the two central facts of reflection and openness to the transcendent values. The notion of person becomes the "foyer of all the problems which define our condition." [70] The person is "a subject who questions himself reflexively concerning his reasons for being and who discovers them in a vocation of perfection that has no limits." [71] As *person* each man becomes himself the bearer of a unique value which is also true objectively (therefore universally) and worthy of imitation.

We can see that Bastide's metaphysics follows the movement of Kant's own practical philosophy. As such it becomes in its very foundations a personalism. As the metaphysician comes upon his postulates by a unique combination of experience and freedom, so the person in the act of spiritual conversion. For the idea of perfection is already suggested in the agonizing experience of the "conscience malheureuse" (man *knows* his state is an unhappy one, and *knows* the reasons for his unhappiness in the *will* to be perfect – to succeed, to know the truth, to lead an existence that is truly

[68] G. Bastide, *De la condition humaine*, p. 365.
[69] Cf. G. Bastide, *Traité*, p. 124.
[70] G. Bastide, "Nature, situation et condition humaine," *op. cit.*, p. 63.
[71] *Id.*

worthwhile). However, he cannot *prove* speculatively these values which can be proposed as ends guiding his whole moral life. Therefore this experience only suggests the eternal and transcendent values. It is only in an act of the *will* (enlightened says Bastide by a profound faith) that man finally engages his existence under these values, an act of the will that postulates them in a heroic and generous wager. The person is thus already engaged at the very foundations of the philosophical life (philosophy being understood as necessarily a practical philosophy, a metaphysics of action, an axiology).

Going back once again to the original affirmation, we can now see it in a clearer light. "Il y a conscience." That is, in the moment of spiritual conversion man is freed from egoism and the empirical foundations of his existence which constitutes him as "individual." By that very fact, man is said to experience himself at a new level of his being, one that is *essentially opposed* to the empirical man (since it tends by its very nature to *deny* that man is empirically limited (like things) and in reality is the opposite affirmation, that is, immanence and transcendence). It is the experience of *spirit* and interior unity, of an immanence that is also a transcendence. Man, in the regime of spiritual conversion, conceives the notion of truth as objectivity and universality.

This original experience, therefore, contains something of that which is "more than just me." It contains objectivity and universality. It contains in some way what is really the object of our search, the "essential man," the truth. But at the same time it is also evident that the truth of this experience is not automatic. For it was given in a suffering generously assumed by a good will that was undaunted by the effort required in seeking the truth. Truth was given only in effort, vigilance, generosity and sacrifice. The idea of objectivity "il y a conscience" was essentially *both* the fruit of my experience and my free assent. It was neither the result of pure nature or pure spirit.[72] The ideal which guided man from the beginning was eminently *practical* and *personal,* an initiative of my *person,* my freedom. Yet it was objective. "Il y a conscience et j'en témoigne."

In Cartesian terms, says Bastide, the "dubito, cogito, ergo sum" are intimately connected, rendering the metaphysical experience personal and free. For the "suspension of doubt is an act of the will, as is also the triumphant affirmation of my proper spiritual reality." [73] Bastide interprets the philosophy of Descartes in the light of Kant's own practical philosophy maintaining that "the Kantian doctrine of autonomy is situated in the direct

[72] Cf. G. Bastide, *La conversion spirituelle,* p. 88.
[73] G. Bastide, *La conversion spirituelle,* p. 89.

continuation of the Cartesian doctrine of freedom." [74] In either case, the free alienation of man is followed by a free assertion of the universal law and the conquest of personal autonomy.

We see there that Bastide's own position as regards axiology is also a free decision of his will in the light of his own experience obtained, we can say, in the generous effort to seek the truth in the company of Socrates, Descartes and Kant. He is one of those who has undertaken "to deliberately place themselves at the heart of the axiological problems and to openly proclaim themselves, without any false shame, philosophers of value." [75] It is here that we find the notion of *truth as value* (known heuristically in the experience of duty in the spiritual conversion) and the notion of knowledge as "way," that is, as a practical method on the way to the truth, from which comes the notion of philosophy as a search. The postulates of Bastide's philosophy are practical certitudes, that is, *values* that are the object of a purified faith and a good will and thereby *constituted* as final reasons for action and knowing the truth.[76] In this context the original truths of philosophy are not given in the evidence "of a theoretical tableau of Being, "but rather they are "to be conquered (even merited) as moral certitudes by the consciousness which agrees to obey the demands of morality. Metaphysics is not only a theory, but a *pratique* which demands conversion, moral engagement, a reflecting will, that is, adherence to the values of spirit." [77]

Therefore, spiritual personalism is "the moral and unequivocal result of moral idealism." [78] For "it is not the Spirit who doubts," and even if it is the Spirit who thinks, "it is I who freely, willingly affirm the irreducible truth. And nothing is more personal than this aspect of the spiritual power." [79] The very notion of spiritual conversion is linked to the liberty of the person, for there is a "real option in the conversion itself." The possibility of conversion, the *idea* of conversion, is certainly born in the experience "malheureuse," but the *actual conversion* in the result of a *free choice,* like the *Cogito* of Descartes. The liberation from alienation was only by way of a negative awareness of the false empirical values coupled with the positive choice to put oneself in the regime of spiritual values and

[74] G. Bastide, *Traité,* p. 152.
[75] G. Bastide, "Nature, situation et condition humaine," *op. cit.*, p. 62.
[76] Cf. G. Bastide, "Nature, situation et condition humaine," p. 62.
[77] *Id.*
[78] G. Bastide, *La conversion spirituelle,* p. 86.
[79] *Id.*, p. 89.

the gradual conquest of autonomy. "In all this it is the *person* which is manifest." [80]

Here we find the central role played by the notion of *responsibility.* It is both a personal and interpersonal factor of the human situation. Following our previous line of reasoning, we see that the central notions of reflection and life in the spirit are eminently *practical* notions founded on the free acts of man. The act of passing from one dialectic (naive faith for example) to another (spiritual conversion) takes the form of a difficult *effort* and as such is underscored by a generous assuming of responsibility. This act is seen by Bastide and others [81] in a metaphysical light, germane to philosophy as such. It is the "source and condition of our moral effort." [82]

This notion is in a sense a *key* one, because it provides an important bridge to a practical humanism as well as the ground for the openness of the person to others and to the world. Up to this point these factors have been somewhat neglected because of the stress on spiritual conversion and the interiority of the spirit. But once we have seen the foundations of philosophy as eminently personal and free, and once we have conceived of philosophy as the free and responsible assumption of our authentic vocation to search for truth, then we have found the place for a philosophy of personalism which will be at the same time interpersonal and openness to the world. For autonomy is never complete. It is a *value* connected with self-knowledge, but essentially dependent on the knowledge which others have already acquired in a world infinitely rich with possibilities. For the imperative of moral consciousness is "to be *au maximum* person, that is, a maximum of value. But this imperative is really a command to seek our own autonomy more and more, something which is realizable only "in the mutual cooperation in all reciprocity and moral effort," of persons mutually aiding one another in this common promotion of the common good, namely freedom.[83] For the ideal is authenticity, that is, the maximum of unity in the maximum of interiorized experience, experience which has been grasped and surpassed.[84]

Here we can situate the connection Bastide makes between *responsibility* and *autonomy*. For the notion of person was contrasted with that of "individual" to escape the supposed contradiction between the uniqueness

[80] G. Bastide, *La conversion spirituelle,* p. 89.

[81] Cf. R. Le Senne, *Traité de morale générale,* Paris, P.U.F. (Coll. "Logos"), 1961 (4th edition), p. 583.

[82] G. Bastide, *Méditations . . .,* p. 155.

[83] Cf. G. Bastide, *Traité,* pp. 164-165.

[84] Cf. G. Bastide, *Méditations,* pp. 154-157.

of person and the universality and objectivity of law. In fact, we saw that it was the free person who, in autonomy, proposes to himself his own ideal in the act of spiritual conversion. It is this ideal which becomes the law of the person (the law of authenticity and unity) and the very realization of the law (gradually and in an incarnated way) is bound up not with the formality of the law, but with an ideal which is to be promoted by all men. "It is not a formal law which we follow (as persons) but an idea which we promote." [85] The uniqueness of our person is the object of our search in union with others. It is not supposed as given ontologically beforehand.[86] The law of unity is not "necessary," since it is the object of our search. It is there to be freely accepted. "The autonomy of the person is to be won and to be inaugurated in view of authenticity." [87]

It is in this framework that we see the true "hierarchy" of persons and their mutual relationship. For "persons are valued hierarchicly according to their spiritual penetartion in the way of unity, "that is, in their own personal *maturity*. It is the person who is "most open and most mature" (that is, able to unify many different points of view) who takes on the character of having the "value of normative law" for others. For it is these persons who become, in a way, the source of value for all humanity.[88]

In this sense is there a *metaphysical responsibility,* says Bastide, on the part of the man who is the source and condition of our moral effort. For those who have proposed as their own ideal the law of unity and the law of personal maturity in the self-knowledge and auto-construction of their person according to the lines revealed in reflection, must be, by that very fact, ready to accept responsibly the implications of the constant effort and suffering implied in the moral effort of reflection. The philosopher takes into his own hands the disunity of the world and, setting for himself the ideals of autonomy, duty and the unity of thought and action, sets out along the difficult road marked out for him. "Man," says Bastide, "is a soldier fighting for the sake of the Good; he is not a courtisan of Being." And he adds: "As person man knows that the Infinite is not to be justified in words, but that Unity is to be inaugurated in the world by action." [89] The law of personal being is "always act in such a way in order to take upon oneself the maximum of responsibility." Bastide's own philosophy of action takes up once again the task of formulating the categorical im-

[85] *Id.*, p. 154.
[86] *Id.*
[87] *Id.*
[88] Cf. G. Bastide, *Traité,* pp. 321-322.
[89] G. Bastide, *Méditations,* p. 157.

perative in terms of the laborious responsibility needed to give value to the universe and to humanity.

3. Understanding

The free assumption of responsibility toward the work of reconstruction always open to man's efforts is, then, one of the central conditions for the authentic exercise of the powers of reflection and as a consequence one of the chief conditions of my existence as person. For my existence takes on value (personal being) in proportion to my own assumption of responsibility in the world. But man can only give what he has come to make his own through effort. For this reason another essential aspect of spiritual personalism, closely linked to the assumption of responsibility, is the act of understanding.[90]

Autonomy cannot be conceived without self-knowledge. But knowledge of self, insists Bastide, is dependent on the communication of consciousness. "Il y a conscience." There are men who mutually share experience and different points of view. The situation of man is a "milieu noétique" as well as an axiological milieu, for men move together in the infinite possibility for authenticity and promotion of spiritual values. The values of the spirit are, by their very essence, communal.[91] Each one seeks that unity which is his duty in company with other persons on whom he depends for the reciprocal aid necessary for self-fulfillment.[92] The unity I am as person depends on the different points of view I have been able to interiorize.

Person, then, implies a "welcoming openness." To such an extent is this true that he does not hesitate to say that reflection (in the strict sense of the term) is impossible for a "closed, individualized consciousness." For if man reflects, says Bastide, it is to be authentic.[93] But authenticity is necessarily openness to otherness in order that it might be assumed in the enrichment of my own personal being. That same "sympathie" which characterized conscious life on the psychological level and which founded the possibility of a "conscience délicate" is now seen in its full metaphysical realization as "understanding."

To understand is to take into oneself another's experience in view of

[90] Cf. G. Bastide, "Compréhension et Valeurs," in *Actes* III Congrès des sociétés de philosophie de langue française, E. Nauwelaerts, 1947, pp. 47-51. Also: "La communication des consciences et l'édification de la morale," in Atti del XII congresso internazionale di filosofia, Sansoni editore, Firenze, 1958, pp. 53-57.

[91] G. Bastide, *Traité,* II., p. 718.

[92] Cf. G. Bastide, *Traité,* p. 166.

[93] Cf. G. Bastide, *Méditations,* p. 144.

attaining autonomy in the effective and mutual building up of personal being. This movement of welcome which characterizes the understanding consciousness not only increases the value of person, but also aims at a mutual provocation to a greater spirituality and eventually to a wider base for mutual unity and understanding. On this level morality becomes friendship and the mutual promotion of perfection. It is putting at each other's disposal a diversity of experiences in a common dialectic of promotion, a union of wills in the convergence of efforts towards the common goal of authenticity and in the common love of spiritual values. Friendship, says Bastide, stems from the very nature of autonomy as the orientation of freedom to the spiritual values.[94]

There is understanding, therefore, as often as interpersonal relationships are presided over by the good faith acquired mutually in spiritual conversion. But this faith, we have seen, is constantly acquired on the ruins of bad faith accompanying every movement of life in which all spirituality is immersed.[95] It depends on the *capacity* of each one to receive multiplicity without a rupture in their own personal being. It depends on the equilibrium of each one to give a just proportion to the different values which constitute the human condition. Understanding becomes the norm for measuring the degrees of authenticity in a twofold way: as a promotion of spiritual values according to the law of duty and according to the mutual respect for other autonomies.[96]

The problem of self knowledge which Bastide has defined as *the* philosophical problem is now put into a new perspective. For the problem of reflection has been seen at various levels: the critical level, the level of self knowledge and self-determination (spiritual conversion and the transfiguration of values) and last of all in the function of self-constitution in the unity of personal being with the power of giving value to a world in need of redemption. We have, in short, the critical metaphysical and ethical functions of reflection. All three functions are bound together in intimate unity.[97]

It is especially Bastide's desire to ground a *practical* philosophy of action that makes him insist on the unity of the three functions. For the problem of self-knowledge, the *total* reflection is given a context which, in the last analysis, is ethical in nature.[98] Understanding is to be conceived in the

[94] Cf. G. Bastide, *Traité*, p. 718.

[95] Cf. G. Bastide, *De la condition humaine*, p. 373.

[96] Cf. G. Bastide, *Traité*, pp. 193-194; p. 293.

[97] Cf. G. Bastide, *Traité*, p. 88; also *De la condition humaine*, pp. 373-375; 326-329.

[98] By total reflection Bastide means a good will which carries through to its complete cycle the need for "total accomplishment" which is opened up in the spiritual

framework of axiology and spiritual conversion. The problem of knowledge is not, for him, the question of sensation, since the latter does not play an intrinsic role in reflection.[99] The question of truth is not put into the context of an "adequatio rei et intellectus" since Bastide rejects the approach to knowledge by the philosophies of representation or participation.[100] The notion of truth, he says, "is never reducible to the purely empirical realm of fact." [101] In the context of spiritual conversion truth is regarded strictly as a common work of *persons* seeking together the authenticity of their witness and confronting one another with their experiences with the sole purpose of mutual enrichment. The norm of truth, we have seen, is the unity of the spirit given heuristically as a goal to be obtained. Knowledge becomes essentially ethical. The noetic activity pertains to "moral activity in general" as a particular mode.[102] It is one with the activity of the sciences and fits into the axiological situation of man as augmenting the dimension of clarity in the axiological field. Noetic activity pertains especially to the logical, rational aspect of existence which is constituted in the act of establishing wider and wider areas of relations. It seeks the true idea.[103] It is "nothing more than the conquest of good faith in the reciprocity of our mutual witness." [104] The fundamental function of noetic life is the constitution of the various sciences in such a way that they will be spiritual functions whose very essence (in authenticity) is the instauration and promotion of spiritual values.[105] Thus it is essentially a *moral* function. Its pole of value is that of the true idea.

The true idea is the proper object of science and as such its function is irreplaceable. It is creative of objectivity (not the so called objectivity given

conversion. That is, if reflection does not proceed from the given to the work (self-knowledge and the self-constitution of one's person in the acts and life of the spirit, that is, in unity) then it is only "half-reflection." Reflection, to be authentic, must end up in an *act* actually promotive of the unity of person, for "l'unité éthique n'est jamais donnée; elle est toujours à faire." The unity, here, to be sure, is not simply logical unity, but the ethical unity of the person. The total reflection, then, is defined by the authenticity of action, an action which a man does who *knows* the *value* of what he does, says and believes. In its triple function, its norm is that unity constitutive of person (unity of knowledge, will and belief). "... dans la connaissance éthique de soi, connaître et agir ne sont, au fond, qu'une seule chose." Cf. G. Bastide, *Les grands thèmes*, pp. 17-25.

[99] Cf. G. Bastide, *Méditations*, pp. 169, 172; also *Traité*, pp. 277-278.

[100] *Traité*, p. 278.

[101] G. Bastide, *Méditations*, p. 164.

[102] Cf. G. Bastide, *Méditations*, pp. 168-169.

[103] *Ibid.*, p. 169.

[104] G. Bastide, *Méditations*, p. 170.

[105] Cf. especially *Traité*, pp. 340-344 where Bastide treats the function of science in an order of spiritual promotion.

in exteriority, since for Bastide objectivity is never "given" to consciousness; it is always won at the end of a long effort.)[106] The objectivity of the sciences, says Bastide, is never radically exterior to the subject, since it is the *raison d'être* immanent to the very effort of consciousness. Truth is in the minds and hearts of men provoking one another to greater and greater perfection. Since science is the effort of conquering that good faith that is also merited in spiritual conversion, it can be regarded as a *duty*, wherein the respect for others in the reciprocal exchange of their mutual testimony requires justice and clarity without which we cannot know who we are, because we would be lacking knowledge of what we are doing, perceiving or saying.[107] For the truth is an aspect of the Good.[108]

Bearing witness to the truth (science, art, morality) is the authentic function of person, the act "par excellence" of my person as value. The broadened notion of reason as understanding (and not merely "raisonante"), says Bastide, can bring together the apparent antinomies of naive realism as regards reason and will. In the order of spiritual conversion, the order of the new faith in the spiritual values, the affectivity moves, opens up and deepens the intellect. The intellect, on its part, enlightens, refines and enriches the affectivity; an affectivity which is more than merely sensual, for after conversion it becomes truly loving.[109] That is, in spiritual conversion we find our most personal liberty (autonomy) aimed at the spiritual values and, because of this direction, realizing itself authentically under the light of the *idea* which permits the affectivity to be truly "généreuse." The understanding becomes the "loving intellect" of Spinoza in its dynamic striving for autonomy.[110] It is the vision of *unity* which makes the different aspects of human activity converge upon a common goal. "To

[106] *Id.*, p. 169.

[107] For Bastide truth is never radically exterior to the subject, since it is the *raison d'être* immanent to the very effort of consciousness. Truth is in the minds and hearts of men provoking one another to greater and greater perfection. The more mature the man of science is in the other axiological areas, so much the more precise will his witness be. For example, in proportion as his witness is impregnated with the category of unity (nourished by prospective and synthetic philosophy), the more science presents itself as *relation*; or in so far as the spirit of the man of science is nourished with the depth that can come only from aesthetics, so much the more will his science be able to furnish the intellectual and structuring element to the existential values. The function of science, in this light, can be said to be "the function of clarity made with analytical precision joined to unifying relation and put in connection with the existential values under the form of justice."

Cf. G. Bastide, *Traité*, pp. 341-342.

[108] "... le vrai est nécessairement un aspect du bien." *Id.*, p. 343.

[109] Cf. G. Bastide, *Traité*, p. 157.

[110] *Ibid.*, pp. 157 and 201; see also *Ethics* by B. Spinoza, translated by A. Boyle,

understand is the function of authentic action in the unity of value to such a degree that if we are able to penetrate the profound essence of this act we ought to see the value of truth take its proper place, where it becomes that aspect of the unique and absolute value by which consciousness manifests its vision of universality by the elaboration of a common witness capable of determining, without seduction or force, the unreserved adhesion of persons of good faith communicating to one another their experiences." [111]

But more particularly, what is Bastide's approach to the concrete problem of knowledge? In the context of all that has gone before, we can now situate this particular problem. Bastide proposes a tri-pole philosophy of relation to explain his own philosophy of knowledge.[112] Viewing understanding as *act* (rather than the result of representation or participation, that is, knowledge as union between subject and object, between an I and a Thou), Bastide proposes a "circuit" between three terms (instead of a linear union, as he says, between subject and object) an I, Thou and object (cela). For understanding, says Bastide, is a promotion of value, not only between a subject and an object, but between *consciousnesses* open to each other as simultaneous points of view looking on the same object and ready to be mutually exchanged.[113] For every experience, he says, is that of an I speaking to a Thou about *something*.

In an axiological framework (for the three terms must be viewed axiologically, not "ontologically") the comprehensive relation is between a *subject of knowledge* who is such precisely in so far as he can assume different points of view other than that assigned him by his own situation; to understand is the power to go beyond my own temporal-spatial limitations as a simple individual and assimilate a multiplicity of viewpoints which can be interiorized and united in knowledge. As such the subject is a *person,* that is, a subject of value, one who can bear witness to unity in giving value through knowledge. Knowledge is the surpassing of my own facticity.

But the *other* is a "co-subject" of knowledge.[114] For he is a co-subject of value, that is, another person. As such he both occasions the disequilibrium in my own consciousness and provokes an effort of unification necessary if I am to *understand* his point of view. I can *close* myself to him if I *will,* but in so doing I close myself to my being as a subject of understanding.[115]

London, pp. 217-224 (prop. XXXI-XIII).

[111] G. Bastide, *Méditations,* p. 173.

[112] *Id.,* p. 174. Also: *Traité,* pp. 277-292.

[113] *Ibid.,* pp. 282-283.

[114] G. Bastide, *Traité,* p. 282.

[115] *Id.,* p. 283.

The object is that about which there is an exchange of view between an I and a Thou. It is the occasion and objective support,[116] an obstacle for the knowing subject provoking good faith. What is *known* (object as known) is not "my object" or "your object" in the sense of an impersonal abstraction, but something *we* have in *common,* in objectivity – but an objectivity which is the objective support of interpersonal relations, since it is the result of a common effort in good faith.[117]

What we have expressed so far seems to be valid for an ethical-sociological view of truth and knowledge. But we must not miss the point of Bastide's intention to express what seems to be for him the unique function of philosophy and knowledge as such. We can recall here that for Bastide spiritual personalism is simply the doctrine of his metaphysics whose object is liberty, act, value and whose method is that of reflection. Bastide criticizes traditional philosophies of being and traditional idealism in so far as they suppose that they can "judge" about a value as ontologically given or psychologically known. For him, this approach is only, at best, a vacillation between subjectivism and objectivism. He seeks a philosophy of value, but one does not claim to "explain" the values or even to "know" them. Bastide's philosophy is a philosophy of action – an action which does not have to seek the values as "given" at the end of our search or as having a reference to our subjective desires. For Bastide, *the act* is the act of understanding, the act "par excellence" of value. In fact, it is precisely in so far as reflection seizes this act *as act* (without confusing the act with its effects) that value is something "always giving, never given, always determining, never determined." [118]

[116] *Id.*

[117] Cf. G. Bastide, *Traité,* pp. 283-284.

[118] G. Bastide, *Méditations,* p. 175. For Bastide philosophy is a search for the *integral* destination of consciousness (Cf. *Le moment historique de Socrate* and *De la condition humaine*) wherein man is constituted as person and value and able to cooperate with others in the act of understanding. It is not the results or effects of human activity that reflection grasps, but the activity iself. For it is the *act* of understanding that is the source of value manifesting itself as truth, beauty and the unity of morality.

This act is the *act of judgment.* To judge pertains to the very constitution of man as a being who thinks. "Man thinks in the act of judgment and judges in the act of thinking" (G. Bastide, "Nolite judicare," Revue internationale de philosophie, 1964, p. 384). "The judgment is the pivot of my thought and, as a result, the foundation of my being" (p. 138 *Les grands thèmes*). The judgment, like reflection, is an instrument of our search for authenticity.

But the judgment manifests different modes and therefore it pertains to philosophy to define and order them in their authentic roles. In general, notes Bastide, we speak of judgments of reality and judgments of value. We must determine, he says, not only their different content, but most of all the *different variations in the very structure*

For value, says Bastide, is born *in the act which establishes the comprehensive relation* (understanding) defined above. Each term of the relation being, in its own way, a pole of value: "We do not understand something except with someone, and we do not understand someone except in relation to something, and we do not understand ourselves except in the presence of someone and on the occasion of something. Man is not man except among men and in the world." [119]

These *three* aspects *together* constitute understanding ("valeur compréhensive") and the three general specifications of Value: *Value as Truth* (emphasis on the relation of subject to the object, therefore the value of truth especially in its manifestation rather than in its intention; translated by the *clarity* with which the object is perceived in the objective relations which constitute it); [120] *Value as the Beautiful* (emphasis on the relation between the I and Thou in the mutual effort at understanding, the value of *friendship*, translated by the profound movement of my personal life in-

of the judgment itself. The two basic attitudes of consciousness determine two basic modes of the act of judgment: one being the judgment of naive consciousness (both judgments of existence and judgments of attribution). Bastide, like Kant, considers these judgments as judgments of appreciation, pre-critical and in reference to subjectivities and the systems of representations as well as systems of value following upon representation. Such judgments are the misuse of its function (pp. 385-387 "Nolite..." *op. cit.*). Such judgments, says Bastide, do not give us "reality" nor do they identify the true values, precisely because of their egocentric orientation and ontological pretensions.

Therefore the basic division of the judgment is not according to reality and value but rather according to *two regimes of consciousness* yielding two kinds of judgments: judgments of appreciation and judgments of comprehension. The *judgment of comprehension* is based on a *new level* of conscious life, a different order of values. It is a judgment of relation rather than a judgment of attribution. Cf. pp. 389-390 "Nolite judicare," *op. cit.*

The comprehensive judgment of relation is a judgment of the second degree of consciousness, essentially analytic and practically constitutive of intelligibility. The metaphysical foundation of this judgment is based on the approach of Kant in his practical philosophy. The foundation is the transcendence of freedom known through the experience of duty *plus* the horizon of the practical postulates of a mutual engagement of persons in the common instauration of a world of spiritual values wherein the autonomy of all is perfected. It is here that we avoid, says Bastide, both the naivité of the judgment of attribution and the relativity of the judgment of comprehension without foundation in metaphysics. For in the regime of spiritual conversion, where philosophy recognizes its role as "fonction fondatrice," the critical judgment of good faith is based on the universality of Value in which the good will becomes conscious of its twofold openness as immanence (principle of legislation) and transcendence (call to perfection practically indeclinable). It is the converted judgment which is *the* judgment of reflection, giving rise to philosophy and morality. Cf. p. 395 "Nolite judicare," *op. cit.*

[119] G. Bastide, *Méditations*, p. 175. Cf. also p. 289, *Traité*.

[120] *Méditations*, p. 176.

The object is that about which there is an exchange of view between an I and a Thou. It is the occasion and objective support,[116] an obstacle for the knowing subject provoking good faith. What is *known* (object as known) is not "my object" or "your object" in the sense of an impersonal abstraction, but something *we* have in *common,* in objectivity – but an objectivity which is the objective support of interpersonal relations, since it is the result of a common effort in good faith.[117]

What we have expressed so far seems to be valid for an ethical-sociological view of truth and knowledge. But we must not miss the point of Bastide's intention to express what seems to be for him the unique function of philosophy and knowledge as such. We can recall here that for Bastide spiritual personalism is simply the doctrine of his metaphysics whose object is liberty, act, value and whose method is that of reflection. Bastide criticizes traditional philosophies of being and traditional idealism in so far as they suppose that they can "judge" about a value as ontologically given or psychologically known. For him, this approach is only, at best, a vacillation between subjectivism and objectivism. He seeks a philosophy of value, but one does not claim to "explain" the values or even to "know" them. Bastide's philosophy is a philosophy of action – an action which does not have to seek the values as "given" at the end of our search or as having a reference to our subjective desires. For Bastide, *the act* is the act of understanding, the act "par excellence" of value. In fact, it is precisely in so far as reflection seizes this act *as act* (without confusing the act with its effects) that value is something "always giving, never given, always determining, never determined." [118]

[116] *Id.*

[117] Cf. G. Bastide, *Traité,* pp. 283-284.

[118] G. Bastide, *Méditations,* p. 175. For Bastide philosophy is a search for the *integral* destination of consciousness (Cf. *Le moment historique de Socrate* and *De la condition humaine*) wherein man is constituted as person and value and able to cooperate with others in the act of understanding. It is not the results or effects of human activity that reflection grasps, but the activity iself. For it is the *act* of understanding that is the source of value manifesting itself as truth, beauty and the unity of morality.

This act is the *act of judgment.* To judge pertains to the very constitution of man as a being who thinks. "Man thinks in the act of judgment and judges in the act of thinking" (G. Bastide, "Nolite judicare," Revue internationale de philosophie, 1964, p. 384). "The judgment is the pivot of my thought and, as a result, the foundation of my being" (p. 138 *Les grands thèmes*). The judgment, like reflection, is an instrument of our search for authenticity.

But the judgment manifests different modes and therefore it pertains to philosophy to define and order them in their authentic roles. In general, notes Bastide, we speak of judgments of reality and judgments of value. We must determine, he says, not only their different content, but most of all the *different variations in the very structure*

CHAPTER VIII

CONCLUSIONS

I. *Introduction*

It has been the purpose of this work to enter into contact with new horizons of thought. The problems of idealism and value philosophy are by no means new to the philosophical stage. But as G. Allport noted some years ago for the field of psychology, the practitioners of this science had thrown the self overboard along with the soul. He was saying that psychology could make little headway in dealing with the more complex human realities until it took seriously the omnipresent factor of "ego involvement." [1] Something along these lines could be said, I believe, for American philosophy.

In France especially the Ego is ever a fundamental preoccupation. While French idealism is always taking on new forms, it remains an important philosophical influence. That is why the conflict between the two great orientations of thought – idealism and realism – is far from being resolved.[2] The study of idealism in its most important sources remains essential for a correct understanding of contemporary philosophy. This is seen rather quickly, for example, if we think of the Sartrean notion of freedom.

This conclusion is divided into three main parts, following in order the principal problems raised in this work: the problem of philosophy as we have received it from Kant and Descartes; the problem of idealism, especially as it is posed in the philosophy of Brunschvicg and subsequently in the philosophy of Bastide; and finally the problem of an axiological idealism. Our own orientation and final conclusions bear upon the question: to what extent does the other possible orientation of thought – that of realism – offer satisfactory answers to the philosophical problems of an axiological idealism?

[1] Cf. P. Blair-Rice, "Children of Narcissus," *Kenyon Review*, 1950 (12) p. 137.
[2] Cf. G. Van Riet, *Problèmes d'épistémologie*, Louvain, 1960, p. 249.

The first problem, it seems to me, has to do with the history of philosophy. Having been first impressed myself with the realist point of view as received from Aristotle and St. Thomas and having penetrated to a certain extent a certain tradition of a philosophy of Being, it has become personally clear to me what has for a long time been clear to many others, namely, that a real gap continues to exist between my own understanding of what realism is all about and the understanding of realism presupposed, for example, by the critique of Bastide. This is true both on the level of metaphysics as well as on the level of noetics. What I recognize most of all in Bastide's critique is pertinent to critical nominalism rather than intellectual realism, or, in line with Kant's philosophy, the presuppositions of a rationalistic approach to being rather than a realist's approach. A realist, for example, would hardly agree with Bastide's description of Ontology as "having for its function the adequate apprehension of the real that I am or from which I am." [3] The same could be said of his definition of the concept as that which "registers passively the analogies of a given spectacle." [4] Like Descartes and Kant Bastide is regularly criticizing what rather pertains to nominalism, rationalism or empiricism. But there is another point of view as will be clear as we go on. And we will have occasion to ask if the agnosticism of nominalism has really been surpassed by an axiological idealism.

As F. Van Steenberghen has pointed out, all modern philosophy has developed in the perspective of the nominalistic rupture of the unity of human knowledge, for it is precisely with nominalism that the universal concept of the intellect ceases to be a faithful transposition of an objective form received by way of sensation.[5] It is in nominalism that we have posed the same problem that faces us in regards to idealism – namely, the relationship between experience and spirit. Certainly, if we really had to choose between the priority of one or the other we might well say that idealism has chosen the better part. But does the problem of philosophy have to be posed in this way? Does the immanent character of spiritual activity have to be in conflict with the passive character of knowledge stressed by the empiricist? It is precisely in the light of the real dangers of positivism that we are in one accord with Bastide throughout his critique of these same dangers to the spiritual life of man, and we cannot help but agree wholeheartedly with the need for acknowledging the creative aspect of spirit. But since philosophy by virtue of its radical nature can neglect no

[3] G. Bastide, "De la situation de l'homme," p. 242.
[4] G. Bastide, *Traité*, T.I., p. 155.
[5] Cf. F. Van Steenberghen, *Epistémologie*, Louvain, 1965 (4th edition), p. 62.

aspect of reality, the question persists as to the fundamental ground of unity as regards the two aspects of sense and intellectual experience.

In turning to Kant and Descartes, from whom modern philosophy receives its principal orientation, our purpose was to see how this problem of the relation between the spirit and experience was posed and resolved. For neither Kant or Descartes intended to deny metaphysics. It is rather the idea of what metaphysics is all about that is important. And this problem – what is metaphysics – has remained central to the thesis of G. Bastide's axiological idealism. Is metaphysics to be conceived primarily as a critique of knowledge, having for its objects the spirit and its immanent laws or is metaphysics to be above all a philosophy of Being, where the word "être" is not simply "spirit," or "Value" or "Being for us" or the logical copula of the judgment but that which grounds and makes possible all these different meanings.

The orientation given to philosophy by Descartes and Kant does not follow this last mentioned sense of metaphysics as a philosophy of Being. For Descartes (who criticizes an empiricism which is bordering on sensualism rather than the realist empiricism of St. Thomas) [6] metaphysics is not endowed with its own proper knowledge or its own proper method. Science is not radically distinct from philosophy but founded on it. Metaphysics is logically the first in the one unique system of knowledge which Descartes envisions. It is the metaphysical justification of science, just as science, in part at least, furnishes philosophy with its own content (as regards space reality).[7]

The unity of spirit, he reasoned, demanded a unity of method and a unity of intellectual object that was to be found only in mathematics. Metaphysics must henceforth concern itself, not with the laws of Being but the ultimate principle of knowledge. And these principles would, in turn, justify a mathematical science of nature.

It makes little difference for our basic problem if, under the influence of Kant's metaphysics, these ideals become values. What is important to remark is that Value is revealed only if we have taken as our point of departure the different modes of knowing, the *rationes cognoscendi*.[8]

Metaphysics still consists essentially in the reflexive method and the examination of our knowledge and the different functions of knowledge.

[6] F. Van Steenberghen, *Epistémologie*, p. 65.

[7] Cf. J. Ladrière, "Philosophy and Science," *Philosophical Studies*," 1958 (8) pp. ...-5.

[8] Cf. G. Bastide, *Traité*, T.I., p. 127.

Metaphysics rests a philosophy of spiritual conversion and its axiological framework remains as problematic as idealism itself.

For Descartes, then, metaphysics cannot be defined in terms of its own proper formal object since the mathematical ideal is the unique ideal for all knowing. Existence or being does not enter his philosophy as a primary intelligible. On the contrary, existence becomes *the* critical problem. The intelligibles are the *a priori* evidences revealed in the Cogito, especially the discovery of spirit (thought) and the infinite, along with the evidence of extension. For Bastide the picture is not essentially different. For even though his *Cogito* is, by reason of his initial project, fitted to a practical metaphysics of action, nevertheless the metaphysical certitudes revealed therein (Liberty, Value, Act) parallel exactly the innate ideas of Descartes' original metaphysics (spirit, Infinite and extension).[9] Again, this is only to intimate once again that the passage from idealism to spiritualism or to axiology is not an essential change in metaphysical viewpoint. We shall note again that Bastide has everywhere tried to bolster the experiential basis of his philosophy of conversion and in so doing has greatly enriched his own moral philosophy, but idealism remains its essential problematic.

What has been revealed so far is that philosophy, in its effort to rejoin reality and the concrete (for the intellectual intuition attains only the idea in Descartes's philosophy) becomes a *search* for reality, in a way far more radical, say, then the philosophy of realism. For in the latter, the subject-object duality, the science-knowledge duality- does not import any real distance between the two elements. The original affirmation of consciousness is at one and the same time a knowledge of reality as well as a knowledge of self, where there is a conscious identity of the subject as knowing and knowing itself, a twofold experience based on a twofold necessary affirmation of the object and of the self, coming from a twofold undeniable presence.[10] In other words, in a philosophy of Being there us no "problem" of passing from the intelligible order to the order of sense object because of the mediation of the fundamental concept of being.[11]

Kant's approach to metaphysics, we saw, leads necessarily to the vision of a practical philosophy. For the kind of knowledge of spirit and the Infinite espoused by Descartes becomes impossible in Kant's critique, impossible that is to an intellectual intuition the existence of which Kant denies. Value, liberty, God are ideals in the sense of practical postulates of practical reason, making room for faith and regulating human activity

[9] G. Bastide, *Traité*, p. 356.
[10] Cf. F. Van Steenberghen, *Epistémologie*, pp. 98-99.
[11] *Ibid.*, p. 132.

to the highest ethical ideal. We saw this same approach in Bastide's axiological idealism. For Bastide Value (authenticity, God), autonomy and spirit are ideals revealed as practical norms of action for the progressive development of the life of the spirit. Outside this practical metaphysics for Kant philosophy can only be knowledge by way of the pure concepts of reason.[12] It is precisely because the concepts are pure, that is cut off from experience, that the way of realism is again closed, more radically now than in Descartes' philosophy.[13] Knowledge becomes almost exclusively the work of the activity of the knowing subject. The weight of the experience-spirit relationship is now definitely in favor of spirit. What affects the sensibility from outside man is a pure diversity deprived of any internal, intelligible structure.

These brief summaries lead us to the basic differences between idealism and realism. For the former the given of experience is pure diversity, incoherent and without form, whereas the spirit is synthetic activity, informing the object known in so far as it is know to us. For realism, reality has an intelligibility all its own. The knowing act of spirit is an active assimilation of the object known, but the object of knowledge (being) is given in experience. For idealism the ideal of truth and its realization in the philosophical search is related to a certain isolation of spirit until it comes face to face, as it were, with itself. Hence the need for a spiritual conversion, the central position given to critique. For idealism the method and problematic, as far as metaphysics is concerned, remains the same; even though the results vary from one to another (for example, the dogmatic doctrine of Descartes, the transcendental doctrine and practical philosophy of Kant, the axiological personalism of Bastide). For Descartes the critique is necessary to solve the problematic of existence, for Kant it is necessary to establish the possibility of the *a priori* synthetic judgments, for Bastide it is necessary in order to discover the spiritual values.[14] In no case is Being presupposed as grounding or directing the critique itself. Just the opposite is true, for the result of the critique (at least for Kant's philosophy) is to place an impassable distance between knowledge and being.

We can say, then, that the original philosophical intention as far as idealism is concerned, the ideal which it proposes for understanding the foundations of knowledge and reality is spirit. Consciousness cannot be reduced to being; being must be grasped by way of spirit. Realism, in the other hand, takes being as its first principle at the heart of which it attempts

[12] Cf. R. Verneaux, *Les sources cartesiennes,* p. 462.
[13] Cf. F. Van Steenberghen, *Epistémologie,* p. 67.
[14] Cf. G. Bastide, "La conversion spirituelle," p. 19.06-6.

to reconcile what idealism opposes, namely, sense experience and the immanent activity of thought. "With the idealists," says Van Riet, "philosophy of spirit corresponds to what is called Ontology by the realists." [15] This is clearly evident in Bastide's philosophy of spiritual conversion. The existential order is seen as ordered to spirit in the light of which it receives its meaning (raison d'être). The first principle of all philosophy is none other than the experience of the spiritual conversion, the experience of autonomy in a kind of total reflection.[16] The problem of man is the problem of his situation in relation to his *raison d'être,* that is, in relation to Value.[17] Being is thus interpreted in terms of final causality, metaphysics becomes Ethics, but idealism remains the central intuition or point of reference.

For idealism, then, the first fact and the original source of truth is of the intellectual order in the act of reflection. For it is here that being (spirit) is revealed to itself as it really is, an immanent activity at the innermost interior of which is discovered the highest transcendence. From the point of view of our present concern, the orientation of an idealist philosophy, it makes no essential difference if this first fact of the philosophical intention becomes existential (the *volonte voulante* of Blondel, the existential *Cogito* of Bastide), the experience of freedom, the spiritual dynamism of spirit in action.[18] For even here the object of the original intention is not being, but an ideal. Only this time the ideal is more the ideal of spirit as self-knowledge in freedom.[19] It is this ideal which gives direction to the philosophical search which is identified with man's very destiny.[20]

Basically we still have the *idea* of Descartes, the main function of which was to underscore the independence of the spirit in regards to the sense world or to anything else not itself spirit and freedom, a constituting power in regards to any object of knowledge.[21]

For realism, on the other hand, being, intelligible in itself, is originally present to the metaphysical intention and the truth of knowledge is grounded on the original structure of consciousness in its twofold, two-poled subject-object characteristic. The noetic description of consciousness reveals this structure as a real duality, where knowledge appears as a

[15] G. Van Riet, *Problèmes d'épistémologie,* p. 256.
[16] Cf. G. Bastide, *Traité,* T.I., p. 140.
[17] G. Bastide, "De la situation de l'homme," p. 246.
[18] G. Bastide, *Méditations,* p. 129.
[19] G. Bastide, *Traité,* T.I., p. 141.
[20] *Ibid.,* p. 140.
[21] Cf. R. Descartes, *Méditations,* III., 15, 17.

modality of being.[22] The subject is revealed in its real intentionality towards an object of knowledge and the object is revealed as that which, in some way, imposes and opposes itself to the subject.[23] Furthermore knowledge is the reality of the *union* of these two essentially *correlative* elements of consciousness. Knowledge implies being, but being does not necessarily indicate knowledge. Being is more radically "primum notum" than spirit.[24] Philosophy, for realism, does not begin with a spiritual conversion, but with the real existence of man in the world at the heart of which is revealed in an originally primitive way being itself. The primitive relationship that concerns philosophy is not the interiority of freedom revealed in conversion (knowledge), but rather the pre-reflective comprehension of being. Consciousness is essentially a noetic-noematic structure.[25]

Idealism, on the other hand, stresses the spirit's knowledge of itself: "... this problem," says Bastide, appears to us to be the one, unique philosophical problem upon which all the others depend." [26] For the idealist, the real is an idea legitimately affirmed and that is why Bastide can relate the whole philosophical intention to the search for spiritual values. For the object of the idea is value or "être pour nous." Thus the passage to the concrete order of human activity is made only according to the principles of idealism and the order of existence is not attained in the realist sense of the term (the order of being). The essence of being is related to the values discovered in the spirit alone. "A being which has no *raison d'être* would be a nothing for consciousness." [27]

Let us conclude this section by affirming once again our intention. So far we have not brought to bear any particular critique of idealism or realism. We have indicated in a general way the principal differences of orientation between these two approaches to philosophy. We have done so in order to clarify our problem at the outset, thus rendering the subsequent critique of greater value. The first clarification regards the philosophy of Bastide as an *axiological* idealism. His philosophy of values or his spiritualism should not distract us from the central point at issue which is his idealism. The fact of its becoming an existential idealism, a meta-

[22] Cf. F. Van Steenberghen, *Epistémologie*, p. 83. Cf. also G. Van Riet, *Problèmes d'épistémologie*, p. 256.
[23] F. Van Steenberghen, *Epistémologie*, p. 84.
[24] *Ibid.*, p. 87.
[25] A. Dondeyne, *Contemporary European Thought and Christian Faith*, p. 31.
[26] G. Bastide, *De la condition humaine*, p. 365.
[27] G. Bastide, "De la situation de l'homme," p. 245.

physics of action will not change the essential critique of idealism as such. No more, say, than the realism present in Descartes' intention or in Kant's empirical realism should distract us from the main problematic of their philosophy which is their idealism.[28] For idealism has, as it were, a built-in defense mechanism against dogmatism and subjectivism and it was operating in Descartes and Kant no less than in the contemporary movements to ground the reflexive method and the method of immanence in a spiritualist or axiological metaphysics. In fact, the critical idealism of Kant already implies in its very interior an empirical realism, not unlike the idealism of Brunschvicg which implies at the same time a definite positivism ... even though the existence of the thing-in-itself is not the same as Brunschvicg's experiential "choc." But as Vernaux points out, this kind of empirical realism (an agnostic realism) is really not a return to realism but the "triumph" of idealism over subjectivism.[29] At the end of our conclusion we will be in a position to ask to what extent an *axiological idealism* is really a triumph as regards moral philosophy of value or a metaphysics of action. The only authentic way to tackle this problem is to face up to the central problematic, which is idealism. I have tried in general during this work not to let myself be distracted from this central problem by the rich contributions one finds in Bastide's philosophy as regards moral philosophy in particular and the psychology of consciousness in general.

If, then, we have come to this point where we have identified the real problem posed by Bastide's philosophy as *idealism* and if, on the other hand, there is in idealism a positive emphasis on the spirit of man as immanent activity (something no authentic philosophy can neglect) that also coordinates within its own doctrine interiorly a certain realism and even existentialism, than we must conclude that the further discussion and critique must be brought to bear, as we have already noted, on the *relationship* between spirit and experience, or as Dondeyne has put it, on the further analysis (beyond idealism as critique) of the idealist's interpretation of the finite character of the intellectual life.[30]

[28] F. Van Steenberghen, *Epistémologie*, p. 250. Cf. also R. Verneaux, *Les sources cartésiennes*, p. 476.
[29] R. Verneaux, *Ibid.*, p. 477.
[30] A. Dondeyne, "Idealisme of realisme," *Tijdschrift voor Philosophie*, 1941 (4), p. 615.

II. Idealism or realism

1. Idealism

We have indicated two distinct kinds of philosophizing. Each philosophy characterizes itself by the choice it makes of first principles and by the way it attaches its conclusions to these first principles.[31] For idealism the first principle, the first intelligible is spirit. Spirit is the source of intelligibility and value imposing itself on brute matter. Outsdide of this reference to man it is without meaning for man. There is a certain radical heterogeneity between matter and spirit. Realism takes being as its first principle. Philosophy is regarded as the effort to determine and make intelligible the different modes of being as knowledge and action. Idealism tends to reduce all existence to thought (in Descartes' sense of the word).

Without denying the several points of agreement between these two philosophical orientations (such as their mutual opposition to a naive realism), it is our intention here to confront the precise points of difference. This critique will then have prepared us for a more fundamental examination of Bastide's axiological idealism. Let us, then, examine first of all the method of reasoning proper to the idealist.

The idealist's point of departure is a critique of naive realism. We cannot speak of an object of thought without reference to a subject. Furthermore, it is said, it does no good to speak of something beyond thought (or value) "for a being without a reason for being would be a nothing as far as consciousness was concerned."[32] Brunschvicg says the same thing: ". . . Knowledge constitutes a world which is for us *the* world. Beyond this there is nothing. Something which would be beyond knowledge would be, by definition, inaccessable, indeterminable, that is to say for us it would be equivalent to nothing."[33]

Turning to the subject the idealist finds something altogether different. He finds that the very notion of subject (in so far as immanent activity) contains a perfection nowhere manifest in the world of things or the world of "object." The subject (thought) manifests the very absolute philosophy seeks, a reality "par soi et pour soi," an immanent activity which proceeds from the agent and remains in the agent as its own perfection (Bewusstsein ie aus sich und für sich sein). Its character is spontaneity and self-

[31] G. Van Riet, *Problèmes d'épistémologie*, p. 263.
[32] G. Bastide, "De la situation de l'homme," p. 245.
[33] L. Brunschvicg, *La modalité du jugement*, p. 2.

sufficiency, a kind of *being itself* wholly different from the dependence noted in the appearance of "object." [34]

In this framework realism is interpreted as the antithesis of the authentic philosophical method, since it begins by asserting the objective reality of the object over thought.[35] This separation of the two orders of thinking and being can at best find only an artificial unity in the unjustified foundation of Descartes' God or in the naturalism of empirical philosophy which reduces intellectual activity to an epiphenomenon of the objective world.

The idealist does not deny the existence of the universe or the reality of experience. But the *role* that the material world plays in his philosophy is the crucial point of our discussion here. For it is precisely because immediate experience is interpreted in terms of naive realism that the idealist insists on grounding philosophy – not on this experience – but on *a priori* conditions which make possible this experience, namely in *consciousness itself,* since it is here that we find existence as activity, perfection and absolute autonomy. For this reason idealism is a critical meditation on the activity of thought reflecting upon itself. "Philosophy is the ideal reconstruction of consciousness understanding itself with all that it contains." [37]

In turning to spirit as the primary intelligible, therefore, idealism, at the same time, diminishes the import of the subject-object opposition registered in the immediate contact with reflective experience. Philosophy, they insist, does not begin on this level. The primary spontaneity of spirit, the original unity of its activity must be the deeper ground founding the possibility of the subject-object opposition. For Brunschvicg this reality takes on the nature of an impersonal consciousness which becomes manifest in the common spiritual life of a plurality of personal consciousnesses. For Bastide this basic reality is the discovery of God in an experience or apperception of Value manifesting itself in the deepest interiority of the self.[38] God is the Spirit of our spirit, the Value of all values.[39] From a realist viewpoint, however, critical idealism finishes in a metaphysical agnosticism.[40]

Yet, as Dondeyne notes, if we take into account the efforts of contemporary idealism to integrate into its own philosophy the world, God and the existential existence of man, if in other words they have posited an

[34] A. Dondeyne, "Idealism of realism," p. 610.
[35] L. Brunschvicg, *La modalité du jugement,* p. 2.
[36] A. Dondeyne, "Idealisme of realisme," p. 613.
[37] Cf. G. Bastide, *De la condition humaine,* p. 3.
[38] G. Bastide, *Méditations,* p. 60. Cf. also p. 45.
[39] G. Bastide, *De la condition humaine,* p. 323.
[40] Cf. F. Van Steenberghen, *Epistémologie,* pp. 68 and 252.

"open Cogito" and to this degree have approached in many aspects a transcendental realism, then we must look beyond the critical method as such for the real differences which idealism continues to manifest in regards to philosophies of being.[41] This is especially true for Bastide's *axiological idealism* where a philosophy of value approaches on many levels, especially in moral philosophy, the analyses we might expect to find also in a philosophy of being.

At the most basic level of our analyses of the ground for the differences in the two philosophical orientations of idealism and realism we are brought face to face with the problem of knowledge, or in other words the problem of finite human truth. What is the essence of truth? For both idealism and realism seek the concrete, real order. Both idealism and realism point to the finiteness of man as indicated by his dependence in knowledge on something outside pure spontaneity. As Kant emphasized, we can *think* by positing in the mind non-contradictory ideas, but this does not imply *knowledge*. Only in rationalism do we find posited a perfect correspondence. What is, then, the relationship between experience and spontaneity?

In part one we analysed briefly Brunschvicg's concept of the judgment and the relationship between the form of internality (the reciprocal immanence of ideas, the unity of the spirit determining its own laws) and the form of exteriority, the "exterior" limit to the ideal spontaneity of spirit.[42] What is important to note is that this very limitation, the "given" of experience, presupposes, for the idealist, the synthetic unity of the spirit. Formally considered the "given" of experience can only be regarded as the simply other than the interiority of spirit. It has no explanation or justification.[43] It is a simple "choc" without any positive content.[44] It is a simple principle of affirmation of the real.

What is to be noted for our present critique is that this view of experience is very much tied up with the understandable rejection of a naive realism, copy theories of knowledge envisioning the spirit as going outside itself to grasp reality. But isn't this interpretation of realism in general itself naive? Perhaps the real plausability of idealism must, in the last analysis, lie in its close correspondence to the facts of contemporary mathematical physics. In other words, at the root of idealism and its interpre-

[41] A. Dondeyne, "Idealisme of realisme," p. 615.
[42] Cf. Part I, chapter II, pp. 80-83.
[43] L. Brunschvicg, *La modalité du jugement*, p. 91.
[44] *Ibid.*, p. 92.

tation of experience lies the ideal of Descartes envisioning the unity of knowledge attained according to the mathematical method.[45]

As a matter of fact the mathematical sciences in particular do continue to manifest themselves as a particularly important region of our experience. To such an extent that it continues to offer itself to many philosophers as a fitting substitute for metaphysics.[46] What is more, the axioms of mathematics have an objective and universal validity for physical reality that goes beyond, it seems, the immediate perception of things on the level of realism. That is, the mathematical project and the life of spirit as conceived by the idealist bear remarkable similarities. In part, at least, both realities are given to us in the dynamic development of their particular histories, histories that are not linear, but complicated, discontinuous and free. It was precisely the "legality" of the new science of relativity that enabled Brunschvicg to come to a new appreciation of the activity and laws of spirit as intimately bound up with its history and experience. In this context he conceived of a new kind of legality with which to relate man's finite autonomy and base the unity of person while leaving in tact his fundamental dualism. That is, the unity of man was not now founded on an *a priori* reconciliation on the speculative level, but in the conscious experience of the good and beautiful in act. The very presence of the effective unity between two opposed realities (nature and spirit) is proven in the state of harmony of consciousness itself, where life offers itself to man's freedom and in the authentic exercise of freedom man finds himself, as it were, liberated by the gift of nature itself.[47]

2. Critique

It would seem to be a striking paradox that spiritualism in France, which had its origins in part as a reaction against the twofold menace of positivism and scientism, should continue to approach in various ways the problem of truth from the mathematical viewpoint. Yet this will be surprising only to those who tend to forget that much of French spiritualism (for example the spiritualism of Le Senne or the axiological personalism of Bastide) is wholly rooted and committed in principal to idealism.[48] The

[45] Cf. Part I, chapter II of this work, note 6. Cf. also G. Bastide, *Traité*, pp. 155 and 195.

[46] J. Ladrière, "La philosophie des mathématiques et la problème du formalisme," *Revue Philosophique de Louvain*, 1959 (9), pp. 165-166.

[47] L. Brunschvicg, *Le Progrès de la Conscience*, T. II, pp. 692-695.

[48] Cf. R. Le Senne, *Introduction a la Philosophie*, pp. 3, 89, 356. Cf. also G. Bastide, *De la condition humaine*, p. 376; *La conversion spirituelle*, p. 70.

principal connection lies in the idea of objectivity common to both.[49] It centers around the role played by the given of experience in the constitution of knowledge. As we have seen it merely occasions, as it were, the conversion of the spirit to itself and to its own nature as a principle constituting the value of its object. "Science is essentially creative of objectivity." "Objectivity is never given to consciousness." "Objectivity is the *raison d'être* immanent to the very effort of consciousnesses." [50]

As such idealism goes beyond radical empiricism, but it remains, from the realist's point of view, on this side of a more authentic philosophy. For the reality of the world has no metaphysical significance. What significance, then, metaphysically can we give to spirit and spiritualism, if we finally conclude that the first fact is not spirit, but man's existence in the world? "Without noticing it, we can pass from the most exaggerated spiritualism to the most absolute materialism." [51]

Idealism, then, can be criticized from the same direction in which realism might criticize empiricism, namely, beginning with its analysis of the "choc" experience.[52] The idealist accepts the distinction between "thinking" and "knowing" as the realist does. But on what basis? How does the "choc" experience limit the spontaneity of spirit in order to acquire knowledge, that is, an idea of reality? With or without application the mathematical notions remain in tact as possibilities for ideal truth. What seems to be implied is what Etcheverry and others have called the "latent realism" of idealism.[53] For the limitation of knowledge (man's finitude) and the consciousness we have of this limitation already points to a broader range of intellectual activity than that of the merely idealist faculty.[54] It seems to imply that we *know* what being is and that at the heart of consciousness we are *aware* of the essential duality of knowledge as a modality of being.[55] In other words there is in my consciousness (upon reflection) an awareness of the *direction* of knowing as going from the subject to the object. The object, in our awareness, is known as limiting, measuring in some way the knowledge I have of it. Knowledge appears as a certain original grasping of being.[56] It is not my spirit which poses being, but being

[49] A. Dondeyne, *Contemporary European Thought*, p. 78.
[50] G. Bastide, *Méditations*, p. 169.
[51] A. Dondeyne, *Contemporary European Thought*, p. 80.
[52] A. Dondeyne, *"Idealisme of realisme,"* p. 627.
[53] Cf. A. Etcheverry, *L'idéalisme français contemporain*, p. 297.
[54] A. Dondeyne, "Idealisme of realisme," p. 627.
[55] F. Van Steenberghen, *Epistémologie*, p. 86.
[56] F. Van Steenberghen, *Epistémologie*, p. 89.

which imposes itself on my consciousness and determines it.[57] In short, it seems that we can in no way identify being with "spirit." The intellect has a transcendental range and we are conscious of this fact.

Furthermore, the "choc" experience is said to be necessary for the affirmation of reality, since the pure spontaneity of the spirit is of itself limited to the ideal order. Concepts without content are empty, as Kant emphasized. But the exteriority aspect of the "choc" experience is itself without content,[58] that is, before contact with the spirit. The conclusion must be drawn, it seems, that the knowing power of spirit extends beyond its mathematical function and that it is a power able to appreciate the given as a "message of reality," that is, it knows the meaning of being and existence, something a mere ideal faculty of knowing (thinking) could never do.[59] All idealism, says Dondeyne, seems to give way under this contradiction between its explicit doctrine and its implicit affirmation of reality known as such in the distinction between "thinking" and "knowing." [60]

The same conclusion forces itself upon our reflection when we consider the relationship between the "choc" of experience and the idea in which reality is known. That these two conditions are necessary for knowledge is no longer a question today, but when we examine the relationship or interpretations of this relationship many different explanations are given. The radical heterogeneity between interiority and exteriority in Brunschvicg's philosophy, even when expressed in terms of a tension of consciousness,[61] leaves unanswered this basic problem. For in the affirmation of reality the truth of the idea does assume the value of reality which it lacks as the product of pure spontaneity of consciousness; the "choc" sensation does accommodate itself and receive meaning from the spirit. This seems to indicate that the spirit is already by its very nature a power directly inclined to knowledge.[62] Therefore the original description of consciousness, it would seem, must include this aspect of the spiritual activity. If the critique is to be exact, it is necessary that the object of the critique be described faithfully. Otherwise the whole value of the critique will be undermined, not only as regards what it leaves out but also as regards that which it attempts to describe. As Van Steenberghen points out, when we study the great historical systems that have tried to come to grips with the problem of knowledge, we are struck to see that the most radical differences of

[57] *Ibid.*, p. 90.
[58] Cf. L. Brunschvicg, *La modalité du jugement*, p. 92.
[59] A. Dondeyne, "Idealisme of realisme," p. 629.
[60] *Ibid.*
[61] Cf. Part I, chapter II, p. 80.
[62] A. Dondeyne, "Idealisme of realisme," p. 631.

opinion are due less to the critique of the immediate evidence of consciousness than to the original description of these evidences.[63]

And this is precisely our problem here. For it is not so much the distinction between sense and intellectual knowledge but the manner of defining these two poles. Descartes, we saw, characterized sense knowledge by its obscurity and passivity; for Kant the sensibility is characterized by its passivity in regards to the action of the sensible upon it. But if we admit this aspect of sense knowing but add that sense knowledge is an activity, an intentionality of the subject towards an object, a taking possession of an object present, an object present to the mind in its own concrete existence and not that simply constructed by the spirit, then we do have a different orientation of thought and an opposition between critical realism and critical idealism. And yet how else can we attain to existence except by way of its immediate sense experience? For the existence of thought is immediately given but only grasped in the apperception of reflection and direct intellectual knowledge does not yield the real existence of any object.[64] The real point of departure of critique, then, seems to be this unique combination of the original affirmation of consciousness as receiving its existential modality from immediate sense experience. Thinking and experience meet each other, each having its own obligation, as it were, to fertilize the other. Both belong to the same original spontaneity of consciousness.[65] The radical separation of the factors, as two completely heterogeneous functions (the heritage of Kant), is the source of all idealism and is no less operative in the axiological idealism of G. Bastide.[66] For the realist experience is not to be defined in terms of the passivity of sensation or in terms of the *a posteriori*. It is rather "all direct knowledge without intermediary." [67] It is the twofold openness of the self to self and to an objective presence in one necessary (but not *a priori*) affirmation containing a twofold original evidence.[68] With its over emphasis on the pure spontaneity of the spirit idealism logically tends to become a closed critical dialectic. It seems in principle to affirm implicitly what it explicitly denies, namely the existential meaning of truth and a transcendental range of the spirit (and not just its formal interiority) in grasping directly reality in one unique affirmation wherein the idea and experience are one.[69] What is

[63] Cf. F. Van Steenberghen, *Epistémologie*, p. 23.
[64] Cf. R. Verneaux, *Les sources cartesiennes*, p. 491.
[65] A. Dondeyne, "Idealisme of realisme," p. 631.
[66] Cf. G. Bastide, *Méditations*, p. 169.
[67] F. Van Steenberghen, *Epistémologie*, p. 77.
[68] *Ibid.*, pp. 98-99.
[69] A. Dondeyne, "Idealisme of realisme," pp. 633-634.

desirable is that idealism might complete its critical analysis and explicitly state the wider horizons of the philosophical project and the basic situation of the existential interiority of consciousness. Even a careful criticism within mathematics itself, as J. Ladrière has shown, can help us regain a metaphysics of finite existence.[70]

In the next section we shall come to grips with the question posed by Baside's axiological idealism in the framework of an *interior transcendence.*[71] No doubt this is a laudable attempt to go beyond the limitations of the impersonal idealism of Brunschvicg and establish an axiological personalism.[72] Yet we shall see that Bastide's personalism cannot escape the problematic of idealism on which it is firmly based. The following exposition of the realist point of view will prepare the way for showing why this is true.

3. Realism

For realism it is precisely this original transcendental existential interiority of consciousness that makes man a person, that is, an "I in the world." [73] This is the original experience. It is not necessary to "search" for the self or discover the self in the recognition of the critical and ontological priority of the subject over the object. It is impossible that the critique of knowledge should procede without some previous idea of knowledge, just as it is impossible to begin philosophy without some idea however hidden of what philosophy is all about, and we might add, without some idea of what *human existance* is all about. This is why the preliminary efforts of a phenomenology of consciousness and a phenomenology of existence is so important. The real value of contemporary philosophy in great part lies here.

Moreover, if we precede without care or humility in this regard or without a will to be simply faithful to the facts we will prejudice our whole work. We have seen how the mathematical ideal as regards metaphysics determined the narrowness of Descartes' viewpoint. The same can be said of Kant as regard the pure concepts of knowledge.

The realism we are defending here does not proceed by asserting the ontological independence of the object reality in relation to the subject reality.[74] Rather it begins by seeking to verify, first on the critical level,

[70] J. Ladrière, "La philosophie des mathématiques et le problème du formalisme," *Revue Philosophiques de Louvain,* 1959 (9), 167-168.

[71] G. Bastide, *Traité,* II., p. 724.

[72] Cf. G. Bastide, "Le malin génie," p. 238.

[73] A. Dondeyne, 'Idealisme of realisme," p. 634.

[74] F. Van Steenberghen, *Epistémologie,* p. 89.

what later becomes the hallmark of realism, namely a certain primacy of the object over the subject. But this primacy is established first of all on the level of my actual consciousness wherein the realist orientation of thought and the primacy of being over knowledge is given as an undeniable fact of my experience bearing with it its own evidence.[75] The evidence of the real which is the point of departure for critical realism is not to be understood as that which is simply opposed to the Cogito in its ontological independence.[76]

What realism does demand is that the original given of consciousness is not limited to the sciences of mathematics or physics as already constituted by the spirit of man. Being is also given and any critique that wants to be integral must take this aspect of the given as part of its object. In other words the *full Cogito* must be our starting point. Granting that a science of mathematics exists in a state most desirable to certain basic tendencies of the human spirit, and granted that metaphysics does not exist in the same way, nevertheless there is a science of metaphysics, that is, there exists a project of man's spirit opening up a horizon of knowledge and experience that is *distinct* from the mathematical project and the kind of knowledge given by that science.[77]

To determine what metaphysics is we do not begin by presupposing a method. This would certainly be to prejudice our cause, as we have seen in the case of Descartes. Bastide sees this very well, at least in principle, as was manifest in the first chapter of part two. From the problematic of the Cogito he proceeds to describe the evidences of the first fact and only after that does a method emerge in the spiritual conversion. With Descartes it was assumed at the outset that the mathematical method was the unique and universal road to truth.

Realism, it can be said, has benefited by the idealist critique in so far as it has itself become much more sensitive to the problems involved in establishing the ground of metaphysics. It has enlarged and refined its own viewpoint precisely in the area of describing faithfully the full content of the *Cogito* and thus it is prepared to meet the idealist challenge on the same ground where dialogue is possible, in the description of the original data of consciousness. For realism has had to enlarge its own vision as regards the precise meaning of the original presence of the object and its relation to the function of consciousness. It is nothing more than an effort to deepen our understanding of the relationship between the given of ex-

[75] F. Van Steenberghen, *Epistémologie*, p. 89.
[76] This is contrary to the opinion of Gilson, cf. F. Van Steenberghen, *ibid.*, p. 90.
[77] J. Ladrière, "La philosophie des mathématiques," pp. 163-165.

perience and the spontaneity of spirit that has been our problem from the beginning. For realism itself has not always avoided the pitfalls of phenomenalism.

Realism, then, seeks to establish the relationship between the original presence of the object to the act of knowledge, a relationship which penetrates the act and is itself part of my original consciousness. The object, in other words, must be known precisely as terminating the act of knowledge *in so far as present.*[78] Thus the formula of Bastide's first *Meditation* "il y a conscience et j'en témoigne" is an excellent and in fact the only starting point, but the subsequent description of the subject-object pole which the formula designates so well is crucial for all that is to follow. In chapter one of part two we saw that Bastide slips quickly into an idealism of consciousness. The object of the original intention lays bare, for Bastide, the problematic situation of the subject in relation to the highest Transcendence, God.[79] In the final section on axiological idealism we will look more closely at Bastide's approach. Here it will be useful to examine more in detail the approach of realism.

For realism it is important to take as the starting point of the critique both the original affirmation of consciousness and the affirmation of the real. For the real, like the *Cogito,* is that which is most fundamentally given in every experience, that which needs no other justification than its own presence. The value of the original sense experience as an experience of the real cannot, in other words, be left outside the original description of the immediately given without by that very fact weakening the critique itself. The *idea* is only a modality of being and must be defined in terms of it.[80]

Why is this so? Because it seems to be an unescapable conclusion of an analysis of consciousness. Not only negatively speaking, that is, from our previous critique of idealism, but positively speaking and even in idealist terms we can say *from the very nature of the spirit's active presence to itself.* As Bastide indicates there is together with every awareness of my most interior self the real possibility for a presence without limit. Even though we cannot agree with him on the nature of this transcendence, nevertheless, the fact that he has assigned it to the act of self-consciousness seems already significant and a point on which we can agree to some extent. My existence as a subject living in the world is founded on transcendence as well as immanence. For the realist, however, this transcendence is the

[78] Cf. A. Dondeyne, "Idealisme of realisme," p. 642.
[79] Cf. Part II, chapter two of this work.
[80] F. Van Steenberghen, *Epistémologie,* p. 235.

possibility, not of experiencing value (God) but it is a possibility without limit of all other things understood as other.[81] For without doubt this act of presence is an active interiority, an active existence coming from an immanent action wherein we exist as persons, that is consciously present to ourselves as a reality in and for ourself, a subject that is a living unity tending towards an even greater unity. Except for this active presence and openness consciousness could not maintain *itself* (as it must) through all the moments of time and *a posteriori* experiences.[82] Existence for oneself as person, in other words, is based on an unlimited act of self presence determined by no content of any particular being. It is transcendental.[83] Thus Bastide is correct in saying that this active self-presence cannot be defined as a this or that or by any finite being content, not even by the content of a being making up a finite "I." [84] The affirmation of consciousness is of another order than all my determinations.

But in the light of idealism it is precisely the nature of this transcendence that must be emphasized here. Realism sees little ground here for having recourse to the experience of Value or the affirmation of the existence of God.[85] For realism the transcendent reality of being correctly understood is the only necessary and sufficient *philosophical* explanation. The value of our knowledge is grounded in the experience of existence.[86] The unlimited act of self presence is seen as an interiority of consciousness with transcendental possibilities which can be naturally and sufficiently expressed by the concrete order which surrounds us and of which we are a part.[87] Being (existence) is the continuous and fundamental situation of all our knowledge, making it possible for us to exist as subjects. The idea of being is no pure idea, but the pure experience as an I in the world. It is this virtual presence of the idea of being that enables realism to undercut the idealist objections against philosophies of concept, for it is precisely here that the realist doctrine of knowledge is seen to be more than a mere representationalist one.[89]

The experience of existence (understood as the primordial, constant and

[81] A. Dondeyne, "Idealisme of realisme," p. 642.
[82] *Ibid.*, p. 643.
[83] *Ibid.*
[84] Cf. Part II, chapter one.
[85] Cf. G. Bastide, *Méditations*, pp. 45 and 60.
[86] Cf. R. Verneaux, *Les sources cartésiennes*, p. 336; cf. Also A. Dondeyne, *Contemporary European Thought*, p. 147.
[87] A. Dondeyne, *Ibid.*, p. 146.
[88] A. Dondeyne, "Idealisme of realisme," pp. 644-645.
[89] A. Dondeyne, *Contemporary European Thought*, p. 145.

final experience implied in all particular experiences and in all the activities of our life) [90] includes, then, an active, *a priori* interiority of consciousness with transcendental meaning. And this experience grounds our existence as person. Again Bastide poses this truth in a way which is striking, but which carries with it the limitations of his idealism. For person is defined in terms of a "witness of consciousness," that is, in terms of the problem my existence is and the duty I have of bearing witness, that is, in terms of my *devoir être* as well as in terms of my being.[91] But, as we saw, this interpretation limits itself to an aspect of human knowledge and to an interpretation of the moral function of knowledge.[92] For realism the finality of consciousness has first and formost as its goal a "possession" as adequate as possible of being.[93] For realism metaphysics is not only a need for truth, a care entrusted to man's responsibility, but it is also a project, a simple "curiosity" to know, an ideal of truth to be realized. Bastide minimizes this latter and more fundamental aspect of the truth project in his desire to found a metaphysics that is an ethics and a philosophy of action.[94]

Yet in the long run it seems that the idealist diminution of the world and the first fact as existence in the world greatly lessens its project as a moral philosophy and metaphysics of action. For the metaphysical intention is stripped of some of its most important meaning and value upon which the very meaning and possibilities of person and personality rest. For it is precisely the experience of existence which "constitutes our participation in being, our way of *having a part* of and *taking part in* the being that surrounds and bears us." [95] Again this is way the realist doctrine of knowledge is not a representationalist one at its deepest source. This presence of man to being and the presence of being to man is, for the realist, the only experience which can found a true philosophy of person, for it is this experience wherein man knows himself as "a power to be, a call to realize himself in realizing more and more our presence in being, particularly through a better understanding of being." Bastide's analysis approaches many aspects of this same intention as described here, except that his tendency to voluntarism causes him to minimize the important aspect of progress in becoming a person through a better *understanding* of being. For the realist this knowledge of being (emphasis on Beings self-mani-

[90] *Ibid.*, p. 147.
[91] G. Bastide, *Méditations*, pp. 6 and 8.
[92] Cf. Part II, chapter four, p. 552 of this work.
[93] F. Van Steenberghen, *Epistémologie*, p. 147.
[94] Cf. G. Bastide, "L'expérience morale," p. 310.
[95] A. Dondeyne, *Contemporary European Thought*, p. 147.

festation) is as important as man's realization of himself and the subsequent self-revelation to others (emphasis on Beings self-actualization in man). That is, the knowledge of being as existence in the world grounds the possibility of revealing myself (after becoming conscious of my own being in the world) as *man.*

Therefore, our critique of idealism and this brief exposé of the realist viewpoint seems to satisfy best the spirit-experience problem by grounding firmly the finite character of human existence in the noetic-noematic structure of human knowledge having for its object reality "whatever it is and as it is." [96] The project of knowledge is directed immediately and constantly to the whole of being which is present but also absent, because it is *transcendental.* Furthermore this presence with absence must be represented by the finite mind. There are no innate ideas nor, does it seem, do we have any direct experience of Value as Bastide intends it. Both the reflective experience and the function of immediate presence of being are grounded in one and the same spontaneity of consciousness and have their root in the same transcendental act of consciousness of which Being is the expression.[97] The universal character of our knowledge is the natural result of the one original transcendental act of consciousness in its inexhaustability. Idealists would not, it seems, be so scandalized by this doctrine if they really understood it apart from associationist doctrines and saw it as "an illuminating analysis of the perceived datum." [98] It is precisely in the framework of the notion of being outlined above, that is, as a "lumen naturale" intimately connected with man's being in the world that the doctrine of philosophical knowledge receives its proper context.[99] The dualism of Brunschvicg and Bastide seems unacceptable.

Bastide's duality of the two consciousnesses [100] takes on meaning perhaps on the psychological and religious level, but the ultimate and synthetic unity which is the source and ground of man's existence as an incarnated spirit cannot be conceived philosophically only in terms of descriptive psychology. The ultimate metaphysical unity is of necessity of the transcendental order. Granted that Bastide has a transcendental in the notion of Value. However it is to be doubted if he has established philosophically its existence and role. Furthermore "self-consciousness, liberty, sentiment and their noematic correlatives-value and being-for-me-are only particular

[96] *Ibid.,* p. 150.

[97] A. Dondeyne, "Idealisme of realisme," p. 646.

[98] A. Dondeyne, *Contemporary European Thought,* p. 142.

[99] *Ibid.,* pp. 144 and 157. Cf. also A. Dondeyne, "L'abstraction," *Revue néoscolastique de philosophie,* 1938 (aôut et février), pp. 5-20; 339-373.

[100] G. Bastide, *De la condition humaine,* p. 369.

aspects of being" and cannot really determine the ultimate unity of being underlying the multiplicity of particular beings and their manifestations.[101] For dualism the problem lies in the original conception of the *Cogito*. The spirit of man is regarded as the source of intelligibility and value. It is the source of meanings which are imposed on brute matter. Matter, outside of its reference to man, has no sense. This irreducibility of the two aspects of our experience leaves us with a dualistic agnosticism.

Realism finds this unity in the notion of existence. But again, it is important to see what is meant by these notions. Bastide's critique of substantialism [102] is really quite acceptable to a realist. But it does not apply to the realism we are talking about here. For *existence* is "the existential act whence spring the fruitful operations thanks to which each subject progressively extends its conquest of nothingness, each according to its type of essences, with increasing liberty as one ascends the scale of being." [103] This notion of Being is understood in a way that is valid for transphenomenal being. It is conceived as "the transphenomenal unity which is the ground of the series of manifestations of the existing thing. This unity is not situated behind or underneath these manifestations, but saturates and envelops them, so that it is, as it were, 'indicated' in them." [104] "The proper act of substance is to *exist*, just as the proper characteristic of existence is to make an existing thing subsist in itself and manifest itself." [105] To become conscious by reflection of all that I am as a subject in the world is the object of metaphysics. That is why, for realism, metaphysics is not only a philosophy of reflection or spiritual conversion. It is also a philosophy of existence. As such it does not part from a vague idea of being nor from a brute outside world, but from the undeniable fact that existence is at one and the same time "spirit and being, idea and experience, a posteriori data and a priori spontaneity, finiteness and transcendence, namely that we exist and live as an I-in-the-world." [106]

III. Axiological Idealism

1. Critique

In this last section we aim to consider Bastide's philosophy from the point of view of his axiology. For like the philosophy of Le Senne Bastide's

[101] A. Dondeyne, *Contemporary European Thought*, p. 138.

[102] Cf. G. Bastide, *De la condition humaine*, pp. 280-293.

[103] E. Gilson, *L'être et l'Essence*, Paris, 1947, p. 309 cited by A. Dondeyne, *Contemporary European Thought*, p. 156.

[104] A. Dondeyne, *ibid.*, p. 156.

[105] *Ibid.*

[106] A. Dondeyne, "Idealisme of realisme," p. 648.

axiology is, in part, an attempt to go beyond the narrow viewpoint of an impersonal idealism. His philosophy is a moral idealism, a practical philosophy, a spiritual personalism.[107]

In chapter III of part one we indicated briefly how the contemporary philosophies of reflection and the philosophies of spirit attempted to ground their philosophies in existence without abandoning the idealist method. At the source of the immanent activity of spirit is revealed the Absolute Spirit. But the Cogito is now an *existential* one. The intellectual pole is not the only source of value.[108] For Bastide it is precisely the notion of value which has the function of "finding again the deepest ethical resonances of the philosophical search without falling into the exaggerations which the philosophies of existence have not always guarded themselves from." [109] For Bastide the notion of value has manifested its "incontestable aptitude to unite in all clarity intellectual analysis and the depth of lived experience." In truth the idealist position rests fundamentally intact.

Idealism rests essentially intact because the first principle is not existence but the spirit. But now spirit is revealed in its autonomy through act. The experience of liberty in a "difficult" total reflection (spiritual conversion and the transfiguration of values) is the "most pure evidence" revealed "in the most secret interiority" of man.[110] This experience of liberty is at the same time the awareness of my existence as person.[111] It is no wonder that in this perspective Bastide relies on the practical philosophy of Kant for his metaphysical axiology. For Bastide's goal is to established a speculative voluntarism and a practical intellectualism. Therefore our critique must ask from a philosophical viewpoint the role of faith and value in philosophy. We must examine briefly the relation between value and truth, value and being. We must pose the question of transcendence and the meaning of authenticity. Finally we must pose the question of the relationship between knowledge and action in metaphysics. We must pose the question of person.

The orientation of contemporary philosophy towards a philosophy of man and towards a practical humanism was already a fertile climate in which to choose value as the metaphysical framework for the autonomy of spirit. As Etcheverry points out, idealism, in so far as it rests faithful to

[107] G. Bastide, *La conversion spirituelle*, pp. 73, 86.
[108] Cf. G. Bastide, *Traité*, I., p. 196; also cf. *De la condition humaine*, p. 319.
[109] G. Bastide, *La conversion spirituelle*, vii.
[110] G. Bastide, *Traité*, p. 140.
[111] *Ibid.*

itself, tends to substitute the objective judgment for reality, relation for the Absolute, function for the given, "in short value for being." [112] For idealism estimes that the sentiment of value is not taken from the real order but is derived from the spontaneity of spirit and from the dynamism of the will. As Bastide puts it: "While science seeks to know the different modes of being of the object, philosophy seeks to become conscious of the *raisons d'être* of the subject." [113] Philosophy is the "practical search for certain values." [114] Man is the author of philosophy in the fullest sense of the word. For value is *a priori* in respect to the subject, expressing as it does the legislating function of the spirit.

This radical opposition between being and value has its most fundamental origins in the philosophy of Kant wherein is introduced the distinction between the metaphysical and moral orders.[115] While it is true that both Brunschvicg and Bastide appeal to the reflexive judgment of Kant in order to bring together nature and spirit in one philosophy of spirit, nevertheless Kant "underlines the fact that such a thought grounds a moral faith and not a real knowledge." [116] We are not surprised, then, to find Bastide turning to a practical philosophy, leaving to science the problem of the different modes of being. "Philosophy (idealist) will abandon, without too many regrets, the domaine of reality to the positive sciences in order to attach itself to epistemological, ethical and aesthetic problems which the sciences cannot resolve." [117] This is precisely the position of Bastide's axiological idealism.[118] The original affirmation yielded the three constituents of philosophy: the true, the Good (Value) and existence (vd. the notion of friendship in chapter IV, part II: the existence of persons in understanding is for Bastide the beautiful).[119] From the outset metaphysics is concerned with duty and becomes Ethics, in the broad sense of the word.[120]

[112] A. Etcheverry, "La valeur et l'être," in *Les Valeurs* (Actes du III Congrès des Sociétés de philosophie de langue française), Louvain, 1947, p. 78.

[113] G. Bastide, *Traité,* T.I., p. 123.

[114] *Ibid.*

[115] Cf. A. Wylleman, "L'homme et la création des valeurs," *Revue philosophique de Louvain,* 1960 (février), p. 89.

[116] *Ibid.* Cf. also L. Brunschvicg, *Le Progrès de la conscience,* pp. 692-701 and G. Bastide, *Traité,* T.I., pp. 712-713.

[117] A. Wylleman, *ibid.,* p. 90. Cf. also the expositions of F. Alquie and J. Wahl in *Expérience,* pp. 29-41 and 409-424.

[118] Cf. G. Bastide, *De la condition humaine,* pp. 324-348; *Traité,* pp. 332-353 and chapter IV, Part II of this work.

[119] Cf. p. 361 of this work.

[120] G. Bastide, *Méditations,* p. 8.

This becomes especially clear when we consider Bastide's analysis of moral experience.[121] For him morality is universal in its extension and "by right nothing escapes it." [122] It has the same extension as consciousness itself and philosophy is nothing more than perfection of this fundamental moral experience.[123] Moral experience, says Bastide, gives sense to everything.[124] It is not necessary here to go into the nature of this experience since we have already discussed in the body or our work the metaphysical dimensions of duty (vd: scruple), the experience of freedom in spiritual conversion and the subsequent transformation of values. The given is without moral value as the constatation of man's alienation brought out. But this is not an experience in the full sense of the word in which Bastide uses it. By experience Bastide means the *act of reflection* (spiritual conversion) which is also a free act and the experience of freedom. They are one and the same certitude of consciousness. Thus the first fact of the metaphysical order is not man's being-in-the-world-with-others. For Bastide and the idealists it is the second level experience of spiritual conversion (reflection). Even more. It is the practical elaboration of the moral idea in act in the elaboration of a moral philosophy, that is, a metaphysics of action.[125] "Without this moral experience all other experiences would be deceptive and in the end illusory." [126] There is no metaphysical experience in the realist understanding of the word.

By reason of its first principles realism must judge this approach to philosophy as partly insufficient. For it is evident that we have not essentially parted from an idealist point of view in the assertion of an axiological metaphysics. It continues to propose, now in ethical terminology, the radical heterogeneity of the given and spirit. But to assert the absolute immanence of value is to compromise real objectivity no less on the practical than on the level of speculative idealism. As Van Steenberghen points out: "As to the ethical or moral finality of knowledge, it finds its point of support in the absolute value of the object of thought which alone is able to fix the absolute norms of morality in function of human person." [127] Let us examine more closely the realist position in this regard.

Existential idealism takes as its first principle the spirit as creative liberty. Spirit is light (spiritual conversion) and autonomy. Metaphysics is the result

[121] Cf. G. Bastide, "L'expérience morale," in *Experience*, pp. 307-323.
[122] *Ibid.*, p. 308.
[123] *Ibid.*, pp. 308 and 309.
[124] *Ibid.*, p. 320.
[125] G. Bastide, "L'expérience morale," p. 315.
[126] *Ibid.*, p. 320.
[127] F. Van Steenberghen, *Epistémologie*, p. 226, note 1.

of reflexive analysis brought to bear on the authenticity of our free acts, for "liberty is not something to contemplate but to exercise." [128] The authentic exercise of freedom in the promotion of the spiritual values is the ideal. This ideal is continually clarified by philosophy in close conjunction with moral activity.[129] Its transcendental is the Good, "pure value" which is experienced as "a call to truth and existence." [130] The value of truth and existence (act) is assured in the experience of Value "which manifests itself in the act of enlightening and creating us, in the act of conferring on us knowledge and being, in the act of impregnating with its own vivifying and rectifying action the activity by which we know what we know and are what we are only because we are authentically what we are in and by Value itself." [131] The ultimate sense and direction of life is present in the experience of God at the heart of the spirit.[132] The spiritual conversion is both a reward and a call to faithful effort.[133] The ideals or values revealed to reflection confer on man the attitudes regulative of his destiny in authenticity. The sciences and aesthetics nourish these ideals in the completion of the reflexive cycle in action.[134] In all its steps axiological idealism is careful to preserve the inventive effort of man in a practical humanism. Objectivity in the final analysis is the result of interpersonal relations.[135]

This in brief is the outline of Bastide's philosophy presented in part two of this work. Despite the richness of its content as regards certains aspects of moral philosophy, we must take exception to the principles at least implied in a philosophy of action such as Bastide's axiology. The central problem again appears as eminently an epistemological one. How, in other words, explain the attitude of consciousness by which we arrive at the authentic values in all certitude? How do we become conscious of ourselves in our freedom apart from an act of reflection understood in the realist sense? How arrive at positing the transcendence of God, that is, how experience Value apart from all knowledge understood as an illumination of the given of experience? Certainly we have posed these questions from a realist point of view, because the problem is essentially the same and we suppose the validity of our previous conclusions concerning the

[128] G. Bastide, *Traité,* p. 141.
[129] G. Bastide, "De la situation de l'homme," p. 242.
[130] Cf. Part II, chapter one, p. 199 of this work.
[131] *Ibid.* Cf. G. Bastide, *Méditations,* p. 60.
[132] G. Bastide, *Traité,* T. II., p. 724.
[133] G. Bastide, *Traité,* T. I., pp. 58, 170, 199-200; T. II., p. 488.
[134] *Ibid.,* pp. 380-381. Cf. Also pp. 340 and 347.
[135] Cf. p. 357 of this work.

realist viewpoint. Axiological idealism continues to underestimate, it seems, the value of *understanding* being. For realism, philosophy is by definition an effort to give a foundation for a *universal* knowledge concerning the fundamental meaning of existence.[136]

The first part of our comments here, then, would only serve to recall what was said earlier concerning the realist notion of the first fact and the intimate relationship of spirit and experience in the framework of which are to be understood reflective knowledge and Being. For if we reject this approach we are thrown back on seeking the foundations for knowledge on something no less problematic, such as sentiment and activity. We cannot help but remark, for example, the obscurity of the essential text on page sixty of Bastide's *Meditations*. Yet it is central to his thesis concerning the primacy of Value over knowledge and action (existence). It seems that in the end we are left once again with the question: how do we experience the presence of Value? [137]

With the primacy of action over knowledge we are left with the curious anomaly that knowledge is only a second level manifestation of existence. Like Descartes we are left with a problem of existence in so far as it can be known and grasped intellectually. To abandon the role of reflective knowledge in philosophy manifests itself invariably in what E. Morot-Sir has referred to as "one of the most serious problems facing philosophy today," namely, the problem of philosophical mystification.[138] The tendency to make the spirit the whole of reality weakens the very notion of spirit ... easily paving the way back to materialism. "Idealism destroys the conviction that consciousness could have of being a spiritual reality." [139] At best we are left with a comprehensive description of the real or a propedeutic for an experience bordering on the mystical or religious. A philosophy of value becomes a promotion of values, a maieutic, a theory of a certain process of action having no science in the strict sense of the word justifying its procedures. Axiology becomes an apologetic of value.

These criticisms could be seen out of context if we do not see them as trying to shed light on the deepest implications of a philosophy of action. In this regard we might recall that like criticisms have been raised concerning the approach of Socrates who remains throughout Bastide's philosophy a dominant guiding force.[140] For Bastide also knowledge is

[136] A. Dondeyne, *Contemporary European Thought*, p. 97.
[137] G. Bastide, *Méditations*, p. 60.
[138] E. Morot-Sir, "Etre et Valeur," in *Encyclopédie française*, p. 19.06-15.
[139] *Ibid.*, p. 19.06-16.
[140] J. Maritain, *Moral Philosophy*, New York, 1964, pp. 15-16.

authentic action and philosophy as a provocation to action.[141] The life in the spirit as action is not essentially different from life in the spirit as reflection. But how are to escape the pitfalls of a new kind of pragmatism, however enriched by an axiological spiritualism? For pragmatism is the "accentuation of the role of action, of the practical life in the discovery of truth or even in the very constitution of truth . . ." [142] It seems, that a philosophy of spiritual conversion understood in Bastide's terms as a "difficult total reflection, rare and difficult to attain" takes us too far outside the field of philosophy. The real revelation of the spiritual conversion does not seem to be grounded on a satisfactory explanation, for the spiritual conversion appears "more the work of man than the philosopher." [143] The remarks of professor Van Riet apropos of H. Dumery are in this regard applicable to Bastide, namely, that he minimizes considerably the real difficulty of a philosophical explanation of the Transcendent and overestimates considerably the revelatory nature of our limited experience of freedom.[144]

In the end then, we are thrown back to our original problem concerning the first principles of philosophy. In the long run the problem is the problem of reflection and of the relationship between the reflective and pre-reflective life of consciousness.[145] Self-presence, points out Van Riet, is not self-knowledge, for the former does not employ judgments, words or concepts: "it is silent, it does not say anything." [146] Reflection does not speak. It clarifies by giving expression. Its fruit is the judgment. *But even this clarifying act is, in regards to itself, pre-reflexive,* presence to self but not yet reflexive knowledge. Only a *new act* of reflection can elucidate it.[147] There is no total reflection. For realism, as we have seen, the spiritual dynamism of spirit, while depending on man for its effective exercise, refers to the real order of being as regards its sense.[148] Does this approach of realism hinder the creativity of spirit? We saw that on the speculative level it did not. In the following section we will examine briefly certain positives aspects of a philosophy of action and a metaphysics of value.

Once we have criticized the idealist approach to a philosophy of value

[141] Cf. G. Bastide, *Traité,* p. 92. Cf. also G. Bastide, *Le moment historique de Socrate,* pp. 272-298.

[142] Cf. F. Van Steenberghen, p. 68, note 2.

[143] Cf. G. Van Riet, *Problèmes d'épistemologie,* p. 292.

[144] Cf. the remarks of Van Riet concerning H. Duméry, *ibid.,* pp. 291-293.

[145] Cf. G. Van Riet, *Problèmes d'épistémologie,* p. 294.

[146] G. Van Riet, *ibid.,* p. 294.

[147] *Ibid.*

[148] *Ibid.,* p. 296.

and action the task rests upon us to show that realism does come to grips in a better way with the difficult moral problems involved in the fundamental question: does my life have a meaning? What is my destiny? What is the realist approach to the question of value, to the question of action and practical knowledge, to the question of authenticity and personal responsibility?

The response of realism is in two parts, one being metaphysical and one epistemological. Let us consider first of all the epistemological question.

We saw that the original affirmation of Bastide's philosophy was from the beginning placed in a moral context, that his original project and philosophical viewpoint was grounded in a primitive and original experience that was explicitly moral, that the particular intentionality of consciousness was concerned with the final end of man (authenticity, God) and the means for arriving at the end (axiology, spiritual conversion). It is precisely in this context that *the* object of Bastide's philosophy is freedom and his method is the manifestation of this freedom in all its authenticity through spiritual conversion.[149] Bastide's philosophy is geared explicitly towards the judgment of value made authentic in the practical action accomplished for the promotion of the spiritual (authentic) values. The search for authentic values as attained by man in his freedom is truly to pose the moral problem.

Realism would have little objection to this approach. In fact we readily acknowledge once again the richness of Bastide's moral philosophy. But our question here is necessarily geared to the relation between knowledge and action, for it is precisely the former that is minimized in axiological idealism. As we have seen, critical idealism tends to metaphysical agnosticism as far as realism is concerned. Yet it is precisely metaphysics and a philosophy of being which must, from the realist point of view, ground a moral philosophy. For realism there is a double intentionality of consciousness (the self-presentation of Being being both self-manifestation and self-actualization) and both must be grounded on a philosophy of Being.[150] Action implies a practical knowledge, a *potential* intelligibility. Reflection can bring to light the intelligible structure of action, not by way of a total reflection wherein action and reflection are said to be one, but only in a *change of attitude*. Here again we are brought at once both to the richness and problematic of Bastide's philosophy: its richness because it is wholly devoted, we might say, to lay bare the practical attitude of consciousness,

[149] Cf. G. Bastide, *Traité*, T.I., pp. 356-357. Cf. also G. Bastide, "De la situation de l'homme," p. 256.

[150] Cf. Van Riet, *Problèmes d'épistémologie*, p. 240.

the practical norms of knowledge and action.[151] Axiological idealism is wholly concerned with faith won by spiritual conversion in the ideality of value.[152] The central intuition of Bastide's philosophy and its principal problem is that of the spiritual conversion, "the problem around which is centered the engagement of the *whole* soul." That is, he is concerned with the *practical attitude* of consciousness. This is certainly an important project, perhaps the most important ultimate project of philosophy. But our point is that he greatly prejudices his task in neglecting metaphysics by submitting to axiology the concrete order of existence. The whole structure of his practical philosophy threatens to fall without this support.

For there is, we maintain, a more fundamental attitude of consciousness than the "practical" one. We are thus brought back once again to our main critique against idealism, that it is a *second-level* construction of consciousness. Philosophy must return to the primitive revealing intuition. It is our experience as subjects in the world that grounds the unity of speculative and practical philosophy, for it is the first access to truth. Idealism, in reducing truth to a single mode, "truncates the being of man and makes his relation to the world unintelligible." [153]

For the human condition is such that man is this primary and primitive relation to the real. Man does not create existence but is simply open to it. Existence is already there with the richness of its content. It is not originally alienation as Bastide maintains. It is just the opposite, for it is a principle of intelligibility, bringing its own light to the problem of man's existence. For idealism, we have seen, it is pure facticity. It only enters the judgment as modality.[154] In itself existence as first grasped by consciousness is non-critical, naive and alienating. "Idealism parts from meanings (Cf. Bastide, values, i.e., *raisons d'être*) [155] and ascends towards the transcendent object (Bastide: Value, the Good); realism parts from the real intelligible and aims at understanding it." [156]

It is this difference of viewpoint on the metaphysical level that greatly colors the differences between the moral epistemology of realism and idealism. Action does tend towards value. But a moral philosophy (as knowledge) must give support to the practical art. The practical axioms of purification and spiritual conversion, based only on the experience of the moral values in themselves, might well tell us *about* a very important

[151] Cf. G. Bastide, *La conversion spirituelle*, p. 74.
[152] *Ibid.*, p. 70.
[153] A. Dondeyne, *Contemporary European Thought*, p. 23.
[154] G. Van Riet, *Problèmes d'épistémologie*, p. 337.
[155] G. Bastide, "De la situation de l'homme," p. 245.
[156] G. Van Riet, *Problèmes d'épistémologie*, p. 340 (parentheses are mine).

moral attitude, but it cannot help us attain it with sufficient moral knowledge coming from reflection.[157] The axiological idealism of Bastide tends in this direction (by underestimating the role of speculative knowledge). The values are not grasped at the heart of being but rather *in the analysis of human activity*. The purpose of philosophy, as with Brunschvicg before him, is to grasp the spiritual values as they reveal themselves in the *process* of revelation rather than in the object of revelation (existence).

Realism does not minimize the necessity of action. Nor does it presuppose that reflection alone is enough to guarantee the authenticity of action. In fact we can say that parallel to the original affirmation of the *Cogito* (the realist cogito) there is also an immediate evidence grounding the authentic practical judgment. Parallel to realism on the speculative level we find that the realist theory of the Good is grounded in existence, but an existence which is a relational and transcendental interiority. On the one hand man is in the world as a presence that is given to him and acknowledged by him. It is a presence of values.[158] On the other hand man transcends the world over and over again by reason of his consciousness and his freedom. As Bastide brings out so well, man has a *responsibility* towards the world. In the midst of the human condition man is autonomous.

Furthermore, as idealism tries to bring out, the world is for man and man is for himself. "The world would have no value except by reason of the fundamental value of our being-consciousness-in-the-world of which it is only the term." [159] Integral realism emphasizes the *relation* in consciousness and not simply the objective term. Realism is not objectivism in the moral order any more than in the speculative order. The moral axiology of realism is also a philosophy of moral invention.[160] But like the interiority of the self the absolute character of value (pointing out our existence in so far as that existence is a self-construction of the self by the self) [161] is engaged in a world which determines it by virtue of the self's essential relation to the world.[162] For Bastide and idealism, on the other hand, it is essentially in the interiority of spirit that our activity of value is elaborated.[163] The two points of view are clearly distinguished: a consciousness

[157] Cf. A. Wylleman, *Tijdschrift voor Philosophie*, 1959 (21), p. 613 (summary in French).

[158] A. Wylleman, "Valeur et existence," in *Les Valeurs*, p. 83.

[159] A. Wylleman, "Valeur et existence," p. 84.

[160] *Ibid.*, p. 85.

[161] *Ibid.*, p. 85. Cf. G. Bastide, *Traité*, p. 90.

[162] A. Wylleman, *ibid.*, p. 85.

[163] G. Bastide, *Traité*, p. 90.

which exists essentially in a world which determines it can exercise and develope its existence but cannot ground or create the value or reality of that same existence; for idealism existence and knowledge have their *raison d'être in Value.*[164] From the realist point of view man "decides, at least in part, on the content and modalities of his existence, but he does not decide on the values (vital, intellectual, moral or aesthetic) which pertain in fact to self-realization." [165]

Therefore for realism it is ultimately in existence that the final end of man and the values towards which that existence is to be orientated are discovered. The good will and the free act, then, are grounded here and not simply in the ideal of autonomy generated by the human spirit.[166] The free act, as a *motivated* and self-justified, morally authentic affirmation does have its own immanent justification just as much as the affirmation of being, but this evidence, as far as the will is concerned, comes only with a certain maturity of consciousness. But again the difference between realism and idealism is that the first principle of morality, the *bonum-faciendum* is not attached to a God discovered at the source of consciousness or to an ideal and obligation legislated by the spirit, but rather to the good of man recognized in its absoluteness, that is, that absolute character of our existence such as it is *given* to us and not merely as we exercise it.[167] We agree wholly with Bastide that the good is tied up with man and the final self-possession which constitutes him as *person,* but this absolute character of human existence must be seen in its relativity to the world and to other persons living in the world. Even the acute analyses of Bastide regarding understanding and friendship lack this existential depth from which morality draws its deepest meaning. For realism the *faciendum* is not so much a *devoir* as it is a wisdom of life dictated by the intelligence and understanding by which we pursue our goal.[168] The obligation of this direction of our existence is more truly founded on our relation with other persons than on the ideal of perfection revealed by the experience of duty and autonomy.[169] For the other possesses an absolute character of existence to be respected like our own. But here again the absolute character of existence as person is something which is given before

[164] Cf. Part II, chapter one, p. 199.
[165] A. Wylleman, "Valeur et existence," p. 85.
[166] G. Bastide, *Traité,* p. 155.
[167] A. Wylleman, "Le bien comme fondement métaphysique du droit et de la morale," in Actas III of the Congresso internacional de filosofia, Barcelona, 1948 published at Madrid, 1949, p. 323.
[168] *Ibid.,* p. 322. A. Wylleman, "Le bien," p. 322.
[169] *Ibid.,* p. 323.

all possible activity. Man has a grandeur surpassing himself.[170] But only realism seems to give this aspect of human dignity the philosophical explanation the experience of our person demands. For by realism we are directed to search for the foundations on the metaphysical level and not merely on the level of human activity.

However, it is only fair to remark that at least on the level of moral epistemology an axiological idealism can in a special way center our attention on certain basic problems. For it is precisely in the area of moral epistemology that we must seek the foundation of our value judgments. It is precisely here that we seek the revelation of the primary values attained by the intentionality of the will.[171] As we noted earlier it was precisely in this desire to establish the solid foundation of moral judgments that Bastide takes from Descartes the spiritualism inspiring his own philosophy.[172]

Like Socrates Bastide has concentrated much of his own efforts in order to come to grips with the problems surrounding moral action. In many ways, as we saw, his own project is not unlike that of Kant.

There is an existential and transcendental necessity in this problematic of human action and Bastide is not the first one to be strongly attracted to its problematic. Newman and Blondel, not to mention others more contemporary, come to mind. Given the nature of the problem we are not surprised to see Bastide seek from the beginning an immediate evidence superior to all doubt in order to ground philosophically the moral judgment. We are not surprised that his idealism developes into a philosophy of spiritual conversion and transfiguration of values in order to explain the real possibility of being able to justify directly each one of our actions. For the nature of the moral problem demands just this kind of solution.

In this context it was as natural for Bastide to turn to a philosophy of liberty as for Sartre or S. de Beauvoir. From there a metaphysics of action and a philosophy of values followed of necessity. Idealism had already made itself available as the unfailing method for "an effective exploration with the whole soul of the major axiological dimensions of consciousness at work," that is, in the practical and authentic moral judgment, where not only knowledge but action is guaranteed, and along with it the meaning of life and the question of man's destiny.

It is here, too, that we understand and benefit from the analyses of man's alienation and man's liberation. For in fact the consciousness of freedom

[170] *Ibid.*
[171] G. Van Riet, *Problème d'épistémologie*, p. 234.
[172] Cf. G. Bastide, *Les grands thèmes*, p. 132.

is arrived at only progressively. The purification of the "conscience malheureuse" is necessary in order that through suffering and contradiction, failure and error man might arrive at that maturity of consciousness, maturity of reason and will, wherein real freedom is born. In this sense, the "total reflection" of which Bastide speeks *is* difficult and few there are, it seems, who care to arrive. Yet in our own times we see and feel that there is a progress in the realization of human responsibility, the dignity of the person and more and more man will be required to make this effort. He will have to assume the responsibility of his freedom which he is demanding today, but he must first come to realize "what price freedom."

As G. Van Riet points out this problem posed by the necessity of action in freedom is not new to our times, even though in some ways it may be more urgent.[173] The solution to the problem was given in terms of conscience as the proximate rule of morality and in terms of the prudential judgment, the source of a personal, incommunicable truth and the final evidence needed for authentic action here and now.[174] However, philosophy being an invitation to begin over again, an effort of personal reflection in the light of the needs and aspirations of our times, I think it can be said that the importance of Bastide's axiological idealism lies especially in its relevance for moral philosophy. It remains for us to consider in our final section some of the positive aspects of Bastide's philosophy in the light of the problematic of moral philosophy.

2. *Orientation for further study: Some positive aspects of Bastide's axiological idealism*

In our critique of idealism we noted its permanent value as a philosophy whose insight and truth lies especially in its emphasis on the immanent character of cognitive life, the interiority and spontaneity of spirit. Here we wish to point up briefly the particular interest and value of Bastide's axiology.

We might well begin by asking again how Bastide himself sees his own contribution to philosophy. He tells us that while other philosophies have given a central position to the notion of the Good (Value), "rarely has it (the axiological method) been employed in a systematic way to the problem of man to whom we wish to apply it." [175] The particular interest of

[173] G. Van Riet, *Problèmes d'épistémologie*, p. 241.

[174] *Ibid.*, p. 244. The author also briefly investigated this problem in his unpublished Master's thesis: *Existential Situation Ethics: A Search for the Real*, pp. 103-125, Chicago, 1965.

[175] G. Bastide, "De la situation de l'homme," p. 245.

Bastide's philosophy, then, is to be found here: he is concerned with the problem of man in his relation to the Good, to Perfection. "There is a problem of man," he says, "it is even the uniquely necessary problem ... the problem of man's situation in relationship to Value." [176] Bastide is concerned with the constant and effective orientation of man's life towards its final destiny.

No doubt we have here themes that are in a certain respect well known. However, I think it can be shown that for all its antiquity, the problem of man and his relationship to his final goal, the problem of the Good as the perfection of Being, the problem of creative liberty and the relationship of consciousness and action, the problem of the will's intentionality, the problem of moral experience and its particular psychology are precisely the areas of moral philosophy that leave much room for further reflection.

Every philosophy is at once a metaphysics, an epistemology and a philosophical anthropology. Man is present to every problematic of Being and Truth. The transcendentals introduce a reference to man, to his intellect and will. In this sense we can say with Bastide and with contemporary philosophy that the problem of man is the uniquely necessary problem of philosophy.

Granted that we have criticized Bastide's philosophy of man in so far as from a metaphysical point of view we prefer to begin with existence rather than spirit as the starting point of philosophy. However, it is in the area of moral philosophy that Bastide's philosophy takes on special interest. For the specific character of moral philosophy is found in the *intention* which gives to man's actions their moral character. And this intention is directed towards the Good as such, or in contemporary terms towards Value.[177] In this sense man alone *acts,* man alone is the free agent of a work produced in view of some value. If, like Bastide, we were to take the moral experience as our first fact, then we could say with him that metaphysics is of necessity a metaphysics of action, that is, of man in his freedom; and that consequently it is necessarily axiology, "since the act itself is the problem and we cannot distinguish between action and passion except through the consideration of Value which confers on the act its authenticity." [178] From the point of view of moral philosophy and its particular problematic we see that Bastide's axiology is precisely to the point. We disagree, however, on the place given to axiology as regards

[176] *Ibid.,* p. 246.

[177] Cf. J. Leclercq, *Les grands lignes de la philosophie morale,* Louvain, 1964 (3rd edition), p. 61.

[178] G. Bastide, *Traité,* pp. 356-357.

philosophy as a whole. Even moral philosophy cannot be reduced to the intentionality of the will towards the Good. The question of the objective reality of Value remains the ground of difference, that is, whether it is Existence or Spirit.

However, these comments do not wholly weaken the value of Bastide's intention: to emphasize the relationship between Value and man's situation. For the value of Bastide's philosophy is to show that the moral good is a *good for man,* that the discovery of the spiritual values are the condition of *man's* self-realization as person and consequently of man's happiness. "The metaphysical function of reflection is to attach moral consciousness to the source of value." [179] Moral philosophy is precisely this, "the science of what is man's good." [180] We deny however that this science can be the exclusive work of reflection alone, that a metaphysics of action is concerned exclusively with "the legislating consciousness." [181]

To further determine the precise areas of value of Bastide's philosophy, then, we can point out the aspects of man's moral good which his philosophy brings to light. We have already noted how Bastide seeks to establish man's relationship to the good. What is more important he seeks to show the moral good (perfection) [182] in its integral role as *the* good for man. For this reason he gives a central place to moral experience: "Without this moral experience (the perception of the spiritual values and man's vocation to perfection) [183] every other experience would be a deception and, in the end, illusory." Previously we took exception to the all-embracing role Bastide gives to moral experience in regards to philosophy as a whole. Here we note the importance of his analyses of moral experience for moral philosophy. In what does this importance consist?

It seems that we can say, first of all, that this importance stems from a much needed effort to return to the *real* essence of the spiritual values in so far as they give a fecundity to the moral life. By this we not only underline the phenomenological descriptions of the cardinal directions of the spiritual values in the promotion of moral life,[184] but especially the relationship established between moral experience and action. The philosophy of Bastide, like that of Rauh and Le Senne, attempts to engage the whole man in life through the progressive perfection of creative and responsible action: "... the notion of value has manifested its uncon-

[179] *Ibid.*, p. 106.
[180] J. Leclercq, *Les grands lignes,* p. 281.
[181] G. Bastide, *Traité,* p. 356.
[182] Cf. G. Bastide, *Méditations,* p. 93.
[183] G. Bastide, "L'expérience morale," p. 320.
[184] Cf. for example G. Bastide, *Traité,* pp. 187-209.

testable aptitude to unite all the clarity of intellectual analysis and all the depth of lived experience." [185]

Previously we noted the danger present in such an approach when detached from a metaphysics of existence. Here we note the importance of these analyses for aspects of morality yet to be fully developed and integrated into moral philosophy, namely man's vocation to action and to the interior life. The development of these areas of research along with a phenomenology of moral experience can do much to help us acquire an *existential awareness* of the fact that the moral good is truly a *good for man.* Let us consider briefly why this is so.

Moral philosophy, it seems, must continue to aim at an *understanding* of the foundations of moral life. In this we cannot afford to abandon the traditional viewpoint received from Aristotle and St. Thomas without falling into the mystifications present in some contemporary approaches to moral philosophy. Morality is also a science. But it cannot rest in the speculative order. It must complete its cycle as Bastide says over and over again, in the practical order.[186] To be sure, we are not advocating a philosophy of action detached from metaphysics. We are simply calling attention to what others have already seen, namely, that the great value of contemporary moral philosophy lies, in part, with its all embracing concern for the practical: "We know that it is in the *work,* the eminently *practical* function, that are elaborated the structures of power, knowledge and willing in which man can alienate himself . . . or find his liberation." [187]

Thus the importance of Bastide's approach to philosophy comes from the fact that he centers our attention on that love (value) which gives direction to life. This love is incarnated in action. It is that which, in great part, reveals reality to us and forms our deepest convictions and ideals. The importance of action in life, we can say, is what underlies Bastide's inspiration to seek the values which give our action authenticity. It underlies his long treatment in the *Traité* of the principle works of man seen in their alienating and liberating dialectics.

Now even when we prescribe certain limitations to moral philosophy as science, we cannot afford to forget that by its very nature this science is dependent, not only on a metaphysics of man but also, for example, on a moral psychology that will open up the interior conditions for the practical realization of moral goals. At this point we can appreciate the possibilities that a philosophy of spiritual conversion and transfiguration of

[185] G. Bastide, *La conversion spirituelle,* vii.
[186] G. Bastide, *Traité,* pp. 380-382.
[187] *Ibid.,* T. II., p. 621; cf. also T. II., p. 3.

values can have for moral philosophy in general. Thus, we noted in our second chapter on alienation the *philosophical* importance for the moral experience of spiritual conversion played by the philosophical scruple, the delicate, disinterested and generous consciousness. Bastide's philosophy is not so much a revelation of something new as it is a much needed emphasis on the *principal* attitudes that characterize the moral life. Basing his central intuition on the fact that man's existence is basically orientated by the dominant intentionality of his will (the motivating force of love), Bastide's philosophy is an effort to point the way towards the comprehension and love of the spiritual values.[188] For it is only in the positive love of the spiritual values that man is turned towards the moral good as a good for himself. Thus the validity of the philosophical scruple is related to the generosity of love and the generosity of love finds its authenticity in its attachment to the spiritual values and ultimately to God himself.

In this context Bastide's philosophy finds another important area of emphasis. The tension at the center of existence and moral experience is the tension of freedom. The love of the spiritual values, in the last analysis, is a free act. True, we disagree with Bastide when he attributes the creation of these tensions to the spontaneity of freedom alone,[189] but what we want to bring out here is the importance for moral philosophy that liberty must play in the constantly renewed effort at spiritual conversion. We must not be lulled into thinking that this is an affair for religion alone. The very future of moral philosophy seems to depend on the integration of the free act of spiritual conversion and the transformation of values into its own proper object. Modern man is becoming more and more moral, since he is becoming more and more conscious of his autonomy. By the same token must he become conscious of the spiritual values and the effort needed to attain them, as well as the responsibility to do so. But this responsibility must be brought home to him interiorly, that is, he must come to see the moral good as being good for him.

But, as Bastide notes, without a metaphysics of action, that is, a metaphysics concerned with the nature of the moral act as moral invention, we cannot effectively incorporate the free act of spiritual conversion into moral philosophy. Here too, once again, the importance of his axiology comes to the fore, since "values are the only means we have for philosophizing on action." [190]

If the primary character of action is not something new to the philo-

[188] Cf. G. Bastide, "La conversion spirituelle," p. 19.06-6.
[189] Cf. G. Bastide, *Traité*, p. 356.
[190] G. Bastide, *La conversion spirituelle*, p. 82.

sophical stage, nevertheless, it must be admitted that contemporary philosophy has called attention to this primacy in a way wholly in accord with the needs of our times and with results that annot but help leave us conscious of the fact of a real progress in philosophical reflection. Let us see how this is so as regards Bastide's philosophy of action.

We saw that from the beginning Bastide places the problematic of philosophy in terms of man's authentic existence which in turn is defined by the orientation of action towards the spiritual values and ultimately towards *the* Value, namely, God.[191] "Unum verum bonum communicabile sui. This is only another way to express what we have called authenticity." [192] But the authenticity sought by Bastide is not realized except in the self-knowledge that man acquires in authentic action.[193] Reflection finds its fulfillment only in the spiritual work. It seems this is what Bastide means when he says that he aims at applying axiology to the problem of man. He wants to reflect upon the incarnation of the spiritual values in works, thus making them truly humain. In other words the *perfection* which is revealed in the spiritual conversion as man's vocation is realized only in the effective constitution of the spiritual works coming from the exercise of an autonomous will. "The ideas are not only representations of objects but above all ideals which command in a normative way both knowledge and action." [194] The causality of the practical reason in the philosophy of St. Thomas plays a similar role, but it seems to be true that all the importance of the practical reason has still to be incorporated into a meaningful moral philosophy of action.[195]

It is precisely in the area of moral philosophy, then, that we see the legitimacy of the primacy which Bastide gives to Value in so far as it tends to approach the notion of the Good. It is in tending toward the good in spiritual works that man realizes himself as person. Man's life tends towards this fulfillment in meaningful activity. All this is rather forcefully summarized in Bastide's notion of the relationship between nature, culture

[191] Cf. G. Bastide, *Méditations*, pp. 15, 45, 59.
[192] *Ibid.*, p. 57.
[193] G. Bastide, *Traité*, p. 141.
[194] G. Bastide, *La conversion spirituelle*, p. 74.
[195] Cf. J. Naus, *The Nature of the Practical Intellect according to Saint Thomas Aquinas*, Gregorian Press, Rome, 1959, p. 202. Cf. also J. Leclercq, *La philosophie morale de Saint Thomas devant la pensée contemporaine*, pp. 137-153. Cf. also the discussion which W. Wallace brings to this question in regards to the work of F. Rahner: The Dynamic Element in the Church (*Das dynamische in der Kirche*, Frieburg, 1958, pp. 22-23) in "Existential Ethics: A Thomist Appraisal," *Thomist*, 1963 (27), p. 507. The author treated this question briefly in his unpublished Master's dissertation *Existential Situation Ethics*, De Paul University, 1965, p. 134.

and morality: "With nature, by means of culture and in view of morality," is his motto.[196] That is, the works of man are meant to increase his own possibilities for meaningful activity as well as that of others. And these works, in so far as they are the fruit of free activity, are the place of man's perfection. It seems to be in this context that we are to understand the heuristic role that Bastide assignes to the philosophies of reflection. For man *is* free to choose from any number of ways of tending towards the Good and his *obligation* is to bear the burden imposed by the unceasing necessity of moral invention.[197] We can benefit, then, from the orientations of Bastide's philosophy in so far as it places action over knowledge as the perfection of man's being in the affirmation of autonomy. The theme is an ancient one, but the expression of this theme in his *Traité* is wholly contemporary to the needs of our time. "In brief, if the perfection of man is expressed by speculative knowledge, man is truly a weak creature; but if it is expressed by the work of art, then man is in possession of all that is necessary in order to realize his perfection. We see that the question is of such importance that it seems difficult to underestimate it." [198]

The perspectives of man's destiny, then, are transformed when seen in the light of creative activity and it is precisely this perspective which Bastide seeks to accomplish in his axiological metaphysics. If we cannot agree with Bastide in his point of departure where moral philosophy tends to be the first fact and the analysis of moral experience the method for arriving at philosophy in general, nevertheless, we can agree with much of the results he obtains in what concerns moral philosophy. For the free act which is the object of his philosophy is the characteristic act of man. The reality of the Good is of the metaphysical order from the realist point of view. Nevertheless, only spirit perceives the Good. Only the rational being can grasp value. Only man can direct his own action. The moral good is, for realism, of the ontological order. Nevertheless, its moral character comes from its relationship to freedom. The moral good is a good for man. It is *the* good for man.[199]

If the notion of value in the philosophy of Bastide does not recover fully its metaphysical foundations, nevertheless it tends to do so, since in the original affirmation the moral character of consciousness is not only determined by duty but more by the vocation to authenticity and perfection.

[196] G. Bastide, *Traité*, p. 233. Cf. also *Mirages et certitudes de la civilization*, pp. 172-207.

[197] Cf. G. Bastide, *Traité*, pp. 487-488.

[198] J. Leclercq, *La philosophie morale*, p. 195.

[199] *Ibid.*, p. 257.

The revelation of the spiritual conversion is the attraction of the Good.

When we consider, then, the needs of our times in regards to moral philosophy, the work of Bastide – philosopher of value and action – merits both respect and consideration. Today we can neither afford to separate the practical from the speculative nor the speculative from the practical. Moral philosophy is a science which seeks to know for the purpose of acting. Man attains perfection in action. His good – *the* good – is realized in authentic activity. For this reason we cannot but listen to Bastide when he says something that tends to characterize his work: "... our work as men is to maintain a conscious equilibrium through a constant effort of invention, that is to say, a just composition of the different values. This perfect equilibrium, this constant finding of ourself (reflection and conversion) will have as its effect the union of existence and thought in order that the ideal might become real, in order that what is given to us might be transformed in a work that is ours. This invention will be wisdom, not a simple state of things, but a continuous creation of a dynamic equilibrium." [200]

Bastide proposes as the goal of his philosophy the application of an axiological metaphysics to the problem of man. In view of the many deviations in moral philosophy in what concerns the union of the speculative and the practical, we cannot but acknowledge the importance of this philosophical intention, for it is true that the metaphysical problems of man's destiny and his relation to the good as a good for him must be the constant source of our reflections in moral philosophy. The same is true of moral psychology of which Bastide's philosophy is rich.

Bastide's preoccupation with action, "the great school of life," [201] must be the model for every moral philosophy, whose special project alone can reveal the horizons and metaphysical values necessary for effective action. In his phenomenology and psychology of moral experience Bastide provides a rich base, then, for renewal in moral philosophy. For our part, we cannot but think that a return to a full realist metaphysics would be a perfect compliment towards such a renewal.

In conclusion, we have during the course of our work tried to follow the philosophical itinerary of G. Bastide. Beginning with the original affirmation of consciousness we saw the development of his philosophy of spiritual conversion within the framework of an axiological personalism. We saw that idealism and axiology, in the philosophy of Bastide, are inseparably joined together into a spiritual personalism.

[200] G. Bastide, "De la situation de l'homme," p. 252.
[201] J. Leclercq, *Les grands lignes*, p. 431.

Our conclusion, following the original inspiration of this study, had for its purpose a confrontation of idealism and realism, for idealism is *the* problem as well as the inspiration of Bastide's axiological idealism. We believe this confrontation of the two points of view has had several results. Perhaps the first to be remarked is that it has been shown that there is an integral realism that can and does come to grips with philosophical problems raised by an axiological idealism. This realism has very little in common with the closed, objectivist realism constantly criticized in Bastide's philosophy. The author regrets that Bastide himself seems to be unaware of the realism we have exposed in our conclusion, for nowhere in his work does he attempt to meet its approach to the problems of spirit and experience, freedom and value.

Secondly we believe our conclusion has correctly established what was already indicated in chapter I, part I, namely, the fundamental links of Bastide's idealism and axiology with the philosophy of Descartes and Kant. For this reason our comments on the origins of modern philosophy applied equally to Bastide's idealism. The purpose of making this connection was to show more clearly that there is really no possible passage from idealism to axiological idealism that does not bring with it the major problems which this passage seeks to resolve, not the least important of which is the problem of man, his person, his existence and his destiny as being-with-others-in-the-world. We believe we have pointed out the weak points of Bastide's philosophy in this regard – both on the level of his idealism and on the level of his axiology.

At the same time we are not unaware of the importance of Bastide's philosophy, especially as regards the renewal of moral philosophy itself.

Throughout our conclusion we have seen exemplified over and over again the importance of first principles as well as the primary importance of the description of the immediate evidences of consciousness. A study of idealism seems to be necessary, not only for avoiding false starts and false problems, but also for the personal deepening understanding of critical and integral realism. For realism has its own dangers. The critique of Bastide is not without foundation as regards some "realist" philosophers who objectivize or who exaggerate the passivity of our knowledge. The grounding of a philosophy of personal responsibility and a moral of invention at the heart of Ontology is not as easy as some have made it out to be. We hope that not the least important of our conclusions was to highlight the relational character of existence and the transcendental existential nature of interiority.

BIBLIOGRAPHY

PART I

I. PRINCIPAL WORKS

The bibliography is divided into two main parts. The first part includes an exhaustive bibliography of the works of Georges Bastide, together with several articles and reviews commenting on his works. The second part includes the primary and secondary sources used in the research and construction of the dissertation, together with a number of contemporary works which pertain to the philosophical tradition of Bastide or which are of special interest because they approach the same problems we have dealt with in this work.

1. *De la condition humaine,* Essai sur les conditions d'accès à la vie de l'esprit, Paris, 1939, 422 pp.
2. *Le moment historique de Socrate,* Paris, 1939, 320 pp.
3. *Les grands thèmes moraux de la civilisation occidentale*, Paris, 1945, 367 pp.
4. *Méditations pour une étique de la personne*, Paris, 1953, 198 pp.
5. *Mirages et certitudes de la civilisation,* Paris, 1953, 339 pp.
6. *La conversion spirituelle,* Paris, 1955, 101 pp.
7. *Traité de l'action morale,* 2 vol. in the collection "Logos", Paris, 1961, 857 pp.

II. ARTICLES

1. "Esquisse d'une axiologie de la personne," *Revue de Métaphysique et de Morale,* 1944 (2), 97-131.
2. "La spiritualité brunschviegienne," *Revue de Métaphysique et de Morale,* 1945 (50), 21-53.
3. "Civilisation et autonomie," *Les Etudes Philosophiques,* 1948 (3), 111-119.
4. "L'itinéraire philosophique de J. Delvolve," *Les Etudes Philosophiques,* 1948 (3), 241-53.
5. "Les problèmes majeurs de l'axiologie," *Les Etudes Philosophiques,* 1948 (3), pp. 84-85.

6. "Le Rire et sa signification éthique," *Revue Philosophique,* 1949 (139), 288-306.
7. "La philosophie de l'action comme critique de la vie et science de la pratique," *Les Etudes Philosophiques,* 1950 (1), 8-17.
8. "La fonction sociale de la philosophie," *Bulletin de la Société de Philosophie de Bordeaux,* 1950 (5), n° 25, 3-13.
9. "Léon Brunschvicg, lecteur de Descartes et de Pascal," *Revue internationale de philosophie,* 1951 (15), 78-99.
10. "L'Esprit occidental de la pensée française," *Annales de la Faculté des Lettres de Toulouse* (1952).
11. "Le Temps, la durée et l'éternité dans la philosophie de Spinoza," *Revista Philosophica,* Coïmbra, 1953 (8), 109-26.
12. "Culture et modernité," *Annales de la Faculté des Lettres de Toulouse,* 1958.
13. "El irracionalismo contemporaneo y la vida social," *Revista de Education* (La Plata), 1958 (4), 1-7.
14. "Le malin génie et la condition humaine," *"Revue de Métaphysique et de Morale,* 1958 (63), 233-245.
15. "Morale et liberté," *Les Etudes Philosophiques,* 1959 (1), 41-52.
16. "Convivre et survivre," *Les Etudes Philosophiques,* 1962 (3), 179-191.
17. "Sur la condition temporelle de l'homme," *Les Etudes Philosophiques,* 1962 (17), 69-80.
18. "The Metaphysical Dimensions of Man," *International Philosophical Quarterly,* 1962 (2), 351-366.
19. "Nolite Judicare," *Revue internationale de philosophie,* 1964 (1), 379-397.
20. "De la condicion del hombre y de las funciones de la philosophia," *Dianoia,* Mexico, 1964.
21. "Naturalisme et spiritualité: Le statut de la réflexion dans la pensée de Teilhard de Chardin," *Les Etudes Philosophiques,* 1965 (4), 409-447.
22. "L'Art et la relation synandrique," *Annales de Faculté des Lettres de Toulouse,* 1966 (March).
23. "L'Esthetisme du lucrèce," *Les Etudes Philosophiques,* Paris, 1967 (22), pp. 143-61.

III. COMMUNICATIONS AT PHILOSOPHICAL CONGRESSES

1. "Subjectivité et transcendence," Société Française de Philosophie, December 4, 1937, published in the *Bulletin de la Société Française de Philosophie,* Paris, 1937 (37), 161-211.
2. "Compréhension et valeurs," Sociétés de Philosophie de Langue Française, Bruxelles-Louvain, 2-6 septembre, 1947, published in *Actes du III Congrès, Les valeurs,* Paris-Louvain, 1947, 47-51.
3. "Les sosies de la liberté," Congrès des Sociétés de Philosophie de Langue Française, Neuchâtel, 13-16 septembre, 1949, published in the *Actes de IV Congrès, La liberté,* éditions de la Baconnière, Neuchâtel, 1949, 44-51.
4. "La fonction morale de la Science," Congrès des Sociétés de Philosophie de Langue Française, Bordeaux, 14-17 septembre, 1950, published in the *Actes de V Congrès, Les sciences et la sagesse,* Paris, 1950, 147-151.

5. "La nature, la conscience et la vie de l'esprit," Congrès des Sociétés de Philosophie de Langue Française, Grenoble, 12-16 september, 1954, published in the *Actes du VII Congrès, La Vie, La Pensée,* Paris, P.U.F., 1954, 25-33.
6. "L'homme et son prochain," Congrès des Sociétés de Philosophie de Langue Française, Toulouse, 6-9 septembre, 1956, published in the *Actes du VIII Congrès, l'Homme et son Prochain,* Paris, 1957, 153-172.
7. "La communication des consciences et l'edification de la morale," Congresso Internazionale di Filosofia, Venezia, 12-18 septembre, 1958, published in the *Atti del XII Congresso,* vol. settimo: *Filosofia dei valori, Etica, Estetica,* G.C. Sansoni editore, Firenze, 1958, 53-57.
8. "Unité, unicité, dialogue," Congrès des Sociétés de philosophie de langue française, 17-19 mai, Paris, 1959, published in the *Actes du X Congrès, Bergson et nous,* vol. II, Paris, A. Colin, 1959 (numéro spécial de Bulletin Sociétés françaises 54), 281-302.
9. "Nature, situation et condition humaine," Congrès des Sociétés de philosophie de langue française, Montpellier, 4-7 septembre 1961, published in *Existence et Nature,* Paris, P.U.F., 1962, 51-64.
10. "L'Expérience morale," XXIV Semaine de Synthèse, 28 mai-1 juin 1962, Centre international de Synthèse, published in *Experience,* Albin Michel, 1964, 307-20.
11. "L'Action de droit comme rectitude ou comme rectification," Colloque des Facultés de Droit, Toulouse, 1964.
12. Allocution, Congrès des Sociétés de philosophie de langue française, Louvain, 22-24 août, published in the *Actes du XII Congrès, la Vérité,* Paris-Louvain (Editions Nauwelaerts), 1965, 13-17.
13. Allocution d'ouverture, XIII Congrès des Sociétés de philosophie de langue française, *to be* published in the II vol. *Actes* du Congrès.

IV. COLLABORATIONS, PREFACES AND PRESENTATIONS

1. "La conversion spirituelle," in the XIX tome of *l'Encyclopédie française, Philosophie et Religion,* Larousse, 1957, chap. II, sec. n° 2, pp. 19.06-3 – 19.06-8.
2. "Introduction à la connaissance de Jean Jaurès," in *Jean Jaurès,* Paris, P.U.F., 1963.
3. Contribution in *Philosophy in the mid-century,* vol. III, "General theory of Value," 3-41, edited by Raymond Klibansky and published in Florence, Italy by La Nuova Italia Editrice, 1958.
4. Bibliographie française, *Morale et philosophie politique* by Georges Bastide, published by the Association pour la diffusion de la pensée française, 1961.
5. *Les Philosophes français,* autobiographie de la philosophie française contemporaine, textes recueillis et présentés par Gérard Deledalle et Denis Huisman, Paris, C.D.U., 1963, 242-261.
6. "Gaston Berger et la philosophie de la spiritualité militante," in *Hommage à Gaston Berger,* Gap, Editions Orhrys, 1964, 39-52.
7. Publication et Préface of the posthumous work of Jean Delvolvé *La fonction morale,* Paris, P.U.F., 1951.

8. Preface to the work *Philosophes espagnols d'hier et d'aujourd'hui* by A. Guy, Privat, 1956.
9. *Leibniz 1646-1716,* Paris, Aubier-Montaigne, 1968. (Introduction and conclusions by G. Bastide).
10. *Le Temps et la Mort dans la Philosophie Espagnole contemporaine,* Toulouse, 1968, E. Privat (Contribution by G. Bastide and others.).
11. *Eugène Dupréel, L'Homme et l'Oeuvre,* Bruxelles, 1968, pp. 41-59, a contribution by George Bastide, entitled: "La pluralisme axiologique d'Eugène Dupréel.

V. COMMENTARIES AND CRITICAL REVIEWS

Blair-Rice, P. "Children of Narcissus, Some Themes of French Speculation," *Kenyon Review* (U.S.A.), 1950 (12), 116-37.

Guy, Alain. "Ethique et civilisation selon Georges Bastide," *Les Etudes Philosophiques,* 1954 (9), 79-90.

–. "L'axiologie personnaliste de Georges Bastide," *Revista filosofica* (Coïmbra), 1955 (5), 157-78.

–. "Las orientaciones espiritualistas en la filosofia francosa contemporanea: René Le Senne, Georges Bastide, Jacques Chevalier," *Espiritu,* 1957 (6), n° 21, 11-22.

–. "Georges Bastide, filosofo de la conversion y del valor," (trad. de M. Teresa Rodriguez), *Crisis,* 1958 (5), 229-32.

Le moment historique de Socrate: G. Bosshard, *Revue de Théologie et de Philosophie,* 1945 (33), 216-218.

Les grands thèmes moraux de la civilisation occidentale:

(anon.), *Revue philosophique de la France et de l'étranger,* 1946 (136), 252-254.

Carreras Artau, J. *Revista de Filosofia,* 1960 (19), 76.

Corvino, F., *Rivista critica de storia della Filosofia,* 1960 (15), 91-93.

Guy, Alain. *Les Etudes Philosophiques,* 1959 (14), 208-209.

Minguet, P. *La Revue Nouvelle,* 1960 (31), 442-443.

I.F. *Revue Bénédictine,* 1959 (69), 416.

Méditations pour une ethique de la personne:

(anon.) *Revue de Métaphysique et de Morale,* 1953 (58), 324-325.

de Certeau, M. *Les Etudes Philosophiques,* 1954 (280), 265.

Geiger, L. B., *Revue des Sciences Philosophiques et Théologiques,* 1954 (38), 289-290.

Perelman, C. *Revue Philosophique de la France et de l'Etranger,* 1959 (84), 255-256.

Reymond, M. *Revue de Théologie et de Philosophie,* 1953 (3), 305-306.

Mirages et Certitudes de la Civilisation:

Borges, J. *Revista Portuguesa de Filosofia,* 1956 (12), 214.

de Contenson P., *Revue des Sciences Philosophiques et Théologiques,* 1956 (40), 330-331.

Dandoy, A., *La Revue Nouvelle,* 1955 (22), 143.
Jacques, E. *Revue Philosophique de Louvain,* 1954 (52), 343-344.
Onimus, J. *Revue Tomiste,* 1958 (58), 578-80.

La conversion spirituelle:

Guy, Alain. *Les Etudes Philosophiques,* 1956 (11), 317-319.
Onimus, J. *Revue Thomiste,* 1959 (59), 787-788.

Traité de l'Action morale:

Decerf, P. *Revue Philosophique de Louvain,* 1963 (61), 705-714.
Dumery, H. *Les Etudes Philosophiques,* 1962 (17), 445-51.
Guy, Alain. Espiritu, 1963 (12), 171.
Montagnes, B. *Revue des Sciences Philosophiques et Théologiques,* 1962 (56), 717-718.
Smith, C. *Philosophy,* 1963 (38), 275-277.
Voelke, A. *Revue de Théologie et de Philosophie,* 1963 (13), 269-270.
–. *Studia Philosophica,* 1963 (23), 212-229.
Watte, P. *La Revue Nouvelle,* 1964 (39), 525.
Zaragüeta, J. *Revista de Filosofia,* 1962 (21), 370-372.

"Le Rire et sa signification éthique":

Iturrioz, J. *Pensamiento,* 1950 (6), 562-563.

PART II

I. PRIMARY SOURCES

Bergson, H. *Oeuvres* (Edition du centenaire), Paris, P.U.F., 1963 (2nd edition), 1602 pp.
Brunschvicg, L. *La modalité du jugement,* Paris, Alcan, 1934 (2nd edition), 246 pp.
–. *Le progrès de la conscience dans la philosophie occidentale,* Paris, Alcan, 1953 (2nd edition), 2 vol., 759 pp.
–. *L'Expérience humaine et la causalité physique,* Paris, P.U.F., 1949 (3rd edition), 601 pp.
–. *Les etapes de la philosophie mathématique,* Paris, P.U.F., 1912, 591 pp.
–. *Ecrits philosophiques:* T.I. L'Humanisme de l'occident: Descartes-Spinoza-Kant, Paris, P.U.F., 1951, 319 pp.
–. T.II. L'orientation du rationalisme, 1954, 336 pp.
–. T.III. Science-Religion, 1958, 249 pp.
–. *"De la vraie et de la fausse conversion," Revue de Métaphysique et de Morale,* 1930, pp. 270-297; 1931, pp. 29-80; 187-235; 1932, 17-46; 153-198.
–. *De la connaissance de soi,* Paris, Alcan, 1931, 197 pp.
–. *L'idéalisme contemporain,* Paris, Alcan, 1905, 196 pp.

Descartes, R. *Discours de la méthode,* Bruxelles, Editions "Labor" (Coll. nouvelle des classiques), 1935, 74 pp.
–. *Règles pour la direction de l'esprit,* trad. by J. Sirven, Paris, Vrin, 1945.
–. *Les principles de la philosophie* (livre premier) trad. by P. Lemaire, Paris, A. Hatier.
–. *Méditations métaphysiques* (Coll. *Les Grands Textes*) trad. by F. Khodoss, Paris, P.U.F., 1966 (4th edition), 315 pp.
Lachelier, J. *Oeuvres,* 2 vol. Paris, Alcan, 1933, 444 pp.
Kant, I. "Critique of Pure Practical Reason," trans. by Carl J. Friedrich in *The Philosophy of Kant*: Immanuel Kant's Moral and Political Writings, New York, Random House (Modern Library), 1946, 476 pp.
–. *The Critique of Judgment,* translated with analytical indexes by James Meredith, England, Oxford University Press, 1964 (4th edition), 179 pp.
–. The Moral Law: *Kant's Groundwork of the Metaphysics of Morals,* translated and analysed by H. J. Paton, London, Hutchinson University Library, 1948, 142 pp.
–. *The Metaphysical Principles of Virtue* (Part II of the *Metaphysics of Morals*), translated by J. Ellington, Library of liberal arts publication, New York, 1964, 174 pp.
–. *Critique of Pure Reason,* trans. by N. K. Smith, New York, Random House, 1958, 335 pp.

II. SECONDARY SOURCES

Alquie, Ferdinand. *La découverte métaphysique de l'homme chez Descartes,* Paris, P.U.F., 1950, 384 pp.
–. *L'expérience,* troisième édition, Paris, P.U.F. ("Initation philosophique" 30), 1966, 102 pp.
Augustine St. *La lumière intérieure,* (Coll. "Les Grands Textes"), Paris, P.U.F.
Baruzi, J. *Philosophes et savants français du XXe siècle,* Paris, Alcan, 1926, vol. I.
Beck, L. W. *A commentary of Kant's critique of practical reason,* University of Chicago Press, 1960, 306 pp.
Benrubi, J. *Les sources et les courants de la philosophie contemporaine en France,* Paris, Alcan, 1933, 2 vol.
Boutroux, E. *La philosophie de Kant* (cours de M. Emile Boutroux professé à la Sorbonne en 1896-1897), Paris, J. Vrin, 1965, 374 pp.
Brehier, E. *Histoire de la philosophie.* Tome I: L'antiquité et le Moyen Age; Tome II: La Philosophie moderne, Paris, P.U.F., 1948 (5th edition).
–. *Etudes de philosophie moderne,* Paris, P.U.F., 1965, 242 pp.
Brun, J. *Socrate,* Paris, P.U.F. (Coll. "Que sais-je" 899), 1966 (3rd edition), 128 pp.
Césari, Paul. *La Valeur* (Coll. "Initiation Philosophique"), Paris, P.U.F., 1964 (2nd edition), 120 pp.
Christoff, Daniel. *Recherche de la Liberté* (Bibliothèque de Philosophie contemporaine), Paris, P.U.F., 1957, 220 pp.
Collins, James, *A History of Modern European Philosophy,* Milwaukee (U.S.A.), Bruce Publishing Company, 1954, 854 pp.

Copleston, Frederick, S. J. *Contemporary Philosophy,* London, Burns & Oates, 1963 (4th edition), 227 pp.

Cousineau, R. H. "Unexplored consequences of existential relation: Relatals of Being and Action," *Revue Philosophique de Louvain,* 1959 (57), 71-79.

Cornford, F. M. *Socrates,* Cambridge, Cambridge University Press, 1964 (reprinting), 113 pp.

Cresson, A. *Les courants de la pensée philosophique française,* Paris, A. Colin, 1927 (4th edition T.I. 1941; T.II 6 th. ed. 1950).

–. *Pascal* (Coll. "Philosophes") Paris, P.U.F., 1962, 126 pp.

d'Ainval, C. *La philosophie de Louis Lavelle,* Louvain, Editions Nauwelaerts, 1967, 366 pp.

Daly, C. "Idealism and Ethics: René Le Senne, "*Irish Theological Quarterly,* 1954 (21), pp. 115-155.

De Finance, J. *Cogito cartésien et réflexion thomiste* (Archives de philosophie, vol. XVI, cahier 2); Paris, Beauchesne, 1946, 186 pp.

–. *Existence et Liberté,* Paris-Lyon, Vitte, 1955, 389 pp.

–. *Etre et agir dans la philosophie de saint Thomas,* Paris, 1946, 371 pp.

–. *Connaissance de l'etre* (Coll. "Essais pour notre temps" 4), Paris-Bruges, Desclée de Brouwer, 1966, 502 pp.

de Jaer et A. Chapelle. "Le noétique et le pneumatique chez Maurice Blondel," *Revue Philosophique de Louvain,* 1961 (59), 609-630.

Delbos V. *La philosophie pratique de Kant,* Paris, Alcan, 1905, 156 pp.

Delesalle, J. "La philosophie de M. René Senne," *Revue Néoscolastique de Philosophie,* 1936 (39), pp. 348-364.

Deleuze, G. *La Philosophie critique de Kant* (Coll. "Initiation Philosophique"). Paris, P.U.F., 1963, 103 pp.

Delvolvé, J. *La fonction morale,* Paris, P.U.F., 1951, 146 pp.

Deschoux, M. *La philosophie de Léon Brunschvicg,* Paris, P.U.F., 1949, 247 pp.

De Waelhens, A. in "Bulletin d'epistémologie," *Revue Néoscolastique de Philosiphie,* 1937 (40), 445-454.

–. "Phénoménologie et réalisme," *Revue Néoscolastique de Philosophie,* 1936 (39), 497-517.

–. "Sur les origines de la pensée de Hamelin," *Revue Néoscolastique de Philosophie,* 1938 (41), 21-45.

–. "Descartes et la pensée phénoménologique," *Revue Néoscolastique de Philosophie,* 1938 (41), 571-584.

–. "Une philosophie de la participation. L'actualisme de M. Louis Lavelle," *Revue Néoscolastique de Philosophie,* 1939 (42), 213-229.

–. "Un symposium de philosophie française," *Revue Néoscolastique de Philosophie,* 1940 (43), 66-95.

–. "Heidegger, Platon et l'humanisme," *Revue philosophique de Louvain,* 1948 (46), 490-496.

–. Comptes rendus: F. Alquié, *La nostalgie de l'être et la découverte métaphysique de l'homme chez Descartes, Revue Philosophique de Louvain,* 1950 (48), 576-580.

–. L'homme, être d'action ou être intérieur," *Recherches et Débats du centre catholique des Intellectuels français,* 1951 (14), 57-69.

–. *La philosophie de Martin Heidegger,* Louvain, Publications Universitaires de Louvain, 1955 (4th edition), 379 pp.

–. *Existence et signification,* Louvain, Nauwelaerts, 1958, 289 pp.

–. *Phénoménologie et vérité,* Louvain, Nauwelaerts, 1965 (2nd ed.), 160 p.

Dopp, J. "Une forme personnaliste de l'idéalisme: la philosophie de L. Lachieze-Rey, *Revue Néoscolastique de Philosophie,* 1935, 454-469.

–. "Le Congrès Descartes," *Revue Néoscolastique de Philosophie,* 1937 (40), 664-679.

Dopp, J. Compte Rendu: H. Gouhier, *Essais sur Descartes,* in *Revue Néoscolastique de Philosophie,* 1937 (40), 650-657.

Dondeyne, A. "Idealisme of realisme," *Tijdschrift voor Philosofie,* 1941 (4), 607-648.

–. "L'historicité dans la philosophie contemporaine," *Revue Philosophique de Louvain,* 1956 (54), 5-25, 456-477.

–. *Contemporary European Thought and Christian Faith,* Pittsburgh, Duquesne University Press, 1963, 211 p.

–. "L'abstraction," *Revue Néoscolastique de Philosophie,* 1938 (février et août), pp. 5-20 and 339-373.

Dupré, Louis "The Philosophical Stage of Man's Self-Discovery," *Proceedings of the American Catholic Philosophical Association,* 1963 (37), 211-223.

Dupreel, E. *Esquisse d'une philosophie des valeurs,* (Bibliothèque de Philosophie contemporaine), Paris, Alcan 1939, 306 p.

Dupuy, M. *La philosophie de Max Scheler. Son évolution et son unité,* Paris, P.U.F., 1959, 2 vol., 441 et 442 pp.

Encyclopédie française, Tome XIX, *Philosophie et religion,* Paris, Larousse, 1957.

Etcheverry, A. *L'idéalisme français contemporain,* Paris, Alcan, 1934, 376 p.

–. "Une orientation nouvelle de l'idéalisme," *Archives de Philosophie,* 1936 (12), n° 3, 341-356.

–. "La valeur et l'être," in *Les Valeurs* (Actes du III Congrès des sociétés de philosophie de langue française), Louvain (E. Nauwelaerts), 1947, pp. 77-81.

–. *Le conflit actuel des humanismes,* Rome, Presses de l'université Grégorienne, 1964 (nouvelle édition), 328 p.

Etienne Jacques. "Eléments pour une morale platonicenne fondamentale. Une lecture de la 'République,' " *Revue Philosophique de Louvain,* 1963 (61), 537-560.

–. "La nature est-elle un critère de moralité?," *Revue Philosophique de Louvain,* 1966 (64), 582-593.

Etudes Philosophiques: numéro spécial: *Blondel,* 1952, (Paris, P.U.F.).

Farber, M. (ed.) *L'Activité philosophique contemporaine en France et aux Etats Unis,* T.II *La philosophie française,* Paris, P.U.F., 1950.

Filosofia dei valori, Etica, Estetica. *Atti del XII Congresso Internazionale di Filosofia,* Venezia, 12-18 septembre, 1958, vol. VII, G. C. Sansoni, editore, Firenze.

Forest, A. "Thomisme et idéalisme," *Revue Néoscolastique de Philosophie,* 1934 (37), 317-336.

–. "La méthode idéaliste," *Revue Néoscolastique de Philosophie,* 1934 (37), 178-201.

–. "L'exigence idéaliste de la philosophie contemporaine," *Revue Néoscolastique de Philosophie,* 1934 (37), 29-48.
–. "L'expérience de la valeur," *Revue Néoscolastique de Philosophie,* 1940 (43), 5-20.
–. *Création et Consentement,* Paris, Aubier, 1943 "La Conversion rationaliste," *Tijdschrift voor philosophie,* 1950 (12), pp. 729-741.
–. "La philosophie de l'esprit," *Giornale de Metafisica,* 1946 (1), p. 283-299.
–. "La présence spirtuelle," *Recherches et débats du centre catholique des intellectuels français,* 1952 (18), 26-30.
–. "De l'idéalisme au spiritualisme," *Giornale de Metafisica,* 1955 (10), 432-439.
Fourez, G. et Jacob, Jean. "Une dialectique de la conversion; l'Action de Maurice Blondel," *Revue Philosophique de Louvain,* 1959 (57), 543-574.
Heidegger, M. *What is Philosophy,* translated with an introduction by William Kluback and Jean Wilde, London, Vision Press, 1962, 97 p.
–. *The Question of Being,* translated with an introduction by William Kluback and Jean Wilde, London, Vision Press, 1958, 109 p.
–. *Essays in Metaphysics,* translated from the German *Identität und Differenz* by Kurt Leidecker, New York, Philosophical Library, 1960, 82 p.
–. *An Introduction to Metaphysics,* translated by Ralph Manheim, New York, Anchor Books (Doubleday & Company), 1961, 182 p.
–. *Chemins qui ne mènent nulle part.* Holzwege, traduit de l'allemand par Francois Fédier, Paris, Gallimard, 1962, 313 p.
Henry, M. "Le concept d'âme a-t-il un sens?," *Revue Philosophique de Louvain,* 1966 (64), 5-33.
–. *L'Essence de la Manifestation* (Coll. Epiméthée), Paris, P.U.F., 1963, 2 vol., 908 p.
L'Homme et son prochain, *Actes du VIII Congrès de philosophie de langue française,* (Toulouse), Paris, P.U.F., 1956, 328 p.
L'homme et ses oeuvres, *Actes du IXe Congrès des Sociétés de Philosophie de langue française,* Paris, P.U.F., 1957 (numéro spécial: *Les Etudes Philosophiques),* 490 p.
Jaspers, K. *The Perennial Scope of Philosophy,* translated from the German *Der philosophische Glaube* by R. Manheim, New York, Philosophical Library, 1949.
Klibansky, R. (ed.). *Philosophy in the mid-century,* 4 vols., Firenze, La Nuova Italia, 1958-1959.
Lachelier, J. *La nature, l'esprit, Dieu* (Coll. "Les Grands Textes") Paris, P.U.F., 1955, 165 p.
Lachièze, Rey, P. *L'idealisme kantien,* Paris, Vrin, 1950 (2nd edition).
Lacroix, J. *Personne et amour,* Paris, ed. du livre français, 1942.
–. *Kant et le kantisme* (Coll. "Que sais-je" 1213), Paris, P.U.F., 1966.
–. *L'Echec* (Coll. "Initiation Philosophique" 69), Paris, P.U.F., 1965 (2nd edition), 116 p.
–. *Les sentiments et la vie morale* (Coll. "Initiation Philosophique" 2), Paris, P.U.F., 1952, 108 p.
Ladrière, J. "Philosophy and science," *Philosophical Studies,* 1958 (8), pp. 3-23.
–. "La philosophie des mathématiques et la problème du formalisme," *Revue Philosophique de Louvain,* 1959 (9), pp. 163-168.

Langlois, J. "Apercu sur 'la philosophie des valeurs,'" *Laval théologique et philosophique,* 1954 (10), 79-95.

Lavelle, L. *La Philosophie française entre les deux guerres,* Paris, Aubier, 1943.

–. *La conscience de soi,* Paris, Grasset, 1933.

–. *Introduction à l'ontologie,* Paris, P.U.F., 1947.

–. De *l'intimité spirituelle,* Paris, Aubier, 1955.

–. *Traité des Valeurs,* Tome I: *Théorie générale de la valeur* Tome II: *Le système des différentes valeurs,* Paris, P.U.F., 1950.

Leclercq, J. *Les Grands Lignes de la Philosophie morale,* Louvain, Publications Universitaires de Louvain, 1953 (edition nouvelle), 445 p.

–. *La Philosophie morale de Saint Thomas devant la pensee contemporaine,* Louvain, Publications Universitaires, 1955, 469 p.

Lefevre, R. *La vocation de Descartes* (Bibliothèque de philosophie contemporaine), Paris, P.U.F., 1956, 288 p.

–. *L'humanisme de Descartes* (Bibliothèque de philosophie contemporaine), Paris, P.U.F., 1957, 284 p.

–. *Le criticisme de Descartes* (Bibliothèque de philosophie contemporaine), Paris, P.U.F., 1958, 340 p.

–. *La bataille du "Cogito,"* Paris, P.U.F., 1960, 236 p.

–. "Du platonisme à l'aristotelisme," *Revue Philosophique de Louvain,* 1961 (59), 197-248.

Le Senne, R. *Le Devoir,* Paris, P.U.F., 1930.

–. *Obstacle et valeur,* Paris, Aubier, 1934.

–. *Traité de morale générale* (Coll. "Logos"), P.U.F. (Paris), 1942.

–. *La destinée personelle,* Paris, Flammarion, 1951.

–. *Introduction à la Philosophie* (Coll. "Logos"), Paris, P.U.F., 1958 (4th edition).

–. "La philosophie de l'esprit," in *L'activité philosophique en France et aux Etats-Unis,* Tome II., 113-131.

–. "Philosophie et spiritualisme," *Revista de Filosofie,* 1935 (avril-juin), 105-122.

Levert, P. "De l'intimité spirituelle," *Revue d'Histoire et de Philosophie religieuse,* 1936 (36), 308-316.

Levinas, E. *Totalité et infini* (Phaenomenologica), La Haye, Martinus Nijhoff, 1965 (2nd edition), 284 p.

–. "Levy-Bruhl et la philosophie contemporaine," *Revue Philosophique de la France et de l'Etranger,* 1957 (82), 556-69.

La Liberté: *Actes de IVe Congrès des Sociétés de langue française,* Neuchatel 13-16 septembre, Editions de la Baconnière, Neuchatel, 1949.

Liberté: *Etudes Philosophique,* no. 1, 1959. (Paris, P.U.F.).

Liberté et Culture: *Les Etudes philosophiques,* avril-juin, 1948 (Paris, P.U.F.).

Luijpen, W. *Existential Phenomenology* (Duquesne Studies), Pittsburgh, Duquesne University Press, 1963 (3rd impression), 362 p.

Madinier, G. *Conscience et mouvement,* Paris, P.U.F., 1939.

–. *Conscience et amour,* Paris, P.U.F., 1938 (3rd ed. 1962), p. 126.

–. *Conscience et signification* (Bibliothèque de philosophie contemporaine), Paris, P.U.F., 1953, 137 p.

–. *La conscience morale* (Coll. "Initiation Philosophique" 14). Paris, P.U.F., 1966 (5th edition), 120 p.

–. *Vers une philosophie réflexive* (ouvrage posthume), Paris, Editions de la Baconnière, 1960.

Maréchal, J. "L'aspect dynamique de la méthode transcendentale chez Kant," *Revue Neoscolastique de Philosophie,* 1939 (42), 341-384.

Maine de Biran. *L'Effort* (Coll. "Les Grands Textes"), Paris, P.U.F.

Maritain, J. *Existence and the Existent,* translated by L. Galantiere and G. Phelan, New York, Doubleday & Company (Image Books), 1956, 153 p.

–. *The Degrees of Knowledge,* translated from the fourth French edition by G. Phelan, London, Geoffrey Bles, 1959, 476 p.

–. *Nef leçons sur les notions premières de la philosophie morale,* Paris, Te qui, 1951, 195 p.

–. *Moral Philosophy,* New York, Charles Scribner's Sons, 1964, 468 p.

–. *Trois Réformateurs: Luther, Descartes, Rousseau,* Paris, Plon, 1925.

Mc Keon, R. "Contemporary French Philosophy," *Proceedings of the American Catholic Philosophical Association,* 1954 (28), 17-36.

–. *l'autorité des valeurs,* Paris, P.U.F., 1957.

Merleau-Ponty, M. *Sens et non-sens,* Paris, Nagel, 1948, 331 p.

–. *Phénoménologie de la perception.* Paris, Gallimard, 1945, p. 531.

Monod, G. "Pensée et action chez Jules Lagneau," *Revue de Métaphysique et de Morale,* 1952 (57), 117-149.

Moreau, J. *Réalisme et Idéalisme chez Platon,* Paris, P.U.F., 1951, 135 p.

–. *La conscience et l'etre,* Paris, Aubier, 1958.

–. *L'horizon des esprits,* Paris, P.U.F., 1960.

–. "Valeur et objectivité," *Les Etudes Philosophiques,* 1953 (8), p. 238-246.

Moreau, J. "Philosophie de l'esprit et philosophie de l'existence," *Les Etudes Philosophiques,* 1955 (4), 166-173.

Morot-Sir, E. "De l'idéalisme à l'axiologie," *Giornale de Metafisica,* 1955 (10), 462-477.

Nabert, J. *Elements pour une éthique,* Paris, Aubier, 1962, 221 p.

–. *Essai sur le mal,* Paris, P.U.F., 1955.

–. *L'expérience intérieure de la liberté,* Paris, P.U.F., 1924.

Naus, J. *The Nature of the Practical Intellect according to Saint Thomas Aquinas,* Rome, Libreria Editrice dell' Universita Gregoriana, 1959, 220 p.

Nedoncelle, M. *Vers une philosophie de l'amour,* Paris, Aubier, 1946, 170 p.

–. "La philosophie de l'action et les philosophies de la personne," *Les Etudes Philosophiques,* 1952 (7), 387-389.

Ngô-Tiêng-Hiên. "La philosophie morale de Frédéric Rauh," *Revue Philosophique de Louvain,* 1962 (60), 542-572.

Nietzsche, F. *The Birth of Tragedy and the Geneology of Morals,* translated by F. Golffing, New York, Doubleday & Company, (Anchor Books), 1956, 299 p.

Nuttin, J. *Psychanalyse et conception spiritualiste de l'homme,* Louvain, Publications Universitaires de Louvain, 1950, 367 pp.

Parodi, D. *La philosophie contemporaine en France,* Paris, Alcan, 1925 (3rd edition).

Pascal, B. *Pensées et opuscules,* publiés avec une introduction, des notices, des notes par Leon Brunschvicg, Paris, Hachette, 1923, 806 p.

Piersol, W. *La valeur dans la philosophie de Louis Lavelle,* Lyon, Vitte, 1959, 191 p.

Platon. *The Dialogues of Plato,* translated by B. Jowett, New York, Random House, 1937.

Paton, H. J. *The Categorical Imperative. A Study in Kant's Moral Philosophy,* London, Hutchinson, 1965 (5th edition), 283 p.

Polin, R. *La création des valeurs,* Paris, P.U.F., 1945.

Presence d'autrui: *Actes du VIII congrès de philosophie de langue française* (Toulouse, 1956), Paris, P.U.F., 1957.

Pucelle, J. *La source des valeurs,* Lyon, Vitte, 1957.

–. *Le règne des fins,* Lyon, Vitte, 1959.

–. *Le Temps* (Coll. "Initiation Philosophique 16), Paris, P.U.F., 1962, 105 p.

–. "Agir et pâtir," *Les Etudes Philosophiques,* 1957 (12), 340-352.

De Raeymaeker, L. *Introduction à la philosophie,* Louvain, Publications Universitaires de Louvain, 1956 (4th edition), 292 p.

–. *Philosophie de l'être. Essai de synthèse métaphysique,* Louvain, Publications Universitaires de Louvain, 1947 (2nd edition), 432 p.

–. "Le sens et le fondement de l'obligation morale," *Revue Philosophique de Louvain,* 1961 (59), 76-91.

Ramirez, E. N., "La filosofia de Louis Lavelle: Dios me es mas interior que yo mismo," *Augustinianum,* 1963 (3), 517-544.

Rauh, F. *L'experience morale* (Bibliothèque de la Philosophie contemporaine) Paris, P.U.F., 1951 (5th edition), 174 p.

Revue de Synthèse: *L'Experience* (XXIVe Semaine de Synthèse, 28 mai - 1 juin, 1962), no. 29-31 of the Revue, 1963 (84); also: Paris, Albin Michel, 1964, 476 p.

Revue Internationale de Philosophie: *La "philosophie de l'esprit,"* 5, 1939; *Descartes,* 12, 1950; *Léon Brunschvicg,* 15, 1951; *Kant,* 30, 1954; *Etudes Platoniciennes,* 32, 1955; *Le bien,* 38, 1956; *La responsibilité,* 39, 1957; *Le jugement moral,* 70, 1964.

Reid, J. L. "Las lineas fondamentales del methode de Lavelle," *Sapientia,* 1952 (7), 186-197.

Ricoeur, P. *Finitude et culpabilité:* T.I: L'homme faillible; T.II: La symbolique du mal, Paris, Aubier, 1960, 164 et 335 p.

–. *Le volontaire et L'involontaire,* Paris, Aubier, 1963, 464 p.

–. "Etude sur les 'Meditations cartésiennes' de Husserl," *Revue Philosophique de Louvain,* 1954 (52), 75-109.

Robberechts, L. "Quelques théories de la liberté. Autour de Jean Nabert," *Revue Philosophique de Louvain,* 1964 (62), 233-257.

Robert, Jean-Dominique, "Reflexions sur l'antinomie idéalisme-réalisme," *Revue Philosophique de Louvain,* 1965 (63), 458-473.

Robert, Jean-Dominique. "Descartes, créateur d'un nouveau style métaphisique. Reflections sur l'introduction du primat de la subjectivité en philosophie première," *Revue philosophique de Louvain,* 1962 (60), 369-393.

Robin, L. *La morale antique,* Paris, Alcan, 1939 (3rd. edition 1963 by P.U.F., Coll. "nouvelle Encyclopedie Philosophique, 178 p.).

–. "Platon et la philosophie des valeurs," *Les Etudes Philosophiques,* 1944, 1-21.

Robinet, A. *La Philosophie Française,* Paris, P.U.F. (Coll. "Que sais-je" 170), 1966, p. 125.

Rodis-Lewis, G. *La Morale de Descartes* (Coll. "Initiation Philosophique" 27), Paris, P.U.F., 1962 (2nd edition), 132 p.

Romeyer, B. "Philosophie de l'esprit," *Revue de Philosophie,* 1935 (5), 347-357.

Ross, Sir David. *Kant's Ethical Theory. A commentary on the Grundlegung zur Metaphysik der Sitten,* Oxford, Clarendon Press, 1954, 96 p.

Ruyer, R. *Le monde des valeurs,* Paris, Aubier, 1948.

Salmon, E. G. "Human knowledge of material and spiritual existence," *Proceedings of the American Catholic Philosophical Association,* 1961 (35), 179-186.

Sartre, J.-P. *L'être et le néant,* Paris, Gallimard, 1943, 722 pp.

Sauvage, M. *Socrates ou la conscience de l'homme* (Coll. "Maitres spirituels") Paris, éditions du Seuil, 1956.

Scheler, Max. *Le formalisme en éthique et l'éthique matérielle des valeurs,* Paris, Gallimard, 1955.

Sellers, R. "The spiritualism of Lavelle and Le Senne," *Philosophy and Phenomenological Research,* 1951 (11), 386-393.

Seve, L. "Panorama de la philosophie française contemporaine," *Pensée,* 1959 (88), 51-80; 1960 (89), 75-89; 1960 (90), 67-90; 1960 (92), 39-68.

Simon, Yves. *Critique de la connaissance morale,* Paris, Desclee, 1934.

Smith, Colin. *Contemporary French Philosophy,* London, Methuen & co., 1964, 266 p.

Smith, R. "Lavelle and Le Senne: University Philosophy in France," *Thought,* 1948 (23), 245-280.

Spiegelberg, H. *The Phenomenological Movement,* the Hague, Martinus Nijhoff, 1965 (2nd edition), 2 vol., 765 p.

Spinoza, B. *Ethics and on the Correction of the Understanding,* London, Dent & Sons, 1963 (latest printing of the English translation by Andrew Boyle in the series: Everyman's Library), 267 p.

Stefanini, L. "Personalismo e ontologia," *Giornale di Metafisica,* 1953 (8), 389-396.

Taminiaux, G. "De Bergson à la phénoménologie existentielle," *Revue Philosophique de Louvain,* 1956 (54), 26-85.

Thévenaz, P. *L'homme et sa raison,* Neuchâtel, La Baconnière, 1956, 2 vol.

Thomas, St. L'être et l'esprit (Coll. "Les Grands Textes"), Paris, P.U.F.

Tonneau, J. *Absolu et obligation en morale* (Conférence Albert-le-Grand), Paris, Vrin, 1964, 126 p.

La Vie, la Pensée: *Actes du VII Congrès des sociétés de philosophie de langue française,* Paris, P.U.F., 1954.

Les Valeurs: *Actes du IIIe Congrès des Sociétés de philosophie de langue française,* Louvain, Nauwelaerts, 1947, 260 p.

Van de Wiele, J. "Les Structures fondamentales de la vie cognitive. Contribution à une anthropologie philosophique," *Revue Philosophique de Louvain,* 1966 (64), 96-129.

Van Riet, G. *L'éspitémologie thomiste. Recherches sur le problème de la connaissance dans l'école thomiste contemporaine,* Louvain, Publications Universitaires de Louvain, 1950 (2nd edition), 672 p.

–. *Problèmes d'épistémologie,* Louvain, Publications Universitaires de Louvain, 1960, 425 p.

–. "Idéalisme et christianisme. A propos de la *Philosophie de la Religion* de M. Henry Dumery," *Revue Philosophique de Louvain,* 1958 (56), 361-428.

–. Compte rendu: J. Moreau, *La conscience et l'être, Revue Philosophique de Louvain,* 1959 (57), 112-114.

Van Steenberghen, F. *Epistémologie,* Louvain, Publications universitaires de Louvain, 1965 (4th edition), 278 p.

–. *Ontologie,* Louvain, Publications universitaires de Louvain, 1961 (3rd edition), 288 p.

–. "Question disputée sur le réalisme immédiat," *Revue Philosophique de Louvain,* 1965 (mai), pp. 209-234.

Veatch, H. *Rational Man.* A modern interpretation of Aristotelian Ethics. Indiana, Indiana University Press, 1962, 226 p.

Verbeke, G. "La doctrine de l'être dans la Metaphysique d'Aristote," *Revue Philosophique de Louvain,* 1952 (50), 471-478.

–. "Thèmes de la morale aristotélicienne. A propos du commentaire des PP. Gautier et Jolif sur l'Ethique à Nicomaque," *Revue Philosophique de Louvain,* 1963 (61), 185-214.

Verga, L. "La 'Philosophie de l'esprit' et le sorti della filosofia," *Rivista de Filosofia neo-scolastica,* 1960 (52), 376-396.

Verneaux, R. *Les sources cartesiennes et kantiennes de l'idéalisme français,* Paris, Beaushesne, 1936, 523 p.

Vialatoux, J. *L'intention philosophique* (Coll. "Initiation Philosophique" 1), 1952.

–. *La morale de Kant* (Coll. "Initiation philosophique" 22), Paris, P.U.F., 1966 (4th edition), 86 p.

Wahl, J. *Tableau de la philosophie française,* Paris, Gallimard, 1962, 178 p.

–. *Le Malheur de la conscience dans la philosophie de Hegel,* Paris, P.U.F., 1951 (2nd edition), 206 p.

Wild, J. "Authentic existence: a new approach to 'value theory,' " in *An Invitation to Phenomenology,* ed. by James Edie, Chicago, Northwestern University Press, 1965, pp. 59-77.

Wylleman, A. "Existentie-Ervaring en Metaphysiek. Beschouwingen bij de philosophie van René Le Senne," *Tijdschrift voor Philosophie,* 1945 (7), 259-276.

–. "Valeur et existence," *Actes du IIIe Congrès des Sociétés de philosophie de langue française. Les Valeurs,* Louvain, Nauwelaerts, 1947, pp. 83-86.

–. "Over de rationaliteit van ons menselijk bestaan," in *Miscellanea Moralia* in honorem eximii Dominii Arthur Janssen, Louvain, Nauwelaerts, 1949, 169-197.

–. "Du bien comme fondement métaphysique du droit et de la morale," in *Congreso internacional de filosofia,* Barcelona 1948, Actas III, Madrid, 1949, pp. 319-325.

–. "L'éboration des valeurs morales," *Revue Philosophique de Louvain,* 1950 (48), 239-246.

–. "Bedenkingen bij enkele hedendaagse opvattingen omtrent de taak van het moraalfilosofisch denken," *Tijdschrift voor Philosophie,* 1959 (21), 587-614.

–. "L'homme et la création des valeurs," *Revue Philosophique de Louvain,* 1960 (58), 88-102.

–. "Le fondement de l'étique," in *Memorias* del XIII Congreso Internacional de Filosofia, Mexico, 1963, 435-444.

Zac, S. *La morale de Spinoza* (Coll. "Initiation Philosophique" 39), 1966 (2nd edition), Paris, P.U.F., 116 p.

Made in the USA
Las Vegas, NV
14 November 2024

11639885R00136